SpringerBriefs in Economics

More information about this series at http://www.springer.com/series/8876

Kanchan Chopra

Development and Environmental Policy in India

The Last Few Decades

Springer

Kanchan Chopra
Formerly, Institute of Economic Growth,
University of Delhi
Delhi, India

ISSN 2191-5504 ISSN 2191-5512 (electronic)
SpringerBriefs in Economics
ISBN 978-981-10-3760-3 ISBN 978-981-10-3761-0 (eBook)
DOI 10.1007/978-981-10-3761-0

Library of Congress Control Number: 2017933476

Printed on acid-free paper

This Springer imprint is published by Springer Nature
The registered company is Springer Nature Singapore Pte Ltd.
The registered company address is: 152 Beach Road, #21-01/04 Gateway East, Singapore 189721, Singapore

For my grandchildren
Ananaya and Aarit

Preface

Issues relating to the environment seem to be caught in an impasse as of now. When we look around, it seems as though they are attracting more and more attention. Little children in different parts of the world seem to be very aware of the environment, the significance of the web of life, interrelationships of species and human and non-human and so on. Curriculums world-wide stress these aspects.

In international forums, climate change, pollution and biodiversity attract attention and so does talk of the planet Earth, our one and only home. However, governments of nation states pay lip service to these understandings and go on nevertheless with 'business as usual' with primary indices of their economic success being GDP rates of growth. Corporates focus on profit too, to the neglect of all else, with a few honourable exceptions. A great deal on ecosystems and the planet Earth is, of course, talked about within the ivory towers of academia.

At the same time, we are told that academics interact very little with the world at large. They only write papers for journals read by a small number of their peer group. New ideas are thus not communicated as widely as they should. This is indeed cause for concern. However, when I look back at 30 years and more in academics, I think that many of us always focused on the policy implications of our work. The following questions therefore arise: Did our work impact thinking in government, corporate and activist circles? If it did not, why so? Did we, academics, learn from them?

Understanding this journey of interaction between different segments of society is itself a study in the evolution of policy. More so, because issues relating to the environment were new both in research and in policy, with activism being a strong voice linking the two. The motivation for writing this brief is purely one of attempting to document this interaction with respect to different sectors relating to the environment.

I have collected many debts in the course of my academic journey. This brief has evolved out of research over three decades but also equally out of talks and discussions with several friends and colleagues. Parts of it have been read and commented on by Vikram Dayal, Purnamita Dasgupta and Nandan Nawn. I am thankful to them for their lucid comments which were very helpful. Over the years, my erstwhile colleagues at the Institute of Economic Growth have contributed to my thinking in substantial ways. The IEG provided an environment for academic innovation and new thinking, and I benefitted in no small measure. Simultaneously, my interactions with a peer group spread across many continents were enabled by my associations with the Beijer Institute of Ecological Economics in Stockholm, the International Centre for Theoretical Physics at Trieste and the South Asian Network for Development and Environmental Economics. The meetings of the International Society for Ecological Economics and the 5-year association with the Millennium Ecosystem Assessment further strengthened these interactions. I owe a great deal to a large number of individuals, far too many to list. I will not even try to do it.

The brief would not have been written without the persistent support of Sagarika Ghosh at Springer. I am thankful to her.

My family has been a constant source of support in my academic undertakings. My husband, Om, has withstood many hours of my absence and preoccupation with ungrudging indulgence. So have my children, Piyush and Priyanka, and their spouses.

However, wise use of our planetary resources is all about holding them in trust for the future. And so, this brief volume is for my grandchildren, Ananaya and Aarit, in the hope that their generation does better than ours on this count as well.

Gurgaon, India
January 27, 2017

Kanchan Chopra

Contents

Chapter 1
Development and Environmental Policy

1.1 Introduction

Policy in India, economic, environmental or any other (as indeed in any country), is the outcome of a process consisting of several steps. Firstly, the underlying political principles outlined in the country's Constitution and the broad pattern of thinking of the government of the day define an overarching perspective. This often results in 'policy documents', with focus on specific sectors of the economy. Such documents are also influenced by academic developments on the issues involved, both national and international, but always (in a democracy) with an eye on votes, the common man's perspective and the position taken by dominant stakeholders. The next steps in the process consist of the framing of Acts and Rules including details of economic and legal interventions (such as taxes, subsidies and judicial processes).

Framing these details is essentially an administrative process, though rooted in prevalent knowledge. The dependence on political positioning and administrative processes holds true in even more glaring detail of environmental policy. Often this happens because the knowledge aspects are controversial and evolving. Such undue significance of political positioning is also often due to the remoteness of environmental issues to the common man and the existence of several vested interests in favour of an extractive approach. At this juncture, civil society could play a significant role by launching parallel political pressures, through knowledge dissemination and, sometimes, grassroots protest movements. Learning from the grassroots, documented over time, or international understandings could also influence the process. In this volume, we propose to study the evolution of environmental policy in India in the last three decades in the context of the influences mentioned above. We do this against the backdrop of a continuing focus on development, an overarching metaphor in the political economy of India.

The analysis is motivated by a set of questions asked within the context of the policy framework enunciated from time to time. Did the policy move in the direction of recognition of the different roles played by the environment? Were

K. Chopra, *Development and Environmental Policy in India*, SpringerBriefs in Economics, DOI 10.1007/978-981-10-3761-0_1

corresponding acts and rules passed to enable implementation? Simultaneously, was there a bottom-up learning that permeated the policy process in a lateral manner due to an understanding of grassroots reality or civil society understanding? Was the process impacted by the existence of environmental movements and protests? And finally, did international pressures or influences shape the policy directions?

In this chapter, we begin with a brief foray into the nature of development, an idea that has dominated the public space for at least the last seven decades. The next section examines the nature of policy responses, one particular subset of human responses to an issue. It also looks at the decision-making cycle and its internalisation of stakeholder responses through an iterative process. This analysis is then viewed in the context of linked sociological systems. The latter sections examine the development process in India and the evolution of environmental issues as areas of concern as development proceeded. Turning points in the evolution of environmental policy are examined and possible drivers identified.

1.2 The Context of Development: The World View

Development, seen as a desired national objective, has overshadowed all else for the last 70 years or more, in almost all nations of the world. In the discourse in the South in particular, the concept has pervaded almost all policy discussion. We can think of at least three interpretations of development in this context: (a) a growth in the availability of goods and services to the average citizen, (b) an increase in his/her capability to acquire the same through better entitlements and (c) better livelihoods to ensure better capabilities.

As expected, the meanings attached to the term 'development' and its interpretation changed from time to time. In the earlier phases, the vision implicit in the nonconflict-ridden and somewhat simplistic Rostowian notions of 'stages of growth' of the 1950s promised all a share in the coming abundance. The dependency school, on the other hand, emphasised the responsibility of the industrial heartland in the North for the poverty of the South. Such a viewpoint introduced a degree of confrontation between the North and the South in the pursuit of development. A new dimension was introduced by the notion of 'development as fulfilment of basic needs'. The Human Development Report of 1991[1] took another step forward when it stated 'the basic objective of human development is to enlarge the range of peoples' choices to make development more democratic and participatory'. The notion of letting people decide their own future rather than defining their needs for them had entered the discourse. Simultaneously, in the eighties and nineties, issues relating to the environment were entering the discourse on a much larger scale than ever before, at least at the international level. After the first Rio conference of 1992, 'sustainable development' became the universally lauded goal. Everyone joined in the hope that policies could be found which would make development humane,

[1] See UNDP (1991).

inclusive and environment friendly. Synergies between development, resource conservation and their wise use provided the byword for good policy, be it in the context of international conventions or national policy pronouncements.

However, increasing populations of nations added to demand for resources. Together with this, increasing inequality and its portrayal in the media focussed on the resource-intensive lifestyles of the rich. Markets catered to these lifestyles and 'sustainability' came to be critiqued as a distant goal incapable of achievement, as long as the dominant system supported market led affluence. Parallel to these developments was the renewed focus on growth and the increase in globalisation. Both these trends claimed that poverty could be reduced through top-down proliferation of growth in production of goods and services, in other words, high rates of GDP growth. By the first decade of the twenty-first century, this had become the perceived way to go. And to accommodate environmental issues into such an approach, the notion of 'green growth' has been introduced, mainly in a top-down manner by national governments and international organisations.[2] In opposition to the concept of sustainable development which emerged out civil society engagement, green growth has been introduced in a top-down manner as a vision to be moved towards by technocrats. If at all 'green growth' as a concept has to provide policy direction, it will have to do more than keep environmental issues in the focus of attention. It should assist in moulding environmental policy in directions that assist in resource conservation and pollution abatement. We still do not know enough to comment on whether green growth can take us far.

Whatever be the shade of meaning that we attach to the terms, it is definitely true that the seductive power of 'growth' and 'development' stays with us.[3] No politician or economist can choose to ignore it, in particular when it is portrayed as leading to lower poverty in low- and middle-income countries. Rist argues that 'sixty years after the international community set its sights on extending development to the South, it has not happened'. One can disagree with the above statement on a number of counts. It is not true that in all instances, development has been an agenda foisted on the South by the international community. Democratically elected governments in the South have owned the agenda as their own. So the onus for its success or failure falls squarely on their shoulders as well. Further, it is also true that some progress in the design of improving the lot of the poorer nations has occurred. Extreme poverty and hunger have been alleviated, albeit to a limited extent. One could claim that this has been at a considerable cost, in particular environmental cost. But that is a different matter.

[2] See the paper by Bleuming and Yun in Dale, Mathai and De Oliveira edited (2016).

[3] For more on this, see Rist (2002). By way of explanation, he says, 'by power to seduce in every sense of the term, to charm, to please, to fascinate, to turn away from the truth, to deceive'.

1.3 Responses and Policy Responses: The Conceptual Underpinnings

Most development plans are accompanied by stated policy objectives. Such policy is understood to mean governmental responses to and plans for development. In general, governmental policy is a subset of a range of human responses to given situations.

Responses are outcomes of human decisions, and they influence and change the key connecting links between elements of development and a range of other systems including ecosystems (otherwise called the environment), the focus of interest in this volume. These responses determine how individuals, communities, nations and international agencies intervene or strategise, ostensibly in their own interests, to use, manage and conserve ecosystems. Depending on the decision-making entity, categorisation of responses could differ. They could be individual, societal, national or international.

Policy responses, one among several kinds of human responses, refer to policy as outlined by an entity with power, legal or social to define the course of action of a social or political entity. The source of authority of the entity could be legal as in the case of national governments or social as in the case of communities with jurisdiction over natural resources. Or it could stem from agreements between national governments on specific issues. Needless to say, policy responses reflect in a sense the aggregation of individual responses.

From a short-term, administrative or political economy perspective, policy-making cycles are said to consist of agenda setting, policy design, implementation and review.[4] Such a view assumes that agenda setting is preceded by taking into account research (and its findings from different stakeholder's perspectives). One would assume also that assessment and monitoring is a part of implementation and review. The Millennium Assessment framework is more comprehensive and treats the dynamic working of each of these, i.e. research, assessment and monitoring are significant components of the decision-making cycle.[5]

Decision-making starts by identifying a problem, followed by collating the research findings in defining and choosing policy options. In setting out the policy options, alternative world views as depicted by the state of knowledge are taken into account. Selection among these policy options is a two-stage process which in the first stage identifies *binding constraints*, which may be political, economic or social, depending on the context. These binding constraints rule out some policy options. As an extreme example, genocide to solve the overpopulation problem would not be an acceptable policy option in most contexts.

From among the feasible options, costs associated with the implementation of different policy options are determined (sometimes intuitively). These determine the *acceptable trade-offs* which determine selection of policies, which are then

[4] See IPBES (2016). The summary for policymakers refers to this as the policy cycle.

[5] See MEA (2005) Volume 3, Report of the Policy Responses Group.

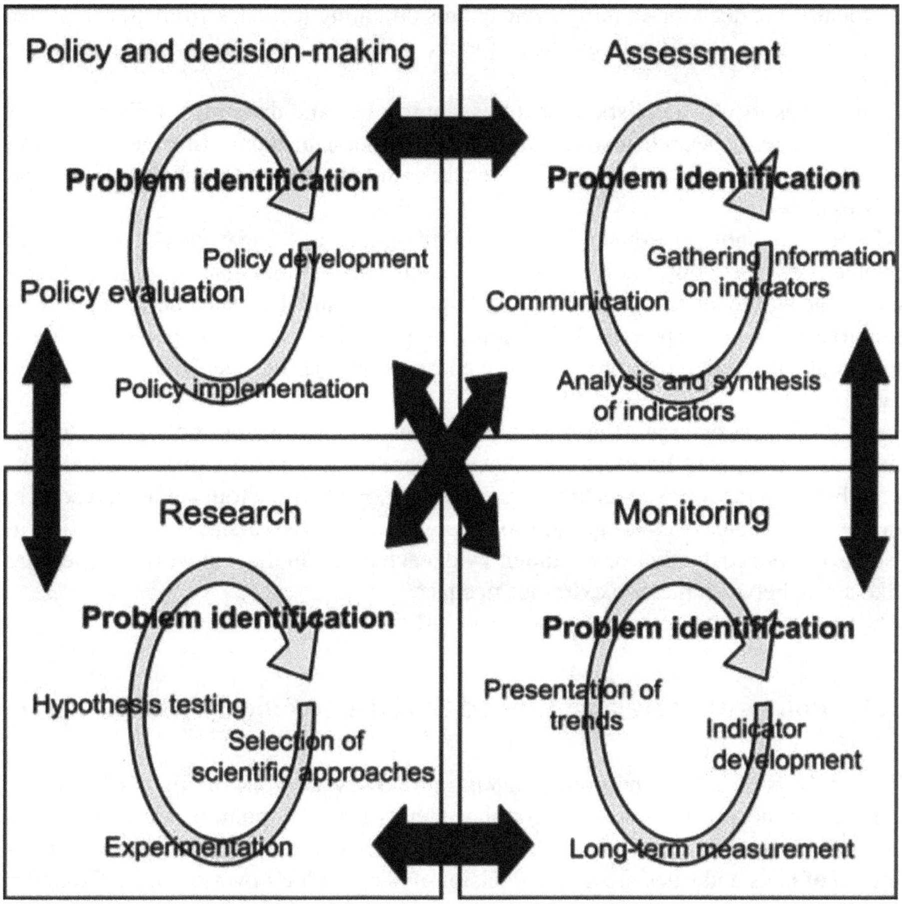

Fig. 1.1 The iterative policy making cycle

implemented (using processes and governance mechanisms available). Finally policies are evaluated for their effectiveness. Monitoring of the successes and failures enables this evaluation and constitutes the feedback mechanism which links one chain of the iterative process of decision-making to the next. It requires feedback from all stakeholders, and if the monitoring is based on partial knowledge or biased feedback, the next component of the iteration may not improve on the earlier one. And the iterative process leads to the identification of another set of problems. These may be targeted at newer issues or older ones so as to improve the effectiveness of earlier policy responses. As shown in Fig. 1.1 (adopted from the MA), research, assessment, monitoring and policy-making are all components of a continuing interactive process to support selection and implementation of responses.

The process is iterative and involves interaction with information providers.

Ideally, the decision-making cycle entails obtaining feedback from all categories of stakeholders. Similar loops exist for the research, monitoring and assessment process.

Each has its characteristic objectives, approaches and dynamics. Under the best circumstances, research insights should yield adequate monitoring networks and indicators of change, to be taken up for assessment towards an informed decision process.

Understandably, the dynamics and timing of each of these cycles do not always evolve in perfect coordination with each other. The dynamic nature of information exchange and feedback to and from these processes and their stakeholders are integral to developing responses. This implies that decision-making processes are liable to change over time to improve effectiveness. A number of mechanisms can facilitate this.

In the above diagram, the multiple ways in which research, policy and implementation are linked are illustrated. Ideally there exist two-way causations and linkages between the four subsquares in the diagram. Each of the four squares, research, policy- and decision-making, monitoring and finally assessment, could function in isolation from each other or in tandem with each other. In the real world, something like a mix between the two extremes occurs.

1.4 Policy-Making and Linked Social-Ecological Systems

The analysis of policy and policy-making processes has gone a long way in social science. Some advances are of particular interest from our point of view. One takes account of the fact that people whose lives policy intends to target through the drawing up of laws and rules are active decision-makers in their own right. As Colander and Kupers put it, 'those very (policy) choices will themselves influence the dynamics of the system, as well as people's tastes and preferences. It won't be the same system once the policies are under way, and that very fact can bring about both opportunities and unforeseen consequences'.[6]

The changed dynamics consequent on policy intervention introduces new institutions of the state as stakeholders, be they the executive, the legislature or the judiciary. There may be different levels of centralisation (or decentralisation) at which these function. Successive changes introduced at different levels result in iterations of interaction and consequences both between these governmental institutions and with other stakeholders, e.g. the resource owners, the consumers and the users of resources. Interrelated economic and social systems make policy drafting and execution a complex affair.

Outside these societal interactions but heavily influenced by the decisions and the events are the ecosystems: the rivers, the lakes, the forests and the fields as well as the urban ecosystems. These bear the impact of the execution of policy and the

[6] See Collander and Kupers (2014) Chapter 1.

growth or conservation that follows. By the very nature of these natural ecosystems, the impact is of different kinds. At times, the ecosystem state changes slowly, and its functioning left unaffected by the increased extractive use, the additional pollution or at times the additional conservation. At other times, the ecosystem may undergo a sudden regime shift and lose its functional capacity, undermining its capability to produce for further human consumption. Ideally policy needs to be able to tell the difference in these two situations, with some degree of certainty. Close association between policymakers and scientists should make this happen.

In this volume we ask how decision-making cycles of policy responses in the context of environmental policy in India have functioned. Have they constituted iterative cycles with learning from one integrated into the other? Alternatively, have they even learnt from empirical evidence, international agendas and progress in knowledge bases or feedback from civil society?

1.5 The Backdrop in India up to the 1980s: Development, Equity and Poverty Alleviation

Development has been at the core of the government's economic policy in India since the 1950s. From the formulation of the First Five-Year Plan in 1951 to the ongoing current Twelfth Plan (2012–2017), development has been the primary concern. In the economic lexicon, equity and poverty alleviation come next as the metaphor around which economic policy has been framed.

Policies and Acts *in the early years after independence* reflect this focus on equity and development. We look at the Plan documents in the first instance. The First Five-Year Plan says in its introduction: 'The urge to economic and social change under present conditions comes from the fact of poverty and of inequalities in income, wealth and opportunity…….. the two have to be considered together'. Both poverty and inequality need to be eliminated simultaneously. As for natural resources, they appear as an asset, a resource, to be exploited. Note the following, from Chapter 1 of the First Plan: 'An underdeveloped economy is characterized by coexistence in greater or lesser degree of underutilized manpower on the one hand and of unexploited natural resources on the other'.

Interestingly, however, even in the First Plan, the chapters on 'Forests and Soil Conservation' do exhibit an understanding of the many services available from nature. In the case of forests, it is stated, 'Forests are important sources of fuel, raw materials…. provide material for defence ……. help in the conservation of soil fertility and play a role in the maintenance of the water regime of the land'.[7]*But these appear only as overarching statements.* The dominant paradigm remained that of harnessing resources, such as water for development, large dams being the centrepiece. The Second Plan and later plans moved in the direction of industrialisation

[7] See Government of India (1952), Chapter 21 for Forests and Chapter 22 for Soil Conservation.

with natural resources being treated more and more as extractive resources, be it coal, iron ore or oil.

The Second Plan was conceived in an atmosphere of economic stability. It was felt agriculture could be accorded lower priority. The Plan therefore focussed on rapid industrialisation with a focus on heavy and basic industries. The Industrial Policy 1956 was based on establishment of a *socialistic pattern of society* as the goal of economic policy.

With a few ups and downs due to extraneous factors (such as armed conflict), the stated objectives in the Plans continued to be growth and poverty eradication. At times employment creation or foreign exchange conservation was thrown in as the situation demanded but nowhere, in these early years, do we find a reference to probable linkages between environmental conservation and poverty alleviation and the need for environmental policy. Forest degradation as an issue receives an occasional mention. Water resources were significant, to be harnessed for agriculture and provision of drinking water was a top priority. Appears occasionally. Achieving higher rates of investment and significant growth in domestic savings continued to be the major objectives of the plans that followed. Poverty alleviation and a better distribution of income were mentioned occasionally. See, for instance, the objectives of the Third Plan in which the following is stated as one of its objectives: 'to establish progressively greater equality of opportunity and to bring about reduction in disparities in income and wealth and a more even distribution of economic power'.

The Fourth Plan (1969–1974) document contains a reference to the lack of an environmental aspect in planning and development[8]. To quote, 'It is necessary to introduce an environmental aspect into our planning and development. At present there is no point in the structure of government where the environmental aspects receive attention in an integrated manner…… these deficiencies have to be overcome before any advance can be made'. It was around this time that the UN Stockholm Summit on the environment was held in 1972, and the Indian Prime Minister in her statement asked: 'Are not poverty and need the greatest polluters?' This is again emblematic of the continued primacy of the fight against poverty over environmental issues in Indian politics. The Fifth Plan (1974–1979) continued the focus on poverty removal (*garibi hatao*) and self-reliance. Promotion of high rate of growth, better distribution of income and significant growth in the domestic rate of savings were seen as key instruments for achieving this.

[8] See Chapter 2 of the Fourth Plan on 'the long-term perspective' for details.

1.6 The Decade of the 1980s: The Rise of Environmental Concerns Within the Government

The decade of the 1980s witnessed the rise of concerns with regard to the environment within the government in India. Prior to this, the Wildlife Protection Act had been passed in 1972, and a few acts and rules on water and air quality existed. These were the Water (Prevention and Control of Pollution) Act, 1974, and the Air (Prevention and Control of Pollution) Act, 1981. The Forest Conservation Act was enacted in 1980 and Air (Prevention and Control of Pollution) Act in 1981. A full-fledged Department of Environment was set up in 1980. But it was in 1984 that a Ministry for Environment and Forests was created. These were like the first green shoots. Around 1985, the National Wasteland Development Board was set up. At the same time, the first plan to clean the Ganga was initiated. The Environment Protection Act came in 1986. But all this was still about steps being taken parallel to the mainstream efforts at development.

At the macro policy level, the Sixth and Seventh Plans were ongoing from 1980–1985 and 1985–1990, respectively. How did they look at these issues? The Sixth Plan focussed on objectives such as an increase in national income, modernisation soft technology, ensuring continuous decrease in poverty and unemployment through schemes for transferring skills (TRYSEM) and assets (IRDP) and providing slack season employment (NREP), controlling population explosion, etc. Broadly, the Sixth Plan could be taken as a success as most of the targets were realised even though during the last year (1984–1985) many parts of the country faced severe famine conditions and agricultural output was less than the record output of the previous year. The Seventh Plan was deemed to be very successful as the economy recorded 6% growth rate against the targeted 5% with the decade of the 1980s struggling out of the so-called Hindu rate of growth of 3%. The imperatives of planning in the country continued to be (overwhelmingly) the achievement of a high growth rate and the creation of employment. It was the decade when liberalisation had been started, though in a piecemeal and partial manner and growth was at the centre of attention.

Nevertheless, indications of an understanding on environmental issues and the need for an overall perspective at the centre on it were also seen. The 1980s was the decade that saw the setting up of the Ministry of Environment and Forests (MOEF) in 1984 and the enactment of the Environment Protection Act (1986). Some analysts claim this happened in the aftermath of the Bhopal Gas Tragedy (1984). Difficulties had been faced in claiming compensation from Union Carbide in the absence of legislation relating to storing, handling and use of hazardous substances and a law to provide immediate compensation to victims of industrial accidents. The focus of the Act on pollution, hazardous circumstances and the like seems to confirm this. The outstanding characteristics of environmental legislation in this period were (a) it was centralised and (b) it viewed the environment as wildlife, birds and beasts and at best water. It was ppiecemeal legislation in these areas in an ad hoc fashion.

In the early 1980s, the First Report of the Centre for Science and Environment (CSE) was published. It focussed on land, water, energy and large dams and, for the first time, provided a detailed description with evidence from the field, of the kinds of environmental degradation that had crept into the country simultaneously with development. But the implications of all this were still to be absorbed by policy-makers, even at the highest levels of decision-making.

1.7 The Decades Since Then

The period between 1990 and 2000 was a relatively good one from the viewpoint of focus on the environment and environmental policy. International understanding took a stride ahead with the Rio Summit on sustainable development. Domestically efforts were on to look for synergies between development and environment. In its objectives, the Ninth Plan (which was operative from 1997 onwards) enunciated that it aimed at, among other things:

(i) Ensuring environmental sustainability of the development process through social mobilisation and participation of people at all levels
(ii) Empowerment of women and socially disadvantaged groups such as scheduled castes, scheduled tribes and other backward classes and minorities as agents of socio-economic change and development
(iii) Promoting and developing people's participatory institutions like Panchayati Raj institutions, cooperatives and self-help groups

The policies, enunciated in the National Conservation Strategy and Policy Statement on Environment and Development and the Policy Statement on Control of Pollution, both spelt out in 1992, were pursued in the Ninth Five-Year Plan. Assigning conservation a high priority both at the central and state levels, the Tenth Five-Year Plan (2002–2007) also sought to tackle environmental degradation in a holistic manner in order to ensure both economic and environmental sustainability. Successive plans[9] continued to mention sustainable development in one manner or the other, but more often than not, the focus continued to be on sustainable growth, meaning thereby maintenance of high rates of economic growth. The period after 2000 in particular saw parallel attention being given to environmental issues.

The Twelfth Five-Year Plan (2012–2017)[10] went further and stated in its foreword, 'The issue of environmental sustainability cannot be ignored. We need a growth process that is consistent with protecting our environment'. Further, its chapter on sustainable development in Volume 1 distinguished it clearly from 'sustainable growth'. Among the economic instruments that it discusses to reach sustainable development are environmental taxes, funds and technology transfers, certificates and obligations. In putting forth an agenda for sustainable development, it states, 'There is a general impression that India is consuming more than what its

[9] For example, for the Eleventh Plan see Government of India (2008).

[10] See Government of India (2013).

ecosystem can sustain, and hence there is a need for programmatic interdisciplinary planning and inter-agency efforts at all levels. A number of national strategies and policies, which inculcate the principle of sustainability, have already been put into place'. The above review indicates that there was a gradual increase in the policy space given to environmental issues over the last few decades.

1.8 Drivers and Impacts: The Present Volume

In the context of this understanding of an enlarged policy space for environmental issues, this brief volume intends to examine the influences that have shaped environmental policy in India and comment on the shape that it could take in the future. Has there been an iterative learning process borrowed from changes in the state of knowledge available? Simultaneously, has the changing character of the Indian citizenry impacted the design of environmental policy?

Among the influences or drivers of environmental policy, four major sets are identified. These are:

- Empirical reality as documented
- International pressures and negotiations
- Environmental protest and justice-related movements
- The evolving theoretical understanding on issues related to the environment

The four chapters that follow analyse each of these influences, sometimes in the context of specific sectors that happen to be important from that perspective. At other times, the perspective is more macro or national.

The impact of the four sets of factors identified above could be of different kinds. There could be an immediate impact in terms of an Act passed by the parliament or an executive order influencing the use of resources. Alternatively, there could be an impact on related sectoral policy which influenced the manner in which future projects were evaluated or granted approval. Finally, a change in the macro policy environment could occur which resulted in a mainstreaming of environmental issues. Each of these impacts has the potential of initiating an iterative process that influences decision-making in the future. The objective is to provide a broad direction for environmental policy in a situation fraught with multifarious challenges.

Having identified possible drivers of change in environmental policy, the analysis in the following chapters illustrates the impact of the drivers on policy in different ways. In the context of empirical reality impacting policy, the sector land and forests are selected for in-depth understanding. Climate change policy illustrates overwhelmingly the influence of international drivers. A more macro approach is adopted for studying the influence of environmental justice movements and of evolving and better knowledge.

References

Bleuming B, Yun S-J (2016) Giving green teeth to the tiger. In: Dale G, Mathai MV, De Oliveira JAP (eds) Ideology, political economy and the alternatives. Zed Books Ltd, London
Collander D, Kupers R (2014) Complexity and the art of public policy, solving society's problems from the bottom up. Princeton University Press, Princeton and Oxford
Government of India (1952) First Five Year Plan. Planning Commission, Delhi
Government of India (2013) Twelfth Five Year Plan, (2012–2017) faster, more inclusive and sustainable growth, vol I. Sage Publications, New Delhi
Government of India (n.d.) Successive plan documents. Planning Commission
Government of India, Planning Commission (2008) Eleventh Five Year Plan (2007–2012) Volume 1, inclusive growth. Oxford University Press, New Delhi
IPBES (2016) In: Ferrier S, Ninan KN, Leadley P (eds) The methodological assessment report on scenarios and models of biodiversity and ecosystem services, summary for policymakers. Secretariat of the Intergovernmental Science-Policy Platform on Biodiversity and Ecosystem Services, Bonn
Millennium Ecosystem Assessment (2005) Ecosystems and human wellbeing, policy responses, volume 3, findings of the Policy Responses Group. Island Press, Washington, DC
Rist G (2002) The history of development: from Western origins to global faith. Zed Books, London
UNDP (1991) Human development report. Oxford University Press, New York

Chapter 2
Land and Forest Policy: Resources for Development or Our Natural Resources?

2.1 The Issue

Land, water and forests dominate the range of natural resources significant in India's development. These resources have also been at the centre of several policy interventions: policy declarations, acts and rules as well as incentivising and restraining tax and subsidy structures. Simultaneously, there exists a plethora of literature on the nature of the use of these resources emerging from the social and the natural sciences. Field reality observed by social scientists and their natural science counterparts has been documented extensively in the last three to four decades. In the last few decades, non-governmental organisations in the development sector have also contributed significantly to the understanding from the grassroots on issues related to these sectors. The questions we ask here in this chapter are: Has the policy direction been impacted by the understandings from this literature? What is the empirical learning policy link? Who are the stakeholders and intermediaries who count?

2.2 The Legacy: Centrally Governed Forest Land and Privileged Private Land

Land, when viewed in the official agricultural statistics of India, is divided into several classes. These categories are net sown area, current fallows, fallows other than current, cultivable waste, pastures and other grazing lands, barren and unculti-vable land, area put to nonagricultural use and forests. They relate mainly to the use to which land is being put, with net sown area or agricultural land and forest land constituting the larger part of the geographical area. One could reclassify the geographical land area in the country from the perspective of rights over it, with a more nuanced perception of rights. Land can be thought of as (a) privately owned mainly agricultural land; (b) forest land which is mainly government owned; (c) common

K. Chopra, *Development and Environmental Policy in India*, SpringerBriefs in Economics, DOI 10.1007/978-981-10-3761-0_2

land which may be pastureland, village land or fallow, both current and other than current; and (d) privately cultivated land within forests. Further, when we distinguish between ownership rights and user rights, the cross classification between the official categories and the property rights-based categories is closer to the field reality. Community user rights over even privately owned land left fallow (current fallows) may exist. The same is true for government-owned forests which allow grazing rights and even limited fuel collection rights to local communities. This spectrum of rights allows for increases in consumption and welfare of the communities outside of the income generation from privately owned land. The details have been recorded extensively in the literature.

In the policy narratives since independence or even before it, two categories in the above classification dominate: forest land and private agricultural land. Forest land constituted a category where state ownership dominated with pockets of private and common forest land. Legal ownership of about 95% of the forest area was vested with the state. Centrally governed forests had been the target of policy statements since the end of the nineteenth century. After independence, they continued to be seen as the source of a range of goods essential for development. In general, at that stage in the development of the economy, natural resources were viewed as resources mainly for use. Conservation of natural resources was mentioned as an objective of policy only in the context of wildlife and national parks and administered by a central government (through its forest department) in continuation of the colonial state's assumption of its 'eminent domain' over the forested landscape. The National Forest Policy of 1952 placed the needs for national and industrial development above those of the local people. Lele and Menon (2014) notes that 'more lands were brought under the category of reserve forests, and silviculture in state forests was even more emphatically aimed at meeting the industrial needs of a modernising India. …remarkably this period was not even marked by major protests or debates, as the newly independent state focussed attention elsewhere'.[1]

Private agricultural land was the other category which dominated the policy narrative during this period. Roughly 30% of land in India consists of net sown area, or land under agricultural cultivation, which is, in the main, privately owned. Its productivity, measured as agricultural output per unit of land, was perceived to be significant for reduction of poverty through generation of farm incomes and for achieving self-sufficiency in food for the country. Right through the earlier decades after independence, the dominant perhaps the only paradigm of agricultural development was built around increasing agricultural productivity of land. Shah (2014) notes, for instance, 'it is important to note the critical role of land productivity in influencing both income poverty as well as human development , where irrigation is seen as the main driver'. From this perspective, therefore, the focus of policy initiatives was on privately owned land which could contribute to agricultural production. Common land did not enter the dominant discourse of policy.

During the Green Revolution era in agriculture which started from the mid-sixties, priority was given to increasing productivity of land to provide for more

[1] See Lele and Menon (2014) pp. 4–5.

food for the population. Using hybrid seed varieties, fertilisers and surface irrigation was considered the way forward. Extracting more provisioning services from the land and water endowment was the priority in the face of an increasing population and political constraints on imports. Food self-sufficiency was achieved; poverty decreased in Green Revolution regions, but these developments bypassed other large areas, in particular, the dryland regions.

In other words, policies with respect to land and water were focussed on the provision of inputs to facilitate adoption of the new agricultural technology. Expansion of irrigated areas and provision of subsidised fertiliser and water were the focus. Canal irrigation was extended to large tracts with large-scale public investment. This was the time which saw the beginning of subsidised and even free power for agriculture. Given the historical importance of agriculture in India, irrigated agriculture has been highly favoured in receiving disproportionately high fiscal inputs and incentives from the government. This was often at the cost of common property, watershed areas and dryland areas[2]. A dominant farmer lobby had voice at the centre and the states, and its views continued to prevail. A significant and even dominant stakeholder group had been created.

Simultaneously, in the early period after independence, the tenets of social justice in land ownership also entered the considerations of policymakers, though in a limited manner. It happened mainly in the 1950s when legislation related to issues such as the abolition of zamindari, the land reforms and the setting up of cooperative farms was put in place. It was not easy. Land was a 'state subject' under the Constitution of India. And an amendment to the Constitution was required to enable the zamindari abolition to be carried through in the states. Even in the process of this focus on 'social justice', the large variety of institutional arrangements which governed the use of land and forests were very little understood. The overextraction from private zamindari forests following the declaration of their intended takeover by the state was not noted. It was not understood that this overextraction reflected an underlying distrust of the impending state control. This may have been due, in part, to the absence of records regarding detailed user-based property rights on forest land. In the event, the initiatives had a limited degree of success.

2.3 India's Common Lands: An Un-understood and Neglected Category

Common land as a category was little understood in the policy arena up to the 1990s. No specific acts or rules targeted common land in this period. A few studies in the 1980s tried to establish the macro picture with respect to common lands by cross classifying accepted land use categories and common land categories. They

[2] See Chopra (2016). Her presidential address in 2004, printed in ISAE (2016). Also see Introduction by Sen (2016) in the ISAE volume of 2016. References to common property resources in agriculture came in the presidential addresses of the Indian Agricultural Economics conference only after 1991.

concluded that CPR area was about 21% of geographical area. When looked at statewise, it varied from 10–11% to 30%, with some higher outlying values too.[3] Further, both ecologists and the few economists who examined issues from a field-oriented perspective concluded that degradation happened when property rights were in the hands of the state with very little concern given to participation of local communities and recognition of their traditional rights.[4] Even up to the late 1980s, these field level realities did not find reflection in government policy.

Simultaneously, poverty reduction in the wake of the agriculture-led growth of the 1960s and 1970s was concentrated in a few regions. Chronic poverty continued to be widespread among both rainfed regions and forests, due to the intrusion on their lifestyles and the absence of an understanding of the nature of their property rights. Pockets of poverty overlapped with those of forest cover.[5] Significant natural resources were found in forests, under state control and ownership for the most part, but also sometimes within watersheds, waterbodies and common lands under varying degrees of common property or open access. It was documented in the literature of the 1980s and 1990s that CPRs (common property land resources) constituted 20–30% of the land area in arid and semiarid parts of the country, that they supported the poor in times of distress and contributed to consumption also in normal times. A consumption of products from forests and waterbodies by the poor prevented starvation and contained hunger, in the presence of poverty. No policy initiatives took this dependence into account. We find therefore that the concentration of agricultural growth in a few of the irrigated river valleys of the country and a lack of understanding of the nature of property and user rights in forested and other common lands of the country constituted a double whammy for the people of these regions. It prevented reduction in poverty by the agency of the new technology, and it took away from them the fall back option of dependence on common lands in times of distress.

As it happened, 'traditional rights' whether of the user rights variety or of the ownership rights and privileges type had evolved over centuries and had been shaped over time, sometimes impacted by the preceding centuries of colonial rule. Interestingly, the British did not tamper too much with the structures that existed in large tribal and forest regions of the country.[6] This complex network of property rights that governed access to and ownership of land was not understood in policy circles, even in independent India. *The only concerns which found expression in the legislation on land of that period related to privately owned land and perceived economic development emerging from it.*

It is interesting to note that this neglect of large sections of land rights happened when rural India was perceived to be of prime importance in the political reckoning of the dominant ruling party. The dominant stakeholders in the rural countryside

[3] See Chapter 2 of Chopra et al. (1990) for estimates.

[4] Jodha(1986), Chopra et al. (1990)

[5] Several studies during that period documented this.

[6] See the study by Upadhyaya et al. (2006) for details of rights, privileges and concessions in the state of Himachal Pradesh.

were owners of agricultural land, and the world view of the government with respect to agriculture fitted into their interests.

2.4 Taking Partial Cognisance of Field Reality: Change Through the JFM and Watershed Guidelines in the 1990s

Following on the Chipko movement of the 1970s and the initial experiments in West Bengal, Haryana and Jharkhand, the significance of managing forests with communities was understood. The decade of the 1990s was significant from the viewpoint of new initiatives in forest and watershed development policy and guidelines. Joint Forest Management, in a number of different hues, was adopted in the early years of this decade. The June 1990 circular from the central government to the states asking them to involve local communities in forest management was an upshot of different developments, some of which we list below:

1. Different initiatives of improved conservation with local participation at local levels, documented by academics and activists.
2. Forward-looking foresters were a part of some of these initiatives, e.g. in Bengal[7].
3. A forward-looking perspective of the government of the day, first spelt out in the National Forest Policy (1988) and then in the Guidelines for Watershed Development Government of India (1992) both of which followed also internalised some principles of participatory development.

The Joint Forest Management initiatives and their recognition by the governments of several states resulted in several varieties of partnerships between the state and people in the management of forests. The rather innocuous-looking DO order of 1990 heralded the beginning of a limited understanding in policy circles. The significance of a range of issues relating to ownership rights, user rights and traditional privileges on forest and common land entered the gambit of discussion in the policy arena. Note that this took place through an understanding of the 'forest land' and 'water' route. Several states adopted one or the other form of Joint Forest Management, and by 2010, the central government claimed that more than one-third of the forest estate in the country was under participatory management.

In parallel, the watershed was recognised as an ecological unit for analysis and action by the Watershed Guidelines of 1992 (as a consequence of the Hanumantha Rao Committee report). These guidelines even mandated the setting up of an institutional structure with peoples' participation at the core, prior to the release of any government funds for the development of watersheds. It seemed that there was a willingness within the government to accept new modes of thinking. The state

[7] Chatterjee, among others, (1996) documents the factors involved in the Arabari experiment in West Bengal.

seemed responsive to the diverse critiques of NGOs, social activists and transnational funding agencies. The watershed programme met with considerable degree of success in different states. In particular, in Madhya Pradesh, the programme was converted into the mission mode. As commented upon by Hanumantha Rao, 'the single most important factor accounting for the positive impact of the watershed development under the government sponsored programme … is community participation and decentralisation of programme administration made possible under the new guidelines. This has come about on account of political and bureaucratic commitment to the new strategy'.[8] The 1990s saw the beginning of some change.

An important, albeit contestable source of that change was the National Forest Policy (1988) which was at the time hailed as a forward-looking one. In stating its objectives, it said that 'the principle aim should be to ensure environmental stability and ecological balance…… The derivation of direct economic benefit must be subordinated to this principal aim'. However, the statement of objectives included several others, without any attempt at prioritisation 'increasing productivity of forests for meeting essential national needs, meeting requirements of fuel-wood, fodder, minor forest produce and small timber of rural and tribal populations' and even 'checking the extension of sand-dunes in the deserts of Rajasthan'.

A contradiction of sorts emerges when we look at this shopping list kind of listing, in particular in conjunction with the different Acts and Rules enacted from time to time. While such a contradiction characterises many aspects of environmental policy, the next section views the forest sector in depth to illustrate the confounding implications and the scope it created for judicial intervention.

2.5 Forests as a Case Study: A Story of Policies, Acts, Rules and Judicial Intervention

Three interlinked components constitute the focus of interventions by governments: overarching policy statements, usually enunciated at the centre; laws passed that give substance to the policy and rules, often laid out both by the centre; and states which guide the nitty-gritty of action on the ground. The National Forest Policy (1988) and the institutional changes represented by JFM and the Watershed Guidelines exemplified the first. However, the evolution of acts and rules in the next two decades tells another story. There existed an overconcern in policy circles with two forest-related issues: its conversion to non-forest land and its extractive potential in terms of fuelwood, fodder and non-timber forest products. Such a focus led to several anomalies creating a space for judicial intervention.

The Forest Act (1980) and the subsequent rules (including the Forest Conservation Rules, 2003) increased sequentially central control over procedures for conversion of forest to non-forest land. Note that the Act of 1980 said: 'No state government or

[8] See Hanumantha Rao (2000). It is a different matter how these worked out in practice. Several writers have commented on it. Note in particular Baviskar(2008).

any other authority, or any other authority shall make, except with the prior approval of the Central government any order directing...............that any forest land or any portion thereof be used for any non-forest purpose..' implying that all proposals for conversion had to go to the central government. By 2003, more detailed procedures for appointment of the committee to approve such conversion had been laid down.[9]

The principles behind the introduction of the JFM and the Watershed Guidelines which referred to more decentralised management and the above centralisation are in direct conflict. There seemed to exist two parallel tracks in policy on forest management. Principles of joint management and community involvement took account of ground reality as studied and reflected in academic and civil society debate. But when it came to enacting law and rules, however, several factors militated. Among them are:

(a) The sheer absence of trust in local communities and their capabilities to manage forests
(b) The inherent faith that the government knows best
(c) The coming together of interests of more vocal groups such as industry and mining
(d) The unshakeable faith that these groups represent development, partly due to the absence of alternative paradigms of development

2.6 The Judiciary in Forest Policy

The conflicting threads in forest and land policy gave rise to possibilities of differential interpretations. This was compounded by the large diversity of situations over which uniform rules were sought to be imposed. In the event, another critical voice became that of the judiciary, represented by the Supreme Court which started taking unequivocal stands. Given the legally enforceable nature of its pronouncements, these had a long-standing impact on public policy on natural resource issues. So much so that a case filed in a court of law in 1995 became an important landmark in the forestry policy debate. For the next decade and more, the Godavarman case of 1995 became the pivot of almost all discussions around forest policy.[10]

Note what Rosencranz et al. (2007)[11] say on the matter, 'In 1995, T.N. Godavarman Thirumulpad filed a writ petition with the Supreme Court of India to protect the Nilgiris forest land from deforestation by illegal timber operations. The Supreme Court expanded the *Godavarman* case from a matter of ceasing illegal operations in one forest into a reformation of the entire country's forest policy. In its first order on

[9] See Government of India (2004).

[10] See Lele and Menon (2014) who wish foresters and policymakers to look beyond JFM, Godavarman and tigers as the three focal points of forest policy.

[11] See Rosencranz et al. (2007) for an in-depth analysis.

the *Godavarman* case, the Court suspended tree felling across the entire country, paralyzing wood-based industries. Despite a series of subsequent orders with far-reaching implications,the case is still pending in the Supreme Court. In the process of hearing over 800 interlocutory applications since 1996, the Court has assumed the roles of policymaker, administrator of policy, and interpreter of law'.

It was claimed that through the *Godavarman* case, the Supreme Court had assumed a legislative role. The consequence of this position taken by the court was, among other things, the December 1996 order which extended the boundaries of forest areas and defined what it called 'forest-like areas'. This interpretation came in conflict with existing legal classifications of land in several states and resulted in several further conjectures, among them by mining and other non-forest interests.[12]

In time, the Supreme Court (SC) also found that the increased micro management of the vast forests of the country had become more and more intractable. *The court had entered into a territory too complex and diversified for its centralised interpretation and control.* In 2002, it set up its own Central Empowered Committee (CEC). Another institution had been created which was to have ramifications for policy in the future.

Conversion of forest land and amounts to be paid for it continued to be the central issue in forest-related litigation. The CEC in particular brought concepts such as net present value (NPV) into the jargon. The SC again appointed an Expert Committee in 2005 to throw light on matters of contention, in particular the understanding that amounts paid for conversion of forest land to non-forest use were miniscule in particular when compared to the value of the ecosystem services of forest land.

The first decade of the twenty-first century thus saw a nod by the highest court of the land in the direction of the new understanding from academia on forests and their ecosystem services.

Though the findings of the Expert Committee[13] were diluted considerably by the time acceptable levels of NPV payments were recommended, a process had been set in motion.

This was the first time after 1990/1992 that new understandings from ecosystem studies had been imported into the policy domain. Additionally, a continuity in inputs from the ivory towers of academe had been ensured. The committee for revision of NPV rates which submitted its report in 2015 bears testimony to this.

One of the consequences of this happenstance was the continuing debate on the distribution of the funds collected under CAMPA (as a consequence of the imposition of NPV for conversion of forest land) between the states, the centre and the local bodies. Local bodies were more or less left out of the reckoning and a great deal of attention given to the distribution between the centre and the states.

---

[12] See the discussion in Khanna (2014), in particular relating to controversies over 'orange areas' in Madhya Pradesh and certain areas notified under Sections 4 and 5 of the Punjab Land Preservation Act (1900).

[13] See Chopra et al. (2006) for details of the recommendations.

Meanwhile, the old mindset of focussing on fund distribution as a measure of success remained. The State CAMPA funds were set up as a result of the 2009 order being passed (amount collected at the centre was 30,000 crores at that time), and the amicus curiae promptly told the court that the fund released to states was more than the combined budget of all state forest departments. The questions arise: Are we measuring success through money collected and dispersed? Or was NPV meant to be an economic deterrent to forest conversion? The original intention behind collection of the funds in CAMPA had been forgotten.

2.7 And What of Institutional Change to Decentralised Community Management?

Old mindsets and earlier administrative structures also continue to come in the way of JFM and watershed programmes. JFM turned out to be a top-down initiative which came before its time, with not enough readiness for it, either at the governmental level or the community level. It was not truly participative in its conception as the forest department held the veto of dismissing the managing committee and the key position of secretary was to be with the forest department. Not enough work had been done with communities as well. They were either not prepared or not interested in working out all the design rules that had been left to their domain. This may even have been, in some cases, due to a lack of trust in the forest department originating in the overall authority that it continued to exercise. The legal basis is also claimed to be weak as the arrangement failed to grant security of rights.[14] In a sense then, it could be said to be flawed in terms of its institutional design.

This almost overriding criticism of JFM in practice (based on various factors such as the absence of legal status for forest protection committees, government's right to dissolve them, unilateral inappropriate sharing, etc.) is in sharp contrast to the early enthusiasm expressed by analysts about it. Poffenberger et al., for instance, had claimed that 'it had brought in a reversal of the alienation of forest peoples' rights, of institutional conflict and of ecological patterns of forest degradation'. They claimed also that it could be replicated across regions and states.

To go back one step for perspective, forest user group committees had existed in selected areas of the country much earlier. The Van Panchayats of Uttar Pradesh, the community forestry of Orissa and joint management initiated in West Bengal and parts of Haryana are examples. In the early phases, it was thought that JFM would replicate them. This expectation did not take into account the long-term sociological, legal and cultural dimensions required for the evolution of institutions.

Further and more importantly, a uniform semi-legal structure binding two unequal partners could not be expected to replace the existing dynamics of power

[14] Some commentators claimed that the short-run benefits offered by JFM do not act as additional incentives as they are no different from traditional rights which some communities enjoyed under '*nistar*'.

relations between communities and the forest department. The consequence as expected was that they succeeded partially in very limited pockets where the change expected of the stakeholders was gradual.

As stated earlier, watershed development programmes were adopted in several states. The mission mode in which it was adopted in Madhya Pradesh was spectacular. Its operation, in particular in the district of Jhabua, was heralded initially as the reinvention of governmental and non-governmental institutions.[15] Baviskar (2008) documents however 'the multiple ways in which the mission is appropriated by the situated knowledge and orientations of these actors.(state actors and villagers). An ecologically-rational rendering of the mission is superseded by the tricky tasks of negotiating with tenurial conflicts, troublemakers and administrative tenets'.[16]

In hindsight, too much was expected from both JFM and watershed management. They were thought of as a kind of 'panacea' for ending conflicts between the forest department and the people and for increasing forest productivity. Extensive literature on policy-making now tells us that 'panaceas' and 'thought of panaceas' often fail, the reason being the complex dynamics of the manner in which different stakeholders respond to the intervention.[17] And the stakeholders in the forestry sector had inherited more power and information. They called the shots in the partnership. Extensive documentation and information dissemination by activists and academics and the process of development and with it the spread of literacy among the population changed the scenario. But this happened slowly and will take time.

2.8 The Tilt Towards Growth: To and Fro Movement

The last decade of the twentieth century and the first one of the twenty-first also saw a great deal happening in the academic arena as far as forests were concerned. Concepts such as ecosystem services of forests had made headway internationally. Academia in India had been exposed to a great deal of this thinking, and individual studies on valuation of forests had internalised these approaches. The late 1990s had seen the World Bank's capacity building programme, an academic initiative which ran across several institutions in the country giving a thrust to the manner in which sociologists, economists and others thought of the environment. It had been a heady time for academic thinking on environmental issues internationally. And forests and water occupied pride of place in matters Indian academics wanted to research on.

A proliferation of stakeholders with voice in forest governance had indeed taken place. And the role of the courts had accentuated the process. *Court intervention being a long-drawn affair added to the number of stakeholders and processes to be followed. Meanwhile, short duration and fast operating market forces create their*

[15] See Agarwal (1998) and Agarwal et al. (1999).

[16] For details see Baviskar in Chopra and Rao edited (2008).

[17] See Brock and Carpenter (2007) PNAS.

own stake in the interest of faster use of natural capital and this increases the degradation.

The role of market forces saw a strong resurgence in the first and second decades of the twenty-first century. The old somewhat hesitatingly created communal and participatory structures and rules remained and were paid lip service to but were being slowly, almost imperceptibly, being compromised with in the name of development. A few examples are given below to illustrate this.

The NPV Expert Committee of 2006 had mandated certain 'no-go' areas where conversion of forest land for no-forest use would not be permissible. In the implementation of the revised report (revised by the CEA), this principle was compromised. Further, in the Verma Committee report (2014), revision of rates for forests was extended to all categories of forests, in effect negating the principle of some forests being irreplaceable. The weak sustainability principle had been accepted, even as the per acre value of forests had increased considerably.

The case of the Western Ghats provides another instance of government priorities moving away from conservation of pristine areas. Several committees over the years have been mandated to 'identify parameters for designating ecologically sensitive areas' in the country: the Sen Committee report way back in September 2000, the Committee on Inviolate Forest Areas in 2012 and, in the context of the Western Ghats, firstly the Western Ghats Ecology Experts Panel (WGEEP), set up by the MOEF in March 2010, and then the High-Level Working Group (HLWG) under the chairmanship of K Kasturirangan, which submitted its report in 2013. Each of the committees recommended that ecologically sensitive areas be left untouched, albeit with differences in detail on extent.[18]

After the submission of each of these reports, the government adopted an approach of silence for a considerable period of time. The Gadgil Committee report was put in the public domain only after a judicial intervention. In November 2013, almost 8 months after the submission of the HLWG report, the MOEF accepted it 'in principle' and decided to go ahead with the implementation of its recommendations. However, in unseemly haste, the MOEF through an order issued on December 20, 2013, stated that a final decision would be taken only after consultation with the states. And this took place, when the views of the state governments had already been elicited by the HLWG itself. As of 2016, the to and fro between state governments and the central ministry continues.

A similar scenario is being played out in the Aravali region of Haryana. The anomalies introduced by depending on economic incentives and valuation exercises emerge clearly when we examine land valuation in peri-urban fringes, such as the Aravalis. Driven by high rates of urbanisation, the demand for land for urban construction and infrastructure pushes the price of land to very high levels. Undoubtedly these are higher than 'traditional' valuation of the provisioning ecosystem services (or sometimes even regulating and recreational) provided by these lands. And so the

[18] For more details on the two Western Ghats committees, see Chapter 4, Section VII Expert Committees, Political Economy and Policy Making: The Western Ghats case. See also Chopra (2014).

tensions at the interface between value of land for different uses and by different stakeholders are rapidly increasing. In the face of a huge demand from urban use, driven by purchasing power, retaining land for agricultural or ecological use is not going to be easy. The underlying asymmetries in the distribution of income, information and power result in a very high ability to pay of urban developers leading to high-demand-driven prices. *Therefore, while valuation of land for different ecosystem services may provide additional inputs, an understanding that there exist 'inviolate areas', whether for ecological or distributional justice reasons will have to be a critical component of policy.* Current environmental problem-solving requires decision-makers, ecologists and economists to use 'ethical rationality'[19] in addition to the focus on 'scientific or economic rationality', which they have frequently employed in the past. How else do we factor in the loss of natural capital or the loss of livelihoods for people?

2.9 Conclusions: Stakeholders, Participation and Complexities of Public Policy

We are inevitably led to the conclusion that participation by a range of stakeholders with diverse interests can be very procrastinating and deleterious to critical components of the environment and natural capital. The unevenness in the distribution of information, power and material resources results in confrontations which end in decisions antagonistic to issues focussing on the long run. Most environmental concerns, in particular those relating to land and forests, fall in this category.

What should be the policymakers' role in such situations? There is no one panacea that one can have on offer. Brock and Carpenter (2007) talk of adaptive learning by decision-makers as they proceed. Collander and Kupers (2014) go further and comment on the art of public policy in complex social-ecological systems. Governments need to understand that they are parts of such complex systems with polycentric decision-making (a la Ostrom (2009)). Their actions or interventions can only set in motion a series of actions by diverse stakeholders; so they need to 'nudge' the system towards desired directions. And it is important to remember that a large part of the government implementing and adjudicating components are themselves interested parties (looking to 'rent appropriation') in this complex system. So the nudging has to be through a combination of economic incentives, legal restrictions and social norms. Each of these works through different mechanisms and within different time dimensions, hopefully taking the gamut of complex systems in the right direction.

[19] See Chopra (2011) for a more detailed discussion.

References

Agarwal A (1998) When leaders deliver: power from the people. Down to Earth, December 31 and The Hindu, October 1998

Agarwal A, Narain S, Sen S (1999) State of India's environment, The fifth citizen's report. Centre for Science and Environment, New Delhi

Baviskar A (2008) The dream machine: the model development project and the remaking of the state. In: Chopra K, Rao C, Hanumantha H (eds) Growth, equity, environment and population: economic and sociological perspectives. Sage Publications, New Delhi

Brock WA, Carpenter SR (2007) Panaceas and diversification of environmental policy. Proc Natl Acad Sci 104(39):15206–15211

Chatterjee AP (1996) Community forest management in Arabari: understanding socio-cultural and subsistence issues. Society for the Promotion of wastelands Development, New Delhi

Chopra K (2011) Managing transformational change: guiding principles from a systems' perspective. Economic and Political Weekly, January 15–22, 2011

Chopra K (2014) Conservation and development in the Western Ghats a tale of two committees and more. Econ Polit Wkly XLIX(11):12–14

Chopra K (2016) Price and non-price reforms in Indian agriculture: a re-examination and some reflections. In: Indian Society of Agricultural Economics (ed) Indian agricultural economy under liberalised regime, vol 3. Academic Foundation, New Delhi

Chopra K, Kadekodi GK, Murty MN (1990) Participatory development: people and common property resources. Sage Publications, New Delhi

Chopra K, Kadekodi GK, Eswaran VB (2006) Report of the Expert Committee on Net Present Value, submitted to the Supreme Court of India

Colander D, Kupers R (2014) Complexity and the art of public policy: solving society's problems from the bottom up. Princeton University Press, Princeton/Oxford

Government of India (1992) Guidelines for watershed development

Government of India (2004) Handbook of Forest (Conservation) Act, 1980, Rules(Conservation), 2003, Guidelines and Clarifications(up to June 2004). MOEF, New Delhi

Jodha NS (1986) Common property resources and the rural poor in the dry regions of India. Econ Polit Wkly XXX(27):1169–1181

Khanna S (2014) The Godavarman case and beyond. In: Lele S, Menon A (eds) Democratising forest governance in India. Oxford University Press, New Delhi

Lele S, Menon A (eds) (2014) Democratising forest governance in India. Oxford University Press, New Delhi

Ostrom E (2009) Beyond markets and states: polycentric governance of complex economic systems Nobel Prize lecture, Stockholm

Rao CHH (2000) Watershed development in India: recent experience and emerging issues. Econ Polit Wkly XXXV(45):3943–3947

Rosencranz A, Boenig E, Dutta B (2007) The Godavarman case: the Indian Supreme Court's breach of constitutional boundaries in managing India's forests. ELR News Anal 37(1):10032–10042

Sen A (2016) Introduction. In: Indian Society of Agricultural Economics (ed) Indian agricultural economy under liberalised regime, vol 3. Academic Foundation, New Delhi

Shah A (2014) Natural resources and chronic poverty in India: interface and policy imperatives. In: Barrett S, Maler K-G, Maskin ES (eds) Environmental and development economics: essays in honor of Partha Dasgupta. Oxford University Press, Oxford

Upadhyaya S et al (2006) "Estimating the economic value of forest land: a methodology: the legal perspective" report submitted to the Supreme Court Committee on NPV of Forest Land

Verma M et al (2014) Revision of rates of NPV applicable for different classes/categories of forests. Centre for Ecological Services Management, Indian Institute of Forest Management, Bhopal

Chapter 3
Climate Change Policy in India

Evolution Through Internationally Driven Changes

Climate change has been termed one of the greatest challenges that humans face today. There is now a consensus among scientists that climate change is indeed underway. Also that it is due to human activities in the form of emission of greenhouse gases, mainly, but not solely from the burning of fossil fuels since the start of the Industrial Revolution in the eighteenth century. While episodes of such variations in climate have happened in the past too, the concern is that equilibrium global temperature and other changes in climate could happen such as to result in catastrophic changes, posing major challenges. Further, the hope is that since the process is human induced, we can act to reverse the trend. That action has however to be undertaken at a global level, with the concurrence of the governments of the nation states comprising our world. This introduces the second challenge in the context of climate change, that of framing a policy which brings on board governments of disparate countries, disparate in terms of economic and social development, as also mindsets in relation to international issues.

3.1 Climate Change Policy: Early Phases

The beginning of serious political attention to the issue of climate change internationally began with a series of conferences in the 1980s which attempted to lay down a process for formalising available scientific evidence and presenting it to the world community through the agency of the United Nations. To this end, the International Panel on Climate Change (IPCC) was established in 1988, through a resolution in the UN General Assembly which recognised climate change as a 'common concern of mankind'. A structure with working groups and a bureau was set up at the IPCC's first session. The structure has remained more or less the same over the years, and the IPCC has now produced five reports, with the last one being submitted and approved by UNFCCC (the United Nations Framework Convention on Climate Change) member countries in 2014. The IPCC is a mechanism for bringing

K. Chopra, *Development and Environmental Policy in India*, SpringerBriefs in Economics, DOI 10.1007/978-981-10-3761-0_3

the best of available science together to act as the anchor for negotiations on this problem of concern to all.

Simultaneously, there was need to set up a single international process for negotiations between governments as well. And, through a separate resolution in 1990, the UN General Assembly established a distinct and unique negotiation process to conduct negotiations on climate change on an international platform. The UNFCCC was adopted in 1992, after 2 years of intense negotiations. To date, 193 countries have ratified the treaty. Since then a two yearly meeting of the Conference of Parties has been held. All parties have agreed to protect the climate system for the benefit of present and future generations of humankind, on the basis of equity and in accordance with their 'common but differentiated responsibilities and respective capabilities'.

It is significant that, right from the outset, the governments of the world were given a significant role in the IPCC process in order to obtain their 'buy-in'. The building up of a credible body of knowledge required the participation of experts from all over the world, and these experts, the reviewers and the authors were almost all selected from lists submitted by governments of UN member states. It is a framework designed jointly by the scientific community, and the governments with the former mandated to make available scientific evidence to the latter. Each IPCC submitted reports on state of the science, its impacts and on response options available. These reports are then approved in plenary sessions of the IPCC where all governments are represented to further ensure their buy-in by the world community. The focus of this initiative was certainly on crafting a policy acceptable to the governments of the world.

Climate change policy evolved in India as a consequence of these international developments, more so in the political sphere. With the setting up of the International Panel on Climate Change (IPCC) in 1988 and the Special Committee on the Participation of Developing Countries in June 1989, India stood in need of knowledgeable negotiators. It was a case of an internationally determined 'top-down' need for taking a position on climate change or adopting a climate change policy.

In the initial years, India was looked upon in global forums as forward looking in issues relating to the environment. As stated by Gupta and Mandal (*2015*), 'India started the UNFCCC negotiations in the early nineties from a position of strength. It had attended the Stockholm Conference at the highest level, it had passed a number of laws to protect the environment, it had some internationally renowned climate scientists, it had strong green activists who had ensured that the 1992 Rio Earth Summit included the right to development as one of the pillars of the new world'.

The first IPCC report (1990) had a significant impact on the negotiations leading up to the United Nations Framework Convention on Climate Change (UNFCCC) and the 1996 report contributed decisively to the formulation and signing of the Kyoto Protocol. The principle of 'common but differentiated responsibility' was the bedrock of this protocol, and the developed countries (Annexe I countries) were to be in the forefront of action on climate. No binding action was envisaged for the non-Annexe I countries (mainly the developing world). This was acclaimed as a huge victory for the developing countries. Then there followed a period of 'wait and watch' followed as several governments (?) including that of the USA failed to ratify and sign the protocol. The protocol was also considered by some scholars to be fatally flawed.[1]

By the first decade of the twenty-first century, negotiations on climate change had become more intense, and positions taken by individual governments had hardened. During these 30 years, Indian climate change policy evolved along several dimensions. Debates around ethics and distributional issues intensified and were heavily lobbied for. Simultaneously, various alignments have emerged among groups of nations. This chapter shall review these dimensions in an effort to assess how international pressures can mould policy.

3.2 Climate Policy Within India: The Indian Position from the 1980s

Climate change policy was not the focus of attention of academics or environmentalists in India in the 1980s. There were several other issues of immediate concern such as large dams, industrial disasters and forest degradation, energy and fuelwood policies and so on. It suited us to relegate climate change to the position of a developed country problem. India held that climate change had been caused by the developed world and should be solved by them. This position fitted into our perception of equity as a significant cornerstone of India's development policy, both domestically and internationally.

In 1991, Agarwal and Narayan of the Centre for Science and Environment (CSE) published a seminal paper which articulated a position most academics and activists sympathised and agreed with. It put equality of per capita emissions at the centre of the concern for climate justice, arguing that the global commons needed to be shared equally. This remained the cornerstone of the Indian position for a long time. At that time, very little attention was paid to the impact of climate change on India. The science seemed ambivalent about the likely effects, and it was agreed that 'the challenge of development was far more significant than the threat of climate change'.[2] The IPCC had divided possible response actions that could be undertaken into two categories: mitigation and adaptation. We rejected undertaking any actions to mitigate carbon emissions as an unnecessary and unjustifiable claim on existing/available resources.

---

[1] See the analysis by Scott Barett (2005).

[2] For a succinct exposition of the Indian position, see S. Lele (2014) in Dubash edited volume.

3.3 India in the World: A Self-Created Isolation (1997–2005)

In this phase, we see a singular lack of a forward-looking perspective on climate policy from all sides of the policy-making spectrum in India. A limited understanding of the realities of global negotiations continued to prevail. The official negotiators depended mostly on an unchanging brief which consisted of two main parts: first, ensure India's right to development is not hampered in any way. Second, maximise the money, technology transfer or any other support available from rich countries.

This lack of an evolving policy regime was a consequence of the absence of an interaction between Indian academia and policymakers. The absence of a close cooperation between academics and policymakers at home ensured that India did not really take advantage of the IPCC process to represent and take forward its perceptions. If it had done so, it might have helped to underscore the developing country perspective in subsequent negotiations. In the event, issues of climate justice were not stressed upon within the IPCC process. Maybe, the IPCC reports were preoccupied with setting up a strong case for the science of climate change, which itself was under attack from sceptics on all sides in the initial phases.

Within the IPCC too, the dominance of natural science meant that the policy science interface was neglected. At the outset, response options, divided into mitigation and adaptation, evoked a sharp response with mitigation being rejected outright by the Indian official position, in line with its policy of 'the western world needs to correct what it created'.

Academics in India too did not rise to the occasion and see the issue of climate change as one of global collective actions. They could not look forward and see that negotiations would fail unless the past was put behind.

Strangely enough, this intransigence in the international context took place when the imperatives of collective action in rural areas were being studied in parallel by many scholars. Issues of the impact of pre-existing inequity and historic injustice among participating agents are endemic in rural society. But it was never asked 'If collective action in rural societies can coexist with these features, is there not an inherent contradiction in stalling global collective action and insisting that the decks be cleared of all historic injustice in international negotiations on the global commons?'

Further, India has been a weak communicator of its position. Its negotiators have been reluctant to speak to the media and civil society representatives, especially if they were not from India. This lack of communication reveals the intellectual rigidity (and perhaps lack of depth) that marked India's position in this phase. It could easily have been corrected with a closer link between the bureaucratic establishments, academia, the media and civil society within the country. In this area in particular, a polycentric approach to policy-making involving different actors (a la Ostrom) would have been the way to go.

3.4 Beginnings of Change: Participation in the CDM and Being a Part of the Solution

The Kyoto Protocol, adopted in December 1997, was acclaimed at that time as a huge success by developing countries. It was based on the principle of 'common but differentiated responsibility' (CBDR) of the nations of the world. Much of the following decade was spent in completing the complex ratification process so that it was ratified only in February 2005 and its first phase was finally determined to run from 2008 to 2012.

Climate science advanced manifold in the period from 1997 to 2008 however, and scientists ratcheted up their warnings, but developing countries failed to initiate effective pressure for more actions from developed countries. Meanwhile, the Clean Development Mechanism (CDM) had been initiated as a part of the Kyoto Protocol mechanism and a shift in India's position took place. This was the first indication that it was accepting mitigation to take advantage of the financial carrot being offered. The requisite institutional structure for the CDM was set up within the country, and over time, India started attracting a large number of CDM projects, second only to China.

In 2008, we see another change in India's stated policy. With the adoption of the National Action Plan on Climate Change (NAPCC) and its eight core national missions running through 2017, India had taken a move towards linking energy security with its development policy and with climate change mitigation and adaptation as co-benefits. Adaptation was linked with building up of coping capacities and resilience, and this link fitted comfortably into a smooth transitioning of the position but with developmental agenda held as still supreme.

With energy efficiency as its focal point, schemes such as Perform, Achieve and Trade (PAT)[3] are also accepted and being taken up for implementation. PAT is indeed structured on the lines of an Emissions Trading Scheme such as the European Union's Emissions Trading Scheme but with energy intensity of production as the target.

From the first decade of the current century, we see a gradual change in India's domestic approach to issues of climate change; a maturing if one may call it so, helped along by more interest of academics and more importantly pushed ahead by the changing international scenario. At international forums, India can justifiably point out towards its efforts at decreasing energy intensity of production and at introduction of renewable sources of energy. Such a stance acquires more significance since the international negotiating scenario has also undergone a change.

This changed stance in policy is best reflected in India's position in the Copenhagen COP of the UNFCCC in December 2009. In the words of the then Environment Minister, 'India has not caused the problem of climate change but it

[3] See Dasgupta, van der Salm and Roy in Ghosh, Mukhopadhyay et al. edited (2016) Nature, economy and Society.

definitely wants to be part of the solution at Copenhagen and beyond'.[4] He termed it as the 'per capita plus approach'. Whereas India's per capita emissions (postulated to reach 3–3.5 tonnes of carbon dioxide by 2030 from the present level of 1–1.2 tonnes) would always remain below that of the developed world, it has started moving on the path of a mix of mitigation measures as part of its NAPCC in sectors such as power, transport, agriculture industry and forestry. An energy intensity reduction target was also announced for 2020.[5] Of course, India insisted that the monitoring review and verification of these will be by Indian institutions, including its purportedly vibrant civil society institutions. By now, India understands that it is one of the countries likely to be hugely impacted by climate change. Of course, the emphasis on finance being provided by developed countries continued to exist.

At Cancun in 2010, India went further and helped in arriving at agreements on contentious topics. It was agreed that 'all countries must take binding commitments, under appropriate legal forms'. While this stance provided negotiating space, at home in India, it was extensively critiqued and seen as a sell-out to the Western nations. It seemed as though domestic stakeholders across the spectrum of political parties viewed it as a sell-out.

3.5 International Stance and Domestic Imperatives: A Contradiction of Sorts

In climate change policy, we see evidence of another kind of phenomenon. Domestically, we seem to be agreed on development at any cost. But the perils of this belief are brought home to us through our international engagements. Policymakers need to engage simultaneously with the two constituencies and chart a path of growth which reconciles the two perceptions. India is gradually moving in that direction with focus on reducing energy intensity, on renewable energy and on low-carbon growth.[6]

This contradiction of a kind between the two constituencies is brought out clearly in the discussion in a recent paper which evaluates expert opinion on climate change policy.[7] The common consensus was that India will not halt the development process but will proactively take steps to mitigate and adapt to climate change. About 67% of experts felt that development needs were too important to be compromised. Further, ' About 73% of the respondents felt that low-carbon growth priorities can be integrated with inclusive growth for better development outcomes, whereas 27%

---

[4] See J. Ramesh (2016) for details of the negotiations.

[5] It was a reduction of 20–25% from 2005 levels by 2020.

[6] See Planning Commission (2014) report on low-carbon growth, the result of an extensive exercise carried out in the Planning Commission. See also Chopra (2011) on the possible focal points in such approaches when viewed from a systems' theory perspective.

[7] See Dutta et al. (2015) for an analysis of expert opinion which clearly illustrates the predicament and the search for ways out of it.

respondents were of the opinion that it was better to focus on inclusive growth and low-carbon growth separately rather than integrate these into a single objective'. Thus, in issues of prioritisation for funding, or where trade-offs between environmental objectives and immediate development needs are involved, decision-making faces difficulties and the longer run perspective may lose out.

Can we afford to focus on inclusive growth and low-carbon growth? Is it even appropriate to bracket the two together? The focus of the Twelfth Plan on inclusive growth is much talked about. Note however for the most part, the discussion of inclusiveness in the Twelfth Plan (2012–2017) is centred on the need for rapid growth, especially in agriculture and manufacturing sectors, without much elaboration of the scope for adoption of a low-carbon path in these sectors. Studies point out co-benefits and costs of mitigation efforts, the centre piece of low-carbon growth. An earlier study indicated (Ghosh *2010*), in the short run, any effort to reduce carbon emissions could lead to a fall in the national income in India. However, a gradual transition to energy from clean sources to mitigate carbon emissions in the long run would not affect the country's economic growth. Similarly, another study (Shukla and Dhar *2011*) showed that it was possible to go with domestic development goals and climate mitigation together as considerable side benefits accrued such as energy security and local pollution abatement. The Dutta et al. (*2015*) study identifies low-carbon interventions in transport and power sectors, easily two of the largest contributors to carbon emissions in India, as those mentioned by experts as having potentially large socio-economic benefits . These could advance inclusive growth through technological and planning interventions. Low-carbon growth and the points of its trade-offs and synergies with inclusive growth need far more critical examination and amplification with research.

3.6 The Changing International Scenario

Two changes mark the international situation now. There has been little success on the most important point India and other developing countries have been trying to make – the equitable sharing of carbon space among every human being in this world. The theory and the justice of this position are unexceptionable. But the problem has been the inability of the world community at large to come up with a formula that can make it work.

The other big trend is that it is no longer a binary climate world, split between developed and developing countries. Several blocs of countries have now emerged, both within and outside the two broad categories of developed and developing nations. These blocs are often overlapping and their shifting as well as relatively constant positions can be confusing.

As put by Gupta and Mandal, 'The world is in the third phase of climate negotiations now. ..... This phase is being marked by a split between the emerging economies and the rest of the developing world. The split has been encouraged by the US and some other rich countries, which point out that China and India, are now the world's largest and fourth largest emitters. The split has enabled rich countries led by the US to effectively dismantle the original UNFCCC pillar of differentiation between rich and poor nations. Despite strenuous efforts by their negotiators, emerging economies such as China and India now have to take a substantial share of the emission control responsibility.'

Further, there is no top-down legal global emission reduction target to be allocated to rich nations. Instead, there are voluntary bottom-up Intended Nationally Determined Contributions (INDCs) by every country. Prior to the Paris Summit in 2015, the INDCs were communicated by all countries, including India. But, as it happens, these voluntary commitments are not enough to limit the global average temperature rise to 2 °C and the greenhouse gas emissions to safe levels. Collective action theory can guide us about why this is so. Given the divergent initial conditions and objectives of the participating entities (countries in this case), this was to be expected. Economic theory tells us that individual countries (agents) acting on their own are unlikely to reach a socially (global) optimal outcome.

We can, however, look at the little progress that has been made post the Paris meeting of the COP. One success that endures is the drawing up of the global technology sharing mechanism. It was India's proposal and it has been accepted by all countries. Also, India has played a key role in preparing the structure of the Green Climate Fund. However, many now see India as a regressive force, in particular since coal continues to be projected as a major source of energy in our future planning scenarios, despite the emissions connected with that use.

In sum, the rich nations of the world have been the dominant stakeholders and drivers of climate policy across the globe. The larger developing country polluters, China and India, have reluctantly understood this, as indeed have other less developed countries. Ideas such as an equal per capita right to the global carbon space describe a far away ideal. Justice has always eluded actualisation. And climate justice is no exception.

3.7 Future Directions for Climate Policy: Co-evolving Institutions

The issue at stake is that policy relating to climate change is viewed in isolation. It needs to be linked to issues such as trade and UNFCCC needs to borrow from the WTO architecture. The linkage between trade and the environment could be incorporated within a new climate treaty to enforce emission limits for trade-sensitive sectors. In this context, trade restrictions applied to nonparticipants would be legitimate and credible, because participating parties would not want non-parties to have trade advantages.[8] Trade, being seen as closer to the short-term interests of

[8] See Walker et al. (2009) for an argument on these lines. To quote, 'International climate agreements must be designed to align national and global interests and curb free-riding.' Borrowing from the WTO architecture, the linkage between trade and the environment could be incorporated

politicians and nation states, would perhaps drive collective action in a more positive direction. Convolution of institutions in different sectors of operation offers opportunities for further progress.

In sum, if policy is to be driven by international forces, it becomes even more complex. The top-down-bottom-up dichotomy continues, and given the strong divergences present between nations and expressed strongly by national governments, the outlook looks pretty dismal.

References

Barett S (2005) Environment and statecraft: the strategy of environmental decision making. Oxford University Press, Oxford

Chopra K (2011) Managing transformational change: guiding principles from a systems' perspective. Econ Polit Wkly, January 15–22 2011

Dasgupta S, van der Salm F, Roy J (2016) Designing PAT as a climate Policy in India: issues learnt from EU-ETS. In: Ghosh N, Mukhopadhyay P, Shah A, Panda M (eds) Nature economy and society: understanding the linkages. Springer, New Delhi

Dutta V, Dasgupta P, Hultmanc N, Gadagc G (2015) Evaluating expert opinion on India's climate policy: opportunities and barriers to low-carbon, inclusive growth. In Taylor and Francis (ed) Climate and development, pp 1–15

Ghosh S (2010) Examining carbon emissions economic growth nexus for India: a multivariate cointegration approach. Energ Policy 38(6):3008–3014

Government of India (2014) The final report of the expert group on low carbon strategies for inclusive growth. Planning Commission, Government of India

Gupta J, Mandal T (2015) Hot air, climate negotiations and India, India Climate Dialogue

Lele S (2014) Climate change and the Indian Environmental Movement. In: Dubash N (ed) Handbook on climate change. Oxford University Press, New Delhi

Ramesh J (2016) Green signals: ecology, growth and democracy in India. Oxford University Press, New Delhi

Shukla PR, Dhar S (2011) Climate agreements and India: aligning options and opportunities on a new track. Int Environ Agreements Polit Law Econ 11(3):229–243

Walker B et al (2009) Looming global-scale failures and missing institutions. Science 325:1345

within a new climate treaty to enforce emission limits for trade-sensitive sectors. New global standards could establish a climate-friendly framework with supporting payments, e.g. for technology transfer, to encourage developing country participation. In this context, trade restrictions applied to nonparticipants would be legitimate and credible, because participating parties would not want non-parties to have trade advantages. Co-evolution of institutions offers a pathway to further progress.

Chapter 4
Rights-Based Approaches: Do Environmental Movements Make a Dent on Policy?

In earlier chapters, we referred to policy statements as overarching principles, which are concretised through the passage of laws and the formulation of rules. Often, the concretisation becomes enmeshed in controversy, due to stakeholder conflicts and asymmetries of power and information.[1] Such controversies are more often than not, resolved to the disadvantage of vulnerable and disadvantaged groups. They then erupt as 'environmental justice movements'. There exists, in different parts of the world, a vast and careful documentation of the consequences thereof. Drawing from the documentation for India, this chapter addresses the following issues: What role can such environmental movements play in the formulation of policy and through what channels? Further, what role have they played in the last three decades in India?

4.1 Environmental Movements

Environmental movements replace deliberation and adjudication by the language of rights, livelihoods or value systems. They usually bring together like-minded stakeholders on issues of common interest. They begin as the expression of a collection of ideas held by a group of people, based either on more advanced knowledge or on common interest. This term includes campaigns led by civil society organisations (like Greenpeace, Centre for Science and Environment) and mass organisations of political parties Kerala Sastra Sahitya Parishad (KSSP), protests by members of a panchayat (Plachimada) as well as Andolans (NBA) and Samitis (*Niyamgiri* Suraksha *Samiti*, *Coca-Cola Virudha Janakeeya Samara Samithy*). At times, a movement may be focussed on one geographical location, while at others the rallying point may be a national or even an international issue. They are

[1] See, for instance, the discussions on land and forest policy in Chap. 2.

K. Chopra, *Development and Environmental Policy in India*, SpringerBriefs in Economics, DOI 10.1007/978-981-10-3761-0_4

confrontationist in character, as indeed are all social movements. David Sills (1968) purports that social movements perform two functions:

1. They contribute to the formation of public opinion by providing for the discussion of social and political problems and through the eventual incorporation of some of the movement's ideas into dominant public opinion.
2. They provide training of leaders who then become part of the political elite and may eventually rise to positions of leading statesmen and policymakers.

When examining environmental movements, three kinds of impact (as postulated in Chap. 1) are particularly relevant. Some movements may have an immediate impact in terms of an act passed by the parliament or an executive order influencing the project at hand. Others could impact related sectoral policy or the manner in which future projects are evaluated or granted approval. Finally, a change in the macro policy environment could occur which results in a mainstreaming of environmental issues. Each of these impacts has the potential of initiating an iterative process that influences decision-making in the future. Through one or more of these impacts, movements reach a point where they change or modify the social order and become a part of it. In other words, they have altered the existing legislative, executive or judicial institutions, even if marginally. The life cycle of the movement then comes to an end.[2]

4.2 Successful Early Movements in India: The Silent Valley and the Chipko Movements

Why do the Silent Valley and the Chipko movement seem trailblazers for the success of environmental movements? We argue below that this happened in different ways; the first success was limited to the project in question, while the latter resulted in more fundamental directional changes in forest policy. The Silent Valley covers a relatively small area of about 89.52 km^2 which is rich in both flora and fauna. Ecologists describe it as the sole surviving bit of evergreen forest in the Sashay ranges. In the words of the renowned ornithologist, Salim Ali, 'it is a very fine example of one of the richest, most threatened and least studied habitats on earth' (from Sugathakumari, 'Silent Valley: A Case Study'). The fact that this area is devoid of any human habitation makes it a rarity among ecosystems in India, an otherwise highly populated country. The area has an 'uninterrupted evolutionary history of almost fifty million years'.

In the 1970s, this remote region in Kerala triggered off one of the most intense environmental disputes ever in the history of India. The Kerala State Electricity Board proposed to build a dam across the Kunthipuzha (Silent Valley Hydroelectric Project or KVSP) to create a reservoir in the Silent Valley and use the water for the

[2] See Sills, David L. (1968).

production of electricity. Almost all stakeholders felt they would benefit. The project would bring electricity to several constituents. There was no human habitation, so issues of lost livelihoods or rehabilitation did not arise. The opposition to the project was based purely on an ecological argument. Several Indian naturalists, supported by European naturalists, wrote in the Journal of the Bombay Natural History Society that this valley should be conserved in its pristine form. Simultaneously, social organisations such as the Kerala Sastra Sahitya Parishad (KSSP) an NGO, which had been working for three decades among the masses of Kerala for growing environmental awareness, pitched in. The campaign to save Silent Valley turned out to be a public education programme in many respects. It is instructive to recall some of the significant landmarks.

In April of 1976, the National Council for Environmental Planning and Conservation (NCEPC) appointed a task force under the chairmanship of the eminent environmentalist Zafar Futehally to study the ecological and environmental problems of the Western Ghats. Based on its report, which categorically stated, 'The taskforce feels very strongly that the project should be abandoned and the area declared a Biosphere Reserve', the NCEPC asked the Government of Kerala to stop construction of the Silent Valley Hydel Project (SVHP) in October of the same year. However, the central government was focussed on energy security and several rounds of discussions between stakeholders ensued. In 1977 and 1978, several scientific studies on the flora and fauna of the Silent Valley were conducted. In 1978, the International Union for the Conservation of Nature (IUCN) also urged the Government of India to give up the hydel project. Local organisations and the media took up the case of the Silent Valley too.

However, the fortunes of the Silent Valley and the hydel project proposed to be constructed saw many ups and downs with changes in governments at the centre, and the MGK Menon Committee was appointed by the then Prime Minister only in August 1980. The Menon Committee submitted its report in December 1982 after thoroughly examining various aspects of the SVHP. This report too emphasised the ecological significance of the Silent Valley, and accordingly, the SVHP was finally shelved in 1983. Thus, at least in the Indian context, the SVHP became the only case in which a hydroelectric project, once sanctioned, was abandoned for purely ecological reasons.

While it is tempting to claim that the success was due to the coming together of activism and advanced knowledge, political leadership at the central level played a critical role. It took about 7 years of struggle at different levels. These were also the initial years of environmental consciousness; conflicts were not so sharp and pressure on resources not so acute.

The name of the second movement mentioned above, that is 'Chipko', comes from the word 'embrace', in Hindi. Reddy (1998) notes that 'in early 1973, the forest department allotted ash trees to a private company, presumably for felling. This incident provoked the Dasholi Gram Swarajya Sangha (DGSS) a local cooperative organization to fight against this injustice through lying down in front of timber trucks and burning resin and timber depots, as was done in the Quit India movement. When these methods were found unsatisfactory, it is said that the villagers hugged or embraced or stuck to the trees in the forest to prevent them from being felled by the contractors…….'. It is claimed that the strategy of 'embracing' the trees to resist the felling of the trees was thought of by the local leader Chandi Prasad Bhatt at a meeting of the Dasholi Gram Swarajya Mandal on April 1, 1973. The name 'Chipko' was derived from the consensual strategy of clinging on to the trees as a non-violent direct action (Nepal, Padam 2009: 135–136).

The Chipko movement was a definitive movement in the history of world environmentalism, as stated by Ramachandra Guha (2006). Before that it was thought that 'the poor were too poor to be green'. After that movement, it was realised that the peasants and tribals had a greater stake in the environment than the aesthetically minded urbanites. For the former, there was an issue of livelihoods and survival linked to forests and water. Parallelly with the movement, several academics and researchers had also initiated studies of the links between the so-called common property resources and livelihoods.[3] But the stark manner in which Chipko brought 'the environmentalism of the poor' into the popular imagination remains unparalleled. Its impact had been on the manner in which environmental issues were looked at in the macro policy context.[4]

4.3 Narmada Bachao Andolan: A Movement with Limited Immediate Success

The Narmada Bachao Andolan (NBA) started as early as the late 1970s. Reddy (1998) notes that 'To start with, this movement was centred around the issue of human rights……. The people who emerged as the main leaders of the movement later (like Medha Patkar) were working towards proper rehabilitation programmes for the dam displaced. Due to improper implementation of the rehabilitation programmes by the state, the human rights activists became the articulators of antidam protests. Their demands included complete stopping of the dam and resettlement and rehabilitation benefits to the oustees……. The movement, however, gained wider public attention with mobilization and organization of oustees (mostly tribals) and the joining of the eminent social workers like Baba Amte, Sunderlal Bahuguna and Medha Patkar. Though its wider public attention was due to its coverage (impact) in three states, the most notable feature of this movement is the international support it received'.

The NBA movement and its appeal to the Supreme Court in 1994 led to a stay order by the apex court in January 1995. It restricted construction of the Sardar Sarovar Dam which had already attained 80.5 m height for 5 years to provide additional time for resettling oustees. The struggle was initially focussed on rehabilitation of oustees but later extended to the environmental effects of the dam. In 1999,

[3] See Chap. 2 for some details of these studies.

[4] Some will claim that it was partly responsible for the introduction of Joint Forest Management in the country. Chapter 2 discusses other parallel influences on policy.

the Supreme Court decision accepted implicitly the first claim but not the second on the ground of insufficient information.[5] Eventually, the NBA was not successful in stopping the construction of the SSP.

However, the success or failure of the NBA cannot be analysed in isolation from what has happened later and is happening continuously in the case of other dams. In the context of Indian policy, the rehabilitation and resettlement policies for 'Project Affected Persons' and the use of the term itself in the context of all projects were some of the indirect impacts of the NBA. The SSP offered many lessons and some hope for people affected by other big dams on the Narmada or elsewhere. The World Bank withdrew its funding of the project and set up the World Commission on Dams, the report of which had far reaching consequences. The NBA, therefore, brought worldwide attention to the issues surrounding construction of large dams and had many ramifications for the future.

4.4 The Vedanta Case in Orissa: The Role of Political Economy

The Vedanta Case, which now has a history of more than a decade of to and fro between different stakeholders, concerns a proposal to develop an open cast bauxite mine on the upper reaches of the Niyamgiri hills in Orissa, India. The project would have had a huge impact on the environment and the livelihood of the local communities, destroying an important wildlife habitat and threatening the traditional way of life of the Dongria Kondh tribe's communities, for whom these mountains are sacred. The initial proposal to open the mine was prepared by Sterlite Industries (SIIL) on the basis of an agreement entered into in 2004.[6] On August 8 2008, the Supreme Court granted SIIL the authorisation for the project, only subject to final approval by the Ministry of Environment and Forests (MOEF). The Ministry constituted an independent panel to investigate the project's impact on the local tribes and the wildlife. In August 2010, a negative report was rendered by the panel. According to the panel, the project was not in compliance with several forest conservation and environmental protection regulations. Consequently, the Ministry denied the project approval.

It is to be noted that around the same time, a senior leader of the ruling UPA government had also told the local tribals that 'his work as their "sepoy" (campaigner/representative) at the centre has just begun.' Was it that this political support at the highest level had resulted in the Ministry's decision? Can we consider this as

[5] 'In a two-to-one decision, it invoked the common law doctrine of latches to rule that the NBA had failed to raise its objections in a timely manner, that the Court was not going to review issues related to design of the Sardar Sarovar Dam itself but only the fundamental rights of the oustees guaranteed under Article 21 of the Constitution of India, and reminded the parties that the decision of a Water Disputes Tribunal (WDT) could not be challenged by private parties once it became binding on the states involved'. See Sahoo et al. (2014).

[6] For more details, see Cirone (2012).

the beginnings of a political voice for the 'ecosystem people', in this case the Dongria Kondh tribals?

Be that as it may, the decision of the Ministry was challenged in the Supreme Court in 2011. Subsequently the court asked for a referendum on the issue in the area, referring to the legal requirement for 'prior informed consent' from the affected parties. All the 12 villages in which this referendum was carried out in 2013 rejected the joint venture of Vedanta and the state-owned Orissa Mining Corporation for bauxite mining in the Niyamgiri hills. In May 2014, Vedanta Resources said it would not mine bauxite at the controversial project in Orissa unless it wins over local communities. However, as reported in Down to Earth, a senior Vedanta official was stated to have said, when the new government took charge at the centre in 2014, 'the next Prime Minister will ease us out'.

Further, as stated by Ashish Kothari (2016), 'Loath to give up a lucrative deal, the State government launched a fresh bid to overturn earlier decisions by approaching the Supreme Court again in early 2016 (through its Odisha Mining Corporation). It had, meanwhile, done everything possible to scare the Adivasis into submission through regular harassment (including imprisonment and killing of tribals) by armed police forces. The Adivasis have stood firm in the face of this repression, and the Supreme Court's recent decision is a vindication of their campaign'.

What are we to make of the factors impacting policy from this case study? The agitation in the Vedanta-Niyamgiri case took place in an environment very different from those earlier referred to, in particular the Silent Valley one which had similar undertones. By the first decade of the twenty-first century, more precise national legal instruments relating to environmental issues had been crafted. India was also a party to many international agreements which could be drawn on in support of ecologically sensitive habitats and indigenous peoples. Note, for example, the Convention on Biological Diversity (1992) and the United Nations Declaration on the Rights of Indigenous People (2007). Both of these are ratified by India and are now part of the Indian legal framework. These were indirectly drawn upon by the expert panel on Niyamgiri set up by the Ministry in 2010 (Saxena et al. 2010) and by the Supreme Court in asking for the first ever environmental referendum held in India in 2013. However, it is political support at the highest level and the prevailing economic thinking which continues to be the critical decision-making factor. It was so in the Silent Valley case and it is so now.

The last word on the Vedanta bauxite project and its newer versions is still to be heard. One expects that the current globalised environment, the emphasis on attracting foreign investment and the increased significance of 'short-term growth rates' will impact the decisions taken in this and other projects. As Martinez-Alier et al. (2016) point out, ecological distribution conflicts associated with rising social metabolism are most clearly evidenced in the eastern part of India. This process will take its toll on the ecological wealth of the country.

4.5 Protests Around Water and Air Pollution

Conflicts around water in India are too numerous to document at length. Water has been at the centre of numerous initiatives, protests and movements. It is indeed difficult to even divide them into a predetermined set of categories. This difficulty is stated succinctly by Gujja in Joy et al. (2008).[7] Analysts often divide these protests into those emerging out of issues of water quantity and quality. This is however a somewhat artificial divide as decreases in quantity tend to aggravate quality issues too. In a limited sense, however, this division helps as the laws governing quality issues tend to be far more stringent, leading, at times, to criminal incrimination of the polluting party. In other words, the polluter pays principle becomes easy to apply to the quality deterioration cases. In India, with industrialisation spreading to the hinterland, release of untreated effluents into waterbodies has become widespread. This takes place in spite of several legal stipulations which are in place. Tanneries, paint factories, textile units, chemical units and several others are equally responsible.[8] Consequently, several peoples' protests against the pollution arise as different water users live in close proximity and both health and livelihoods get impacted by it. Fewer conflicts are centred around ecology of lakes and rivers: when they are, livelihoods are a part of the picture too.

Some local water pollution-related movements have resulted in closures of plants: examples that come to mind are Grasim Industries and the Coca-Cola plant in Kerala and Ghodawat Industries in Kolhapur. This happens partly because the protests are against bad implementations of laws that are already in place. Non-compliance, if proved, invites criminal penalty as per law. There is no scope for mediation or deliberative negotiation. Such a situation sometimes alienates sizable public opinion in the country. The National Environmental Policy (2006), some would say justifiably, recommended the opening of pollution issues to mediation under civil law and the facilitation of voluntary compliance. Such mediation would, however, once again bring to the fore the role of different stakeholder groups and of the asymmetries of power and knowledge between them.

Water as a resource figures in several sectors linked to agriculture, in particular as more than 80% of fresh water in India is used by it. Watershed development plans and policies are often configured around water. Large dams and displacement as well as ecological disruption caused by them have been contentious all over the world. Structural interventions and transfers of water over large distances have been preferred policy interventions in this sphere. The impact of these on access for contending users and uses is often overlooked and leaves scope for innumerable kinds of protests and even large-scale movements.

Though the Bhopal Gas Tragedy was a turning point in the understanding of environmental issues in India, ambient air pollution has not been the rallying point for environmental movements on a large scale in India. Perhaps this is because of

---

[7] See Joy, K.J. et al. (2008)

[8] See the review by Appaswamy in Joy et al. (2008).

the limited physical expanse of the issue. In-depth study of the issue by several academic and activist organisations followed the early initiative of the CSE in Delhi. There is evidence of policy having been directly impacted by these initiatives.

4.6 Local Movements and the National Agenda in India: Did They Impact It?

The cases we selected for more detailed scrutiny, the Silent Valley, the Chipko movement, the Narmada Bachao Andolan and the Vedanta-Niyamgiri case are all localised in nature. In the case of water too, we saw that there exist a multitude of movements around specific local concerns. Rootes, Christopher (2007) points out the significance of the study of local environmental groups and movements in the following words: 'Local environmental campaigns are ubiquitous and recurrent, even in times when environmental issues are not salient on the national agenda. Yet their relationship to trans-local environmental movements and issues has been relatively neglected. Local environmental campaigns are variously related to national and local organizations, and the peculiarities of place are one factor in that variation. But place itself acquires meaning through campaigns, and communities forge identity even as they mobilize against threats of their survival. The relationship between local campaigns and global environmental issues is problematic, but the ways in which local mobilizations often combine issues of environment, economic justice and democracy mirror the emerging agenda of transnational environmentalism (Rootes, Christopher 2007: 722)'.

Environmental justice movements across the world have been documented carefully by Martinez-Alier and his colleagues.[9] They put together in immaculate detail how development projects in Latin America, in the USA and in parts of India have been at the cost of livelihoods and lives of the poor, mostly indigenous people. Development is a cost-transferring process with the extraction of minerals, oil, etc. transferring the environment and livelihood costs to the poor, who live at the margins of commodity frontiers. Such documentation of the commonalities across different developing countries is critical in drawing international attention to the magnitude of the injustices involved.[10]

Parallel with the above process, short-run impacts of environmental movements on policy may take place through different routes. There may be a realignment of stakeholder positions. The judiciary and the executive take note and create precedents which then gradually change the nature of future engagement. Such developments are often the consequence of facilitation through careful documentation and

[9]While this has been ongoing work for some time, the Environmental Justice Organizations, Liabilities and Trade (EJOLT) project gave an impetus to it. See Martinez-Alier (2012) and Martinez-Alier et al. (2016).

[10]The EJOLT project has documented about 2000 conflicts and produced an atlas of country and thematic maps (www.Ejolt.org).

analysis by experts. Such analysis helps to bring these issues to the attention of policymakers in a structured fashion. Such a process is sometimes institutionalised through mandatory requirements for expert consultation. At one stage or another, each of the cases studied above involved the constitution of expert committees which may have had an effect, howsoever marginal on the political decision-making. The role of committees as conveyors of the implications of people's movements and purveyors of the state of the knowledge is illustrated well in recent times by the Western Ghats case.

4.7 Expert Committees, Political Economy and Policy-Making: The Western Ghats Case

The Western Ghats was the site of the 'Appiko movement', initiated by local youth in the 1980s in opposition to teak plantation in the Uttar Kannada district of North Karnataka. It had a modicum of success at that time, but the steady onslaught of commercial and industrial interests continued to erode the ecological integrity of the Western Ghats, in spite of a series of protests by several groups. However, by the first decade of the twenty-first century, there existed a dominant public opinion in the country that ecologically sensitive areas (ESAs), including those in the Western Ghats, needed to be protected. Successive pieces of legislation in the last 20 years had also endorsed such an understanding. It seemed that the motivation to conserve at the cost of reckless development existed in several quarters. It was in this vein that the Western Ghats Ecology Experts Panel (WGEEP), chaired by the eminent ecologist, Madhav Gadgil, was set up by the MOEF in March 2010. The committee, after due diligence, submitted its report in August 2011. For some time after this, there was complete silence on the part of the MOEF, which had set up the committee in the first instance. The report seemed to have been forgotten by the Ministry and was made public only in May 2012 after a High Court injunction asking for the same. The reasons for this unwarranted delay can only be conjectured. Perhaps some of its recommendations tilted towards conservation and local-level decision-making which had not found favour with the powers that be or with other dominant stakeholders such as industry.

The story took another turn with the constitution of a second committee called the High-Level Working Group (HLWG) under the chairmanship of K Kasturirangan.[11] The HLWG (popularly referred to as the Kasturirangan Committee) was mandated to examine the implementation of the Gadgil Committee report with a view to holistic development. In a carefully nuanced report, the HLWG recommended that the area to be conserved as ecologically fragile be somewhat smaller than that recommended by the WGEEP earlier. However, it recommended a complete ban on mining, quarrying and sand mining, 'red' category industry thermal

[11] For a detailed comparative analysis of the two reports, see Chopra (2014).

power projects and large urban developments within this area. In these ecologically sensitive areas (ESAs), all projects were to be undertaken after prior informed consent of the villagers. Further, a set of economic incentives were to be set in place for movement towards green growth and sustainable agriculture. In other words, the report envisaged a moving together of the five state governments in the region in pursuance of some common goals in relation to the Western Ghats.

In the wake of the submission of this report, almost all government, civil society and media attention was focussed on the identification of ESAs and the bans imposed therein. Other aspects of the recommendations were completely overlooked. Also, there was criticism from both sides of the spectrum of stakeholders. To begin with, restive voices in civil society immediately claimed that the case for conservation had been compromised, both with regard to the extent of the ESAs and the primacy of local-level decision-making. It completely overlooked the recommendation that Gram Sabhas were to be the drivers of development in ESAs.

State governments responded negatively to the restrictions and bans on some activities within ESAs. These, predictably, related to industries and urban development projects. The restrictions were dubbed as 'antidevelopment'. And this, when all the report was asking for, was an alternative paradigm of development for some parts of the Western Ghats.

Clearly, multiple stakeholders have emerged with powerful voices in the Indian polity, and it is not easy to reconcile their interests. The question that inevitably arises can be posed as follows: Is a movement towards thoughtful conservation and development possible? Are we as a nation at all willing to implement policies that ask for some degree of restraint in the exploitation of our natural resources? Or are we going to pursue a pattern of development which concentrates on the maximisation of present gains of the privileged few to the detriment of the interests of vulnerable people and ecologically fragile areas?

It seems from the above that internalising the learnings of environmental grassroots movements into existing institutional structures is an uphill task. In a deeply divided social and economic milieu, where unequal access to information and wealth is ubiquitous, deliberations will have their shortcomings. There is, in fact, a focus on 'the two cultures' when referring, in particular, to the environment-development debate.[12] One cannot but conclude that a political voice for nature and its wise use has to emerge before policymakers treat the considered and well-researched findings of experts and academics with the care they deserve.

[12] See Jairam Ramesh (2010), for a succinct exposition of the state of the debate and the policymakers' consequent dilemma.

4.8 From Peoples' Movements to Elected Representatives: At Local and/or State Levels

The emergence of a dedicated 'Green Party' seems a long distance away in the Indian context.[13] At times, however, a local expression of concern and anger can find a hearing in representative legislative bodies. A notable example of this is Plachimada panchayat in Palakkad district of Kerala, where a Coca-Cola plant had polluted and depleted groundwater, drying up wells and adversely affecting agricultural productivity and livelihoods. The people of Plachimada forced a proper inquiry into these losses, which showed that they amounted to Rs. 260 crores. On the basis of this evidence, the Panchayat rescinded the company's licence. The panchayat evoked its constitutional rights, arguing that as a local elected government it had the duty to protect the well-being of its citizens. It had the right to cancel – or refuse permission for – anything that affected its citizens adversely. The company's counterargument was that the panchayat was subordinate to the state government, which had granted it the licence, and that it could not operate out of its domain. The High Court of Kerala rejected this argument, affirming that people at the grassroots level do have the authority to decide on the course of development in their own locality.[14]

Kerala also witnessed a considerable politicisation and polarisation as a consequence of the two Western Ghats reports, the WGEEP report and the HLWG report. In the wake of violence in some areas in 2013, several MLAs took stands on the kinds of development envisaged. We find then that people's movements in some cases have made dents into representative democracy, as one would expect. At others, these environmental movements impact policy via the indirect route of expert panels and committees. Both are welcome processes, albeit slow at times.

4.9 Conclusions

Environmental justice movements, to have an impact on policy, have to associate themselves with institutions of the judiciary, the executive or the legislature. At times, the executive ordains that expert committees give relatively unbiased views be set up. The reports may or may not be heeded, once they come. So, the executive can be compelled to act only by the legislature through newer laws or by the heavy hand of the courts. Unless the process reaches its logical conclusion within the domain of the political economy, it remains an 'also ran' in the arena of policy.

---

[13] One finds a reference to a manifesto for a Green Party around 2014. See Taghioff (2014).

[14] See Gadgil (2014) for a review of the case.

References

Chopra K (2014) Conservation and development in the western ghats a tale of two committees and more. Econ Pol Wkly 49(11):12–14

Cirone M (2012) (CEDAT, Universitat Rovira (Virgili)), The vedanta case in India, EJOLT fact-sheet no. 46, p 8

Gadgil M (2014) Western ghats ecology expert panela play in aive acts. Econ Polit Wkly XLIX(18):38–50

Guha R (2006) How much should a person consume: thinking through the environment. Permanent Black/Black Kite, New Delhi

Joy KJ, Gujja B, Paranjape S, Gaud V, Vispute S (eds) (2008) Water conflicts in India: a million revolts in the making. Routledge, London (Gujja and Appaswamy papers in this volume)

Kothari A (2016) Decisions of the people, for the people and by the people. The Hindu, May 18, 2016

Martinez-Alier J (2012) Ecological distribution conflicts and economic growth. In: Bandhopadhyay J et al (eds) Environmental governance: approaches, imperatives and methods. Bloomsbury Publishing India Private Ltd., New Delhi

Martinez-Alier J, Temper L, Demaria F (2016) Social metabolism and environmental conflicts in India. In: Ghosh N et al (eds) Nature, economy and society: understanding the linkages. Springer India, New Delhi

Nepal P (2009) Environmental movements in India: politics of dynamism and transformation. Authorpress, Delhi

Ramesh J (2010) The two cultures revisited: the environment-development debate in India. Econ Polit Wkly XLV(42):13–16

Reddy RV (1998) Environmental movements in India: some reflections. J Indian School Polit Econ 10(4):685–695

Rootes C (2007) Environmental movements: from the local to the global. Environ Polit 8(1):1–12

Sahoo T, Prakash U, Sahoo MM (2014) Sardar Sarovar Dam controversy- a case study Glob J Financ Manag 6(9):887–892. ISSN:0975-6477

Saxena NC, Parasuraman S, Kant P, Baviskar A (2010) Report of the four-member committee for investigation into the proposal submitted by the Orissa mining company for bauxite mining in Niyamgiri, 16 August 2010 (submitted to the Ministry of Environment and Forests, Government of India, New Delhi)

Sills DL (1968) International encyclopaedia of the social sciences, vol 14. The Macmillan Company and the Free Press, New York

Sugathakumari. Silent valley: a case study

Taghioff D (2014) Green party of India: manifesto downloaded from http://taghioff.info/manifesto

Chapter 5
Does a Good Knowledge Base Influence Policy-Making

5.1 Prologue

Are ideas, sometimes welded into theory, significant in shaping policy? While the practical world of political economy may not think so, we have it on the authority of John Maynard Keynes, the architect of modern macroeconomic policy that they are. Note the following:

> The ideas of economists and political philosophers, both when they are right and when they are wrong, are more powerful than is commonly understood. Indeed, the world is ruled by little else. Practical men, who believe themselves to be quite exempt from any intellectual influences, are usually slaves of some *defunct* economist. Madmen in authority are usually distilling their frenzy from some academic scribbler *of a few years back*. I am sure that the power of vested interests is vastly exaggerated compared with the gradual encroachment of ideas.[1]

Note, however, that he said 'defunct economist' and 'academic scribbler *of a few years back*'. So, according to him, we expect policy to follow theory but with a lapse of time. Kaushik Basu (2016) reiterates Keynes when he states, 'the most important thing I learnt during my more than 3 years in government was the profound truth of Keynes' observation. Ideas, how people think, the beliefs hardwired in them, the mental models people carry in their heads, are more important in shaping our lives than most of us realize, and more so than vested interests'.[2]

Further, many analysts, including Basu, maintain that good policy can only come from good theory. In this chapter, therefore we examine the evolution of environmental policy in the context of the parallel theoretical developments in the last 30 years or so. To put it in another way, can the absence of good policy be attributed to the absence of a good theoretical understanding? Or is it that we need to

[1] See Keynes, John Maynard (1936) the General Theory of Employment, Interest and Money, London, Macmillan.

[2] See Basu, K. (2016). In his treatise on the art of policy-making in India, however, the environment or policy relating to it finds no mention.

K. Chopra, *Development and Environmental Policy in India*, SpringerBriefs in Economics, DOI 10.1007/978-981-10-3761-0_5

understand the impact of knowledge at different levels, initially on policy as drafted in an overarching manner and then on the drawing up of rules and laws which govern actual affects at the project and grassroots levels? This chapter shall examine these issues. It looks at different theoretical understandings of the environment and evaluates their effect, if any, on environmental policy, as well as on the details of laws and rules which give form to that policy.

5.2 The Natural and Social Science Anchor

The natural sciences are basic to an understanding of global, national and local environmental questions. Be it climate change or air and water pollution or ozone depletion, the existence of scientific evidence alone can enable us to determine safe environmental standards or threshold levels for irreversible change. It is in a manner of speaking a requisite first step. At times, direct policy implications follow. For example, when harmful effects of a chemical (such as, e.g. for DDT in the 1960s) are proved and brought to light beyond doubt, it is introduced by law into the list of 'banned commodities'.

However, when it comes to drawing up a feasible response in the form of environmental policy, one needs to understand how human societies function, view the environment and respond to changes in its different dimensions. Social science is therefore expected to have the most direct impacts on policy. On a day-to-day basis, economic and sociological impacts are at the centre of most considerations of policymakers.

The approaches of these two disciplines are, however, somewhat different when it comes to treating the environment. Economists, in general, develop models, whereas sociologists rely on what has been termed as 'analytical description' by Agarwal (1997). In the latter approach, both qualitative and quantitative factors that impinge on outcomes are comprehensively spelt out, without being constrained by the structure that formal modelling imposes.[3] In other words, conceptual frameworks lead directly to conclusions.

To understand better the difference, let us first attempt to differentiate between concepts, theories and models as separate categories.

5.3 Concepts, Theories, Models and Environmental Policy

The development of knowledge takes place along different routes and results in different levels of generalisation. We begin with concepts, sometimes documented in a stylised, abstract form, often referred to as 'theories'. Models, empirical or theoretical, may be used to establish or repudiate these theories. In the words of Ostrom, 'A specific *theory* is used by an analyst to specify which working parts of

[3] See Agarwal (1997) for an example.

a framework are considered useful to explain diverse outcomes and how they relate to one another. Micro level theories including game theory, microeconomic theory, transaction cost theory, and public goods/common-pool resource theories are examples of specific theories …….. *Models* make precise assumptions about a limited number of variables in a theory that scholars use to examine the formal consequences of these specific assumptions about the motivation of actors and the structure of the situation they face'.[4] In other words 'models' are qualitative or quantitative descriptions of key components of a system and of relationships between those components. Models are often focussed on particular issues; take, for example, constrained optimisation models or statistical models. Such models have long dominated thinking by economists. Environmental economists too use them extensively. They have provided the background for a number of policy solutions to problems of resource management and pollution abatement.

Economic theory, for example, has for long treated environmental effects of production and consumption processes to be an 'externality'. Providing incentives for private actors to internalise the full costs of their actions was long thought to be the theoretical solution to the externality problem. The primary advocate of this view was Arthur Pigou, who in *The Economics of Welfare* (1920) proposed that the government should impose a tax on emissions equal to the cost of the related damages at the efficient level of control. These proposals and the exact form they took were based on more precise models. Coase (1960) provided an alternative approach based on bargaining between interested parties. But the conditions required for it to be satisfied are so many that some of them are unlikely to hold for most environmental problems. The detailed modelling showed that private negotiation will not – in general – fully internalize environmental externalities. The argument is further substantiated by the cleavage between private and social costs and their respective accrual to different sets of stakeholders.

The theoretical foundation for the use of the analytical device known as benefit-cost (or net present value) analysis comes from the Kaldor-Hicks criterion, a derivation from the Pareto principle and a test of whether total social benefits exceed total social costs. In practice, these seemingly simple principles of economic theory have guided environmental policy with law stepping in where absolute bans, based on overarching scientific evidence, were deemed necessary. One example of law stepping in is the case of protected areas in which bans on some kinds of economic activity inevitably exist in most countries.

In general then, governments have designed pollution taxes based on the externality principle and other environmental policies based on the Kaldor-Hicks principle. In other words, economic models have been their guiding polestar. Today, economic models of pollution underlie constructed markets for pollution, including those for emission rights.

This approach has of course been roundly criticised by both sociologists and ecologists. Ecologists critique it as 'a permission to pollute'. The implicit argument

[4] See Ostrom (2009).

of ecologists is that it is difficult, rather impossible to order species or ecosystem or levels of pollution by significance or extent of harm they cause. Causing harm to any species is ethically indefensible. Sociologists, on the other hand, focus on inequalities in access to power and wealth of different stakeholders. They take environmental justice arguments as applied to stakeholders as their rallying point and seem to favour strife and confrontation as the way out. It can also be concluded that both ecologists and sociologists favour overarching well-implemented laws to protect both spaces and people who are vulnerable.

5.4 Conceptual Frameworks

Frameworks go beyond theories and models. Models and theories are nested in frameworks which attempt to set up a scheme of thinking that provides space for diverse pedagogies and focuses the sight of the policymaker on all aspects of the problems involved. We argue in the pages that follow that such frameworks have a greater and more lasting impact on decision-making and policy, in particular on environment. They provide space for alternative modes of viewing environmental issues.

Ostrom (2009) provided one kind of framework, 'the institutions and development' framework which focussed on the existence of a range of institutions between the market and the state which influenced peoples' actions. The framework contains a nested set of building blocks that social scientists can use in efforts to understand human interactions and outcomes across diverse settings. The context, the action arena and the outcome were the key constituents of this framework which policy needed to take into account.[5]

The Millennium Ecosystem Assessment (MA) (2003, 2005) provided a more overarching framework than the one mentioned above. It sought to bring together the understanding from different disciplines into a single conceptual framework. The MA constituted a paradigm shift in framing the issues, bringing nature in not as a receptacle for pollutants and/or a resource but as a series of ecosystems with their contributions to human well-being. Understandings of the nature of the human impact on the environment were made more precise, sometimes more stark. The conceptual framework of the Millennium Ecosystem Assessment provided multiple pathways for the links between human well-being and ecosystems to be viewed. These pathways left the scope for different disciplinary perspectives to be accommodated. In sum, the best available knowledge was brought together, in the belief that it would have a bearing on decision-making. Here, information to and feedback from stakeholders is at the centre of the decision-making cycle which conceptualises the process of policy-making.[6]

---

[5] See Ostrom (2009) and Dayal (2014) Chapter 2 for details. Our interest here is in the policy relevance of the framework.

[6] See Chap. 8 of Millennium Ecosystem Assessment (2003, 2005) for details.

While the MA provided a fairly comprehensive conceptual framework for the relation between ecosystem services and human well-being, it also projected scenarios for the future and possible policy responses. It had conceptualised human well-being as multi-faceted and had accepted the division of ecosystem services into provisioning, regulating, cultural and supporting.

The MA found that over the past 50 years, humans have changed ecosystems more rapidly and extensively than in any comparable period of time in human history. This has resulted in a substantial and largely irreversible loss in the diversity of life on Earth. While acknowledging that these changes made to ecosystems have contributed to substantial net gains in human well-being and economic development, it pointed out that these gains have been achieved at growing costs. It emphasised that these problems, unless addressed, will substantially diminish the benefits that future generations obtain from ecosystems. Further, the degradation of ecosystem services could grow significantly worse during the first half of this century and is a barrier to achieving the Millennium Development Goals or any other development goals.

The MA held that 'The challenge of reversing the degradation of ecosystems while meeting increasing demands for their services can be partially met under some scenarios that the MA considered but these involve significant changes in policies, institutions and practices that are not currently under way. Many options exist to conserve or enhance specific ecosystem services in ways that reduce negative trade-offs or that provide positive synergies with other ecosystem services. *Ecosystem degradation can rarely be reversed without actions that address one or more indirect drivers of change.* These indirect drivers were classified by the MA as: (a) population change (including growth and migration) (b) change in economic activity (including economic growth, disparities in wealth, and trade patterns) (c) sociopolitical factors (including factors ranging from the presence of conflict to public participation in decision-making) (d) cultural factors and (e) technological change'. *Collectively these factors influence the level of production and consumption of ecosystem services and the sustainability of the production.*

In recent years, the framework for conceptualisation provided by the MA has led to several other developments. See, for instance, the understanding with respect to planetary boundaries;[7] international, sometimes intergovernmental initiatives have also followed. Examples include The Economics of Ecosystem Services and Biodiversity (TEEB) and the Intergovernmental Science-Policy Platform for Biodiversity and Ecosystem Services (IPBES). The IPBES has recently brought out its latest report with a summary for policymakers.[8] It carries forward and improves on the MA's framework. These developments should help to keep the focus on biodiversity and ecosystem services alive and aid in continued documentation of the state of knowledge on these issues for the benefit of policymakers.

[7] See Steffen, W. et al. (2015) for planetary boundaries and Millennium Ecosystem Assessment (2003) for the conceptual framework referred to.

[8] See IPBES (2016).

Simultaneously, another impact of the MA has been the focus on valuation of ecosystem services. The term and its easy link to the accepted terminology in economics have spawned valuation studies and schemes for payments for them. The dominating valuation language is that of monetisation. Such an approach can be a double-edged sword. If carried beyond its limits, it can result in indefensible policy decisions. There exist languages of rights, of the sacredness of nature and so on, which are beyond the metric of valuation in terms of money and policy needs to draw from all of them. As a conceptual framework, the MA included all this, but follow-ups in policy and research have been and always will be selective.

At another level, deep ecologists have criticised the focus on ecosystem services and their valuation, among them Macauley in *Nature*[9] saying that 'they represent a harmful diversion from a more traditional focus on the intrinsic and aesthetic values of nature'. The panel of the MA responded to this somewhat partial understanding by saying that though 'Historically, conservation has largely relied on the considerations of intrinsic value that McCauley sees as the only solution. This has been manifestly insufficient as a response to the biodiversity crisis. And, it is particularly short-sighted in the world's poorest regions where considerations of intrinsic and spiritual values are often trumped by the needs for survival. It is time to add other approaches based on these ecosystem services to the mix'. Ideally, both intrinsic and anthropocentric values of nature should find a place in policy.

5.5 Concepts in Environmental Policy Formulation: Sustainable Development, Sustainability and Resilience

Some concepts capture attention of the public and the policymaker even before they have been integrated into theories, policies or frameworks. One such concept in the context of environmental policy has been 'sustainable development'. As a concept, it had its origin in the policy discussions way back at the time of the Rio Summit in 1992. At that time, it seemed like a panacea that would resolve all problems. It could at least be looked upon as a vision for the future. Its definition as 'development that would meet the needs of the present without compromising the ability of future generations to meet their needs' was initially welcomed by all. However, the question arose of how this was possible, both at the macro level and in particular situations. A whole literature developed around 'trade-offs and synergies in development', some of it in India itself.

It came in for criticism as a concept and as a guiding principle for practice not providing concrete guidelines in actual situations. Even so, its popularity in policy circles continued, and it has become a catch-all phrase to stand for a vision of development that is equitable and environment friendly. So in 2015, we find the UN

[9] See McCauley, D.J. *Nature* 443(7):27–28 (2006) and the MA panel's response in the same volume of Nature.

replacing its 'Millennium Development Goals' by 'Sustainable Development Goals'. And we have a listing of indicators for countries to pursue, sometimes without questioning the internal consistency of these with each other.

The academic discourse continued alongside, and two concepts which came out of it were 'resilience of ecosystems' and 'sustainability of the linked socio-ecological systems'. Both hold promise of being projected as providing signals for policymakers. Both had their origins in 'systems thinking'. Both in effect attempt to answer a very practical question which could be framed as: 'How do we know that a certain change (perhaps as a consequence of an investment project) is good or bad for the natural or social system?'

The concept of resilience which came from ecology provided the answer: the policy perturbation should not affect the resilience of the system understood as 'the property of an ecological system to withstand shocks while retaining core functions'. A resilient system, however, may or may not be of use to humans. It could exist and be valued for its intrinsic value, again as perceived by human value systems or otherwise. Social sciences, on the other side, privileged the concept of 'sustainability'. Sustainability has strong societal connotations—what needs to be 'sustained' remains a prerogative of human perceptions and preferences.

Clearly, the origins and orientation of sustainability are more anthropocentric than those of resilience. Sustainability implies equity and justice within and across generations, human societies and species. Although intergenerational equity finds more attention in the popular discourse on sustainability, it can be understood only by recognising intra-generational equity as a determinant of sustainability. Without adequate attention to equity and justice in the present, sustainability will be limited to just an ecological or a conservation goal.

Further, while a healthy natural environment is indispensable to human well-being, it is also true that a socially just society is better equipped to conserve its natural resources. In a highly inequitable society, ecological sustainability, even if achievable, would most likely be short-lived. Deep and multipronged (social, economic, political) inequities drive aspirations for resource-intensive lifestyles, while undermining alternate values and knowledge systems of disadvantaged communities.[10]

We conclude therefore that 'resilience' and 'sustainability' together can provide directions for environmental policy. Both concepts emerge out of a systems approach, one which views social-ecological systems as complex adaptive systems. When used in the context of specific locales such as wetlands or lakes, they provide guiding principles. Walker and Salt (2006)[11] document applications in different contexts across the globe.

[10] For a recent exposition, see Purushottaman et al. (2016).

[11] See Walker, B. and David Salt (2006).

5.6 More Concepts: Vulnerable People and Vulnerable Places

Another manner in which the application of these principles from systems theory to policy can be illustrated is by focussing on 'vulnerability'; the existence of vulnerability in some parts of the system reduces its resilience and also impacts adaptability of the system, in particular in times of change. Reducing vulnerability in parts of the system contributes to its overall health and capability for renewal, thereby leading it towards newer equilibriums at higher performance levels. In managing conflict between stakeholders in transformational situations, the guiding principles which emerge from this systemic view are:

- Identify and protect vulnerable people within social systems.
- Identify and protect vulnerable places within land and water ecosystems.

To expound on the two principles relating to vulnerable people and vulnerable places, I can do no better than to refer to a set of studies across six countries. These studies looked at the impact of trade liberalisation on rural poverty and the environment, through the prism of the impact on the poorest people and the most ecologically sensitive regions in those countries.[12]

To elucidate, identifying vulnerable groups and the kind of vulnerability they suffer is a matter of examining absence of options and adaptability in the face of shocks to the system. A study on aquaculture and shrimp processing in West Bengal, which documents the impact of growing shrimp export on all stakeholders from prawn seed collectors to exporters of processed shrimp, has interesting implications on these lines. All stakeholders have gained from the export activity, but the options they face and the uncertainties they encounter differ in nature and degree.[13] Shrimp processing and exporting factories face uncertainty in international prices and also by way of sudden unanticipated changes in non-tariff restrictions imposed by importing countries. Aqua culturists face uncertainties in leasing land, water quality issues and the ever-present possibility of outbreak of diseases. Policy needs to view each stakeholder's uncertainties and evolve responses, giving primacy to the most vulnerable among them.

Within ecosystems, in a similar strain, one needs to identify 'vulnerable places'. In other words, we need to distinguish between ecosystems which provide just services (such as a catchment or watershed which provides clean water downstream) and those which constitute a unique biodiversity-rich habitat and are in addition a source of support to human and other life on the planet. The first kind of ecosystem can be subject to the calculus of benefit and cost as there may be other sources for the provision of the same services; the second kind supports life itself. The

[12] See Cook et al. (2010). The countries included are Chile, China, India, Madagascar, South Africa and Vietnam and the sectors covered aquaculture, sugarcane production, forest and salmon.

[13] See Chopra et al. (2009) for more details and implications for policy.

Millennium Ecosystem Assessment (MA) conceptual framework[14] outlined in depth the reasons why these systems which support life itself should be given special treatment. The NOAA panel in the USA had argued along similar lines. It is now more and more accepted worldwide that these areas are treated as 'no-go areas' for development projects disruptive of their uniqueness. Hence there is a need to legislate and place critical areas that host entities of incomparable value (EIV), as *no-go* areas prior to giving out prospecting licences to ensure that the economic value does not trump the noneconomic value of other entities in the region.

5.7 More Conceptual Approaches: 'De-growth' and 'Radical Ecological Democracy Green Growth'

From certain quarters in academia, we also learn of radical conceptual developments. It is said that we need altogether new methods of organising economic activity. 'Radical ecological democracy' and 'de-growth' can be taken to represent two such approaches. They critique the system, political, economic and financial, and call for a paradigm shift which alone they claim can lead to a more careful use of resources and protect from unabated pollution.

Radical ecological democracy can be viewed as an extension of the Gandhian approach to development. It argues for decentralised political governance and goes beyond the 'representative democracy' that India has to a more radical direct democracy. It is argued that such an approach will lead to a different paradigm of development than the top-down one which has created degradation and unsustainable use of resources together with inequality of a very high order.

On the other hand, the newly emerging concept of 'de-growth' has several possible interpretations. One, possibly the intuitive one, is of shrinkage or a reduction in GDP or the production of goods and services? If we accept this interpretation, will an overall reduction in the production of goods and services be feasible or desirable in the current context? The second and probably more compelling argument for de-growth (in its quantitative interpretation) comes from the impact that accelerated growth may have on resource use and the state of the environment. It has been argued at length that the scale of growth has to be limited, to enable humanity to operate within safe planetary limits. This is, however, a generalisation at a global level. The regional picture varies with some areas evincing capability of growth. Also, whether or not the impact of growth is a harmful, one depends on the kinds of technology used and the institutions in place for guiding and driving it.

However, if de-growth, interpreted in a measurable sense, is about *consumption de-growth*, then some kinds of consumption definitely need to be curtailed. This would target the upper-income stakeholders in the development process. The notion of a 'sustainable consumption line' (Srivastava and Kothari 2012) certainly needs to

[14] See Millennium Ecosystem Assessment (2003) for the conceptual framework.

be taken forward and operationalised in countries characterised by unequal access such as India. But then the pathway to limiting consumption has to be spelt out.

In other words, both these concepts and several others do not take into account the path dependence of systems. We need to charter the way by which we reach the vision we believe in is reached. While such academic exercises serve a very important purpose, they cannot provide guidance for policy in their current forms. With the understanding that these will take time to first get convincingly articulated and then made acceptable in the prevailing political economy, we do not discuss their implications here.[15]

Closer to the policy fraternity is the concept of 'green growth'. Different definitions of green growth have been attempted. Following the Rio+20 conference and the document on 'the future we want' which emerged from there, the UNEP and other UN agencies have initiated several efforts focussed on policies and indicators for green growth for different countries which 'acknowledge the unique geographical and socio-economic contexts that exist in them'. In this vein, a recent document on indicators (UNEP 2014) lays down processes to be followed in setting up indicators rather than providing the indicators themselves.

It can be claimed that in some interpretations, green growth could converge with de-growth. In pursuance of this approach, a country such as India, for example, may proceed in the following manner in order to pursue green growth which will amount to selective de-growth or environment-friendly growth:[16]

- Scenarios for the future with sectoral technologies and institutions which help movement towards resource-efficient and socially inclusive green growth at state or regional levels[17]
- Scenarios for the future which envision low-carbon growth as the major component, at the national level in the context of significant international issues such as energy use
- Macro-level indicators which move attention away from GDP-centric thinking

5.8 Developments in India: The National Environmental Policy (2006), Green Accounting and Low-Carbon Growth

In 2006, the Government of India produced a document called 'The National Environment Policy'. Whereas sector-specific policies had existed and numerous acts purported to lay down rules to protect the environment,[18] this was the first time that a policy for 'the environment' was being put in place. The National Environment Policy, 2006, was the outcome of extensive consultations with experts in different

[15] See Srivastava and Kothari (2012) and DeMaria et al. (2013).

[16] For more details, see Chopra (forthcoming).

[17] For one such study which builds a scenario for a hill state of India. Himachal Pradesh see Chopra and Das (2010).

[18] A number of reviews exist. See among others Sankar (1998 and 2001).

disciplines, central ministries, members of parliament, state governments, industry associations, academic and research institutions, civil society, NGOs and the public.

Interestingly, some state-of-the art theoretical concepts, e.g. the themes of resilience and vulnerability, find a mention in it. See, for instance, the following:

> The poor are also more vulnerable to loss of resilience in ecosystems. Large reductions in resilience may mean that the ecosystems, on which livelihoods are based, break down, causing distress. The loss of the environmental resource base can result in certain groups of people being made destitute, even if overall, the economy shows strong growth.

As a part of the principles underlying the policy, two are mentioned: (a) the precautionary approach to deal with areas where knowledge may not be enough or uncertainty high and (b) the existence of 'entities with incomparable value'. The principle of legal liability is also accepted with the suggestion that civil liability be added along with existing criminal liability (which has not worked as per the policy) to ensure that the ' polluter pays' principle can be implemented. It is stated that 'Civil liability for environmental damage would deter environmentally harmful actions, and compensate the victims of environmental damage'. Further, 'conceptually, the principle of legal liability may be viewed as an embodiment in legal doctrine of the "polluter pays" approach, itself deriving from the principle of economic efficiency'.

A two-pronged approach seemed to underlie the policy: that of using economic principles up to a point and falling back on caution where incomparable value or uncertain knowledge existed. The statement seemed to be taking into account the current state of knowledge. Also, as a part of strategies and actions to follow up on the policy, a revisit of the regulatory regimes prevalent in relation to the environment was suggested.

Of late, initiatives were taken to bring the national statistical and planning systems in line with developments in green accounting. These took the form of expert group reports. The Green Accounting Committee Report (2013) was one such effort which attempted to introduce alternative wealth-based concepts of welfare into the national statistical system.[19] Another was the Planning Commission Report (2014) on low-carbon growth. Alternative scenarios were studied to provide the nature of trade-offs if a 'green growth' path was to be followed.

Such reports are however only, at best, inputs into policies which themselves are broad statements of intent, to be followed up with laws and rules which when followed ensure that correct executive decisions are taken. A few acts enacted in the same period were also forward looking, e.g. the Forest Rights Act (2006) provided for community forest rights and promised to undo historical injustices. The FRA (2006) sought to push the process towards better articulation of objectives and criteria. It requires the state to define criteria for Critical Wildlife Habitat and further demonstrate that coexistence of local communities with wildlife is not possible, before moving towards a rehabilitation process. This was different from the

[19] See Government of India (2013) and (2014). No follow-up on either seems to have taken place.

Wild life Protection Act (1972) which gives the state the power to declare an area as a national park or wildlife sanctuary and then evict people out of it. Similarly, the multidimensional recommendations of the Tiger Task Force in 2005 created a ray of hope. All these initiatives have taken place at a time when a larger narrative of 'growth' which privileged development projects of all kinds pervaded in the economy. And this had its own impact. The last decade for instance has seen a huge rise in forest land being handed over for dams, mining, roads and other projects.[20]

5.9 Looking Forward in India: Mixed Signals

As has been succinctly pointed out by J. Ramesh, there is, in India, a focus on 'two cultures' when referring, in particular, to the environment-development debate.[21] Development practice is the third dimension which attempts to bring together lessons from science but can do so only within the framework of policy as implemented on the ground through the filter of governance. This is true at all levels of governance: local, national and global. There is indeed a kind of lagged acceptance of some ideas from scientific research with a lag of 10 or 12 years by which time thinking has moved forward and policy still falls short.

Further, feedback learning from policy implementation is itself the moving force behind the progress of some aspects of social science. All this happens in a somewhat piecemeal fashion with very little of an analytical framework to define it. A co-evolution between the development of both the natural and the social sciences and the design of policy from a systems' perspective seems a far cry at the present moment of time.

All the same, this to and fro movement has taught us a great deal about the inter-linkages between environment and development. The learning has contributed to planning for several sectors such as forests, mining and water. Discerning analysts of the media have noted the steady increase in space newspapers are giving to issues of the environment.

The Indian agenda on environment stands at the crossroads. Two kinds of processes are operating, albeit at different rates. There does exist a gradual understanding in different sections of the impending environmental crises. Grassroots conflicts, their documentation, judicial intervention and slowly evolving legal codes illustrate an intention to take note and introduce regulation of damaging economic activity. Other elements in the system, moving at a much faster pace, demand faster growth in the shorter run. These are driven by unconstrained market forces, irresponsible industrialisation and urbanisation. As it happens, the dominant political economy

[20] See Das (2012) for evidence and details.

[21] See Jairam Ramesh (2010), for a succinct exposition of the state of the debate and the policymakers' consequent dilemma. Jairam Ramesh was Minister for the Environment, giving therefore an insiders' view from the government as well.

often stresses development, employment and more jobs, often at the cost of longer-run sustainability. Projects need to be cleared fast. Bureaucratic delays are not accepted as readily as they were in the past, and there is cause for concern that this accent on speed may be at the cost of the environment. It is instructive to look at the recent changes documented by an editorial in the EPW (2016).[22] It seems that in several cases, dams in hill regions of Uttarakhand, Forest Rights Acts implementation and moratorium on industry in heavily polluted areas or wetlands regulation acts, compromises are being made to ensure fast implementation of projects, overruling earlier advice on caution.

Which way will the balance tilt? Will a judicial mix of development and environmental protection, of speed and caution, be possible? It is anybody's guess.

References

Agarwal B (1997) Bargaining and gender relations, within and beyond the household. Fem Econ 3(1):1–51

Basu K (2016) An economist in the real world, the art of policy making in India. Penguin/ Viking, London

Chopra K (forthcoming) In Gerber J-F, Raina R (eds) Articulating green growth and degrowth: can they converge?

Chopra K, Das S (2010) India environmental outlook 2030: opportunities for growth in the ecologically fragile hill states: a study of Himachal Pradesh. Report submitted to the World Bank

Chopra K, Kumar P, Kapuria P (2009) Biodiversity, land use change and human well-being: a study in the Indian Sundarbans. Oxford University Press, Delhi

Coase RH (1960) The problem of social cost reprinted in Sankar, U (ed) Environmental economics. Oxford University Press, New Delhi

Cook JA, Cylke O, Larson DF, Nash JD, Stedman-Edwards P (2010) Vulnerable places, vulnerable: trade liberalisation, rural poverty and the environment. Edward Elgar Publishing Limited, London/New York

Das S (2012) Pressure for conversion of forest land to non-forest use in India. In: Anon (ed) Deeper roots of historical injustice. Rights and Resources Initiative, Washington, DC, pp 159–234

Dayal V (2014) The environment in economics and development, pluralistic extensions of core economic models. Springer, New Delhi

Demaria F, Schneider F, Sekulova F, Martinez Alier J (2013) What is degrowth? From an activist slogan to a social movement. Environ Values 22:191–215

Economic and Political Weekly Editorial (2016) Choosing speed over diligence. Econ Polit Wly 51(23)

Government of India, Central Statistical Office (2013) Green accounting in India, report of the expert group

Government of India, Planning Commission (2014) Final report of the expert group on low carbon strategies for India

IPBES (2016) The methodological assessment report on scenarios and models for biodiversity and ecosystem services. Summary for Policy Makers, IPBES

Keynes JM (1936) The general theory of employment, interest and money. Macmillan, London

McCauley DJ (2006) Selling out on nature. Nature 443(7):27–28

[22] See EPW Editorial 'Choosing Speed Over Diligence' Economic & Political Weekly, Vol. LI no 23, June 4, 2016.

Millenium Ecosystem Assessment (2003) Ecosystems and human well-being: a frame work for assessment. Island Press, Washington, DC

Millenium Ecosystem Assessment (2005) Ecosystems and human well-being: synthesis. Island Press, Washington, DC

Ostrom E (2009) Beyond markets and states: polycentric governance of complex economic systems. Nobel Lecture, Stockholm

Pigou AC (1920) The economics of welfare. Macmillan, London

Purushothaman S, Ravi C et al. Harini Nagendra Manu Matha et al. doi:10.18472/SustDeb.v7n1.2016.17424

Ramesh J (2010) The two cultures revisited: the environment-development debate in India. Econ Pol Wkly 45(42):13–16

Sankar U (1998) Laws and institutions relating to environmental protection in India, MSE Occasional Paper No. 2

Sankar U (2001) Environmental Policy. In: Sankar U (ed) Environmental economics. Oxford University Press, New Delhi

Srivastava A, Kothari A (2012) Churning the earth, the making of global India. Viking/Penguin Books

Steffen W et al (2015) For planetary boundaries

UNEP (2014) Using indicators for green economy policymaking

Walker B, Salt D (2006) Resilience thinking: sustaining ecosystems and people in a changing world. Island Press, Washington DC

Chapter 6
Addressing Environmental Issues of the Future

6.1 The Picture Circa 1990: Where Did We Begin from?

Environmental policy in the last three decades in India evolved in an overarching political context which privileged growth and globalisation, more so since 1991 for 25 years of the three decades under consideration. The preceding decade of the 1980s had, however, witnessed the rise of some concerns with regard to the environment within the government in India. A full-fledged ministry had been set up, and an unconventional agenda on land and water management had started to unfold from within the government. Dialogue with other stakeholders was the order of the day.

A document, written in 1989, by two of India's most articulate and respected environmentalists, Ramachandra Guha and Madhav Gadgil, is worth recapitulating. It presents a wish list of sorts. Guha claims it was a kind of 'activist document', not published then but reprinted in his book of 2006.[1] The authors thought that the political situation, with a (then) new government at the centre, heralded a search for an alternative path to development, some of the constitutive elements of which could be as follows:

- *Decentralisation of decision-making* and a much more open, accountable system of governance. The centralised bureaucratic system had led to much of the short-sighted, destructive development.
- Acknowledgement of the *right of the citizens to know.* Further, detailed project reports and information relating to rehabilitation, afforestation, etc. to be in the public domain.
- *Open scrutiny as the characteristic of all government programmes at all scales,* including small village level programmes.

[1] See Guha (2006) p. 267–273 for the details.

K. Chopra, *Development and Environmental Policy in India*, SpringerBriefs in Economics, DOI 10.1007/978-981-10-3761-0_6

- Grant of *the right to productive work to large numbers of our poorer citizens*, work that focusses on sustainable development of our natural resources and on eco-restoration.
- *Good management of the local resource base, through a properly organised right to work programme*.

In retrospect, as we scan the time since then, some of these so-called elements of an alternative development process, more friendly to the environment, have been put in place, at least partially. This was done in the first decade of the twenty-first century. The Right to Information Act, the Forest Rights Act, the National Rural Employment Guarantee Act and movements towards Panchayat's control of natural resources are in place. The NREGA mandates that natural resource-based projects be given priority.

However, the conflicts between environment and other priorities in the policy domain have not become any less sharp. For one thing, the document by Gadgil and Guha itself focusses on the rural sector and on natural resources therein. These constitute a subset of the issues that demand our attention today. In particular, this vision ignores the changing relationship between the people whom Gadgil referred to as the 'ecosystem people' and those he called the 'omnivores'.

A part of this changed dynamic arises out of the changed orientation of the Indian economy in 1991 and after. The din of 'development' and globalisation has grown even louder. Large corporates have grown, the extractive nature of industry has taken its toll on minerals and resources, and lifestyles of the rich have reached hitherto unheard of levels of opulence. Simultaneously, in the age of quick communication, the 'ecosystem people' have access to images of these. Their aspirations have also grown beyond their villages and their local resources. In one sense, this is good. There is better access to employment and consumption, at least for those who can migrate. But the unbridled opulence of the rich and the super-rich results in a high degree of inequality and is resource intensive. Social and environmental sustainability is threatened.

Urbanisation has brought with it its own set of environmental disasters and problems. Air and water pollution and badly designed cities are to be found all over the country. This has resulted in a new set of challenges and opportunities. In facing these challenges, we can learn from the manner in which environmental policy floundered and evolved in the past three decades.

Simultaneously, one cannot ignore the fact that the environment and problems arising out of it occupy far more media and public attention than they did earlier. A content analysis of the media would validate this. Almost every day, national newspapers carry stories on one or the other major environmental issue. This is all very good. But the question that arises is: to what extent has the evolution of environmental policy contributed to this? What can we learn for the future direction of development in India and its implications for the environment and resources?

6.2 Evolution of Environmental Policy in India: A Quick Review

In the preceding chapters, we have identified four kinds of influences as having impacted environmental policy in India in the last three decades. These are (a) early experience coupled with learning from the empirical evidence, (b) international pressures, (c) environmental movements and (d) new theoretical and conceptual developments. We argue that each had a limited impact, sometimes working in diverse directions.

In India, arresting land and forest degradation has been a major concern of environmentalists. At the same time, land and forest policy constitutes an area of long-standing interest and governance in India. Governments are, therefore, expected to be aware of the issues and problems in this area. We saw, however, in Chap. 2, that the awareness which existed was a biased one. The colonial stance of viewing all land as private land for cultivation and all forests as state property continued well after independence. A nuanced understanding of the property rights regimes on land and the multiple functions of forests was missing. So, there was a great deal of floundering on the policy front. Some movements in right directions, sometimes initiated by simple executive orders took place, soon to be scuttled as the implications of a wider replication threatened the elite control over resources. Initial isolated experiments with land and water management by communities (such as the ones in Sukhomajri and Ralegan Siddhi) led its nationwide replication through JFM, which nevertheless kept the forest department in a position of unwarranted privilege. It was only in 2006 that the Forest Rights Act brought in a different rights-based perspective. There was progress, though slow.[2]

Climate change policy stands in contrast with the above. For long it was not a national priority. International circumstances drew our attention to it. In early phases, a somewhat uncompromising stand that 'it was a developed country problem to be resolved by them' was adopted in international forums. This changed, somewhat reluctantly, in the first decade of the twenty-first century, mainly as a consequence of cues from outside the country and the financial sops offered by the Clean Development Mechanism (CDM) initiative. Whatever we did in this arena seemed to be a follow-up on international pressure, at least till about 2007–2008. Later, some initiatives such as acceptance of nationally intended determined targets for emissions have emerged, partly as a consequence of efforts led by India. Of late, in setting up the structure for climate finance too, India has played a role. These are welcome, forward-looking steps, albeit small ones. Over the years, we see a steady though reluctant change in official attitudes from scepticism about the science, to an agreement to look at mitigation, then thinking of being proactive, etc. The understanding that climate change was a concern for India, including its poor, led to the

[2] See the discussions in Chapter II on Joint Forest Management (initially introduced by a departmental D. O. in 1990) and other approaches.

mandate that India should be a part of the solution, even though it had not created the problem.[3]

Within the country, environmental justice movements have sometimes pushed policy in the direction of judicious conservation. However, to have an impact on policy, such movements have to ensure that their concerns are taken on board by institutions of the judiciary, executive or legislature. This has not always been easy. At times, when confronted by such environmental movements and as a temporary alleviating measure, the executive ordains that expert committees examine concerned issues from their perspectives. However, the subsequent reports may or may not be heeded. In effect, the executive can be compelled to act only by the legislature through newer laws or by the heavy hand of the courts. Unless the process reaches its logical conclusion within the domain of the political economy, it remains an 'also ran' in the arena of policy. Examples of all types of movements exist in India and are reviewed in Chap. 4.

In the political economy context of India, academia has almost always taken a backseat. The only exceptions one can think of belong to the period immediately following independence. At that time, the focus was on development planning with very little understanding of possible trade-offs or synergies with the environment. By the mid-1980s, when issues of land and water management came to the fore, the tradition of a kind of lagged acceptance of some ideas from the research community had been set up. However, this generally took place with a lag of 10 or 12 years by which time thinking had moved forward and policy still fell short.

Further, feedback learning from policy implementation is itself the moving force behind the progress of some aspects of social science.[4] All this happens in a somewhat piecemeal fashion with very little of an analytical framework to define it. A co-evolution between the development of both the natural and the social sciences and the design of policy from a systems' perspective seems a far cry at the present moment of time.

In the final analysis, even if appropriate institutions are set in place to provide policy inputs, the final call has to be taken by the government of the day. And this involves lengthy inter-ministerial confabulations. Witness the long and bitter incriminations between two ministries on the issue of 'go' and no-go areas for coal mining around the period of 2009–2010.[5] Some details bear repetition. To quote Ramesh,

> The ministries of coal and environment and CIL (Coal India Limited) agreed to work jointly on an exercise to map coal reserves and forest cover across nine major coal fields to determine where mining could be carried out. (The go areas as against the no-go areas where it could not be). After the exercise was completed,[6] the coal ministry backed out, perhaps as the areas that remained closed to mining activities were far more than they had anticipated!!

[3]This was part of the mandate given by the then Prime Minister to the Environment Minister in 2009. See Ramesh (2015).

[4]For details see the decision making process outlined in Chopra et al. (2005).

[5]See the record in Chapter 8 of Ramesh (2015).

[6]With inputs of satellite-based digitised maps from the Forest Survey of India (FSI) and inputs from the Coal Mining and Development Institute (CMPDI)

So much for the use of the latest knowledge inputs into policy. It is indeed true that at times, there are hard decisions to be made, choosing between development and conservation, between the present and the future.

6.3 State of Knowledge on Policy Choices and How They Should Evolve

The analysis of policy and policy-making processes has gone a long way in social science. In the context of complex economic, social and ecological systems, policy drafting and execution is a lengthy affair. Interventions by different levels of government add a new element to the dynamics. And, as Colander and Kupers put it, 'those very (policy) choices will themselves influence the dynamics of the system, as well as people's tastes and preferences. It won't be the same system once the policies are under way, and that very fact can bring about both opportunities and unforeseen consequences'.[7]

The changed dynamics consequent on policy intervention introduces new institutions of the state as stakeholders, be they the executive, the legislature or the judiciary. There may be different levels of centralisation (or decentralisation) at which these function. Successive changes introduced at different levels result in iterations of interaction and consequences both between these governmental institutions and with other stakeholders, e.g. the resource owners, the consumers and the users of resources. Outside these loops but heavily influenced by the decisions and the events are the ecosystems, the rivers, the lakes, the forests and the fields as well as the urban ecosystems. These bear the impact of the execution of policy and the growth or conservation that follows. By the very nature of these natural ecosystems, the impact is of different kinds. At times, the ecosystem state changes slowly, its functioning left unaffected by the increased extractive use, the additional pollution or at times the additional conservation. At other times, the ecosystem may undergo a sudden regime shift and lose its functional capacity, undermining its capability to produce for further human consumption. Ideally policy needs to be able to tell the difference in these two situations, with some degree of certainty. Close association between policymakers and scientists should make this happen.

Simultaneously, policy execution results in interaction with stakeholders in the social system. In these interactions, stakeholder perceptions about their interests (present and future) and their access to political and economic power are most significant. The institutional environment determines this access and the resulting significance given to the voice of different groups. In general, the more the level of decentralisation, the more the possibility of decisions that are the outcome of deliberative democratic processes. Also important is the nature of power relations between the participants in the deliberative process. Do the agencies of the state in

[7] See Collander and Kupers (2014) Chapter 1.

their interaction adopt a principal-agent approach or try to identify 'polycentric' centres of decision-making?[8] Most of the time, they follow the top-down (principal-agent) approach and do not ascribe to the latter. Note the manner in which Joint Forest Management Committees functioned, once the agenda had been adopted by the Indian government on a somewhat large scale. In many cases, the forest department continued to exercise control over decisions taken. The so-called solution or panacea for forest degradation had faltered, creating a new set of issues to be dealt with.

This course of events was somewhat expected, given the nature of the Indian polity. It had, nevertheless, its positive effects. In general, even if we are never able to fully anticipate the subsequent effect which the introduction of a deliberative process brings about, it will enable more transparent understanding of the issues involved. Venues for facilitating a changed behaviour by all entities, both government and resource users, may also emerge. To provide institutions for preference-changing behaviour to emerge is an important contribution of the process. And as Norgaard (2008) has maintained, 'the lines between *scientific* ways of knowing and *democratic* ways of learning and choosing continue to blur as scientists acknowledge the role of judgement in science'.[9]

The inescapable understanding that we get from the analysis of social-ecological systems is that there is no one panacea that a policymaker, located in a remote echelon, can dispense. Panaceas often lead to significant problems. Ostrom made this point repeatedly in her studies spanning natural resource systems in different parts of the world, in particular South Asia.[10]

The way ahead is in adaptive learning with different kinds of change being factored in. Note, for instance, the following kinds of change.[11] We quote from Brock and Carpenter (2007):

- Ecosystem change ongoing at multiple scales, from the slow weathering of rock or percolation of groundwater to life cycles of microorganisms measured in minutes. This change has both repeated and novel components
- Social–ecological change, although usually gradual and predictable, is sometimes rapid, extensive, and unpredictable. These extensive changes, or regime shifts, may be difficult or impossible to reverse. Some regime shifts have significant consequences for ecosystem services, livelihoods, and human well-being.
- Any institution that is implemented evokes a reaction from people and ecosystems, which then co create a system that may become different from the one that the institution was intended to manage. The reaction may take days or decades, and the resulting co created system may be substantially new. For any proposed institution, an analysis of the reaction of the social-ecological systems must be considered, and this dynamic must be estimated and predicted, before the ultimate outcome of the proposed institution can be evaluated. This analysis is the heart of adaptive management and the source of potential panacea traps.

[8] For details of the polycentric approach to decision-making on the environment, see E. Ostrom's Nobel lecture (2009). Also for early origins of the idea, see V. Ostrom, Vincent, Charles M. Tiebout and Robert Warren (1961).

[9] See in this context Chopra (2016) on the role of values and valuation in policy-making in an unequal world.

[10] See, among others, Ostrom's Nobel lecture (2009).

[11] For details, see Brock, William A. and Stephen R. Carpenter (2007).

Brock and Carpenter also illustrate how a 'panacea' approach to policy can result in either too much extraction or too much conservation. Closer home we see examples from policy shifts in the Ranthambore and the Keoladeo National Parks. In Ranthambore, park managers planted *Prosopis juliflora* because it grew quickly in poor conditions. They felt it would meet the fuelwood needs of the villagers and reduce 'the incredible pressure' on the park. They failed to see that *Prosopis juliflora* is an invasive species and will harm the ecology of the park in the long run.[12]

Adaptive management with monitoring and learning from deliberative processes along the way is recommended by most analysts as the way forward. At times, sophisticated techniques can be used in the process to ensure that the process does not converge to a panacea. A scenario analysis of possible future states can help in different identifying aspects of future uncertainty that could unfold with different policy choices. Both the Millennium Ecosystem Assessment (2005) and the IPBES (2016) emphasise the significance of scenario analysis.

We argue in this section that following an adaptive learning process needs a few prerequisites. We must understand the difference between the fast-moving and the slow-moving elements in complex adaptive social-ecological systems. Often the systemic change is required to impact both the slow-moving variables and the fast-moving ones. Examples of the first are the nature of institutions, peoples' preferences and social norms. Similarly, examples of the fast-moving variables are higher growth rates, and fast changing consumption patterns impact the SES. The challenge before policy- and decision-makers is to finds ways and means of tackling with both.

To quote from the Millennium Assessment (2005):[13]

> Ecosystem dynamics will never be completely understood, socioeconomic systems will continue to change, and drivers can never be fully anticipated. It is important therefore that decision-making processes incorporate, wherever possible, procedures to evaluate outcomes of actions and assimilate lessons learned from experience. Debate on exactly how to go about doing this continues in discussions on adaptive management, social learning, safe minimum standards, and the precautionary principle. But the core message of all approaches is the same: acknowledge the limits of human understanding, give special consideration to irreversible changes, and evaluate the multiple impacts of decisions as they unfold.

In India, we are far from such an understanding. At the larger conceptual level, policy documents tend to take note of changes in thinking but in the fine print (mainly in formulating laws and rules), the political compulsions of growth and fast project clearance take over. An example of this can be found in the Government of India report of 2014.[14] When it reviews the Forest Rights Act and recommends exceptions only in the context of 'linear projects', one can understand the significance of roads, gas pipelines, etc. and the need to give priority to them. Perhaps the

---

[12] Dayal (2007), on the basis of an analysis of future scenarios and their impact on different stakeholders, suggested adaptive management of the park, with adaptation, monitoring and learning with respect to the *Prosopis juliflora.*

[13] MA (2005) Responses volume

[14] See the Government of India (2014) report set up to review acts administered by the MOEFCC.

doing away with Gram Sabha approval for some projects termed 'linear' projects is also understandable. But, the inclusion of mining in this category is inexcusable. Also, this does not inspire confidence in the executive.

Then, the current focus on the speed of clearing projects by the MOEFCC is also understandable but not at the cost of overlooking environmental degradation. In the light of these tendencies to misinterpret and confuse on the part of the executive, the current trends of the judiciary playing a significant role shall continue.

6.4 A Few Underlying Dilemmas and Their Implications

It is significant to understand, however, that policy-making and implementation take place in society, wherein several dilemmas exist and perhaps will continue to do so. We examine some of these below, in particular those that influence environmental issues.

One is the issue of preference for the present over the future. Economists have long struggled with the why and wherefore of it. It impacts environmental issues critically. Time scales of ecological events are, at times, in terms of centuries, whereas economists think at best in terms of two or three decades and politicians in terms of a maximum of 5 years (or the election cycle). How do we resolve issues relating to a unified complex social-ecological system in such a situation?[15]

The second has to do with the treatment of agents situated unequally with respect to wealth, power or knowledge. The more equal a society is with respect to each of these attributes, the better is likely to be the implementation of adaptive learning cycles and deliberative processes in practice. The existence of polycentric centres of decision-making with competing relationships can only flourish in equitable situations. Else we go back to the patron-client relationship of a top-down decision-making process. Some would even say that the nature of the state militates against any such purposeful deliberation. Kashwan (2013) argues that the greening of a Machiavellian state is only possible if environmentalists in developing countries are able to create a constituency that brings together 'the environmentalism of the poor' and 'the findings of the scholarship on the commons' and require governments to act. He maintains that independently these stakeholders are not able to ensure 'the Machiavellian state to act'. Be that as it may, a political voice for the environment is definitely the need of the hour.[16]

The third dilemma concerns the nature of governance, partly following from and overlapping with the first two. A sense of dissatisfaction with environmental governance however remains. There has been a considerable to and fro in decisions taken and almost consistent poor implementation. The first meant that two steps taken in one direction were followed by three taken in the other. The two conflicting cultures pervading our development discourse have been commented upon, and the

---

[15] Some progress has been made by recent work on determining 'safe planetary boundaries' for human activities but areas of concern remain.

[16] For conclusions on such lines, see Chap. 4 on environmental justice movements in India.

way forward seems contentious. The second (poor implementation) meant that the MOEF was seen as the last bastion of the permit and licence raj and 'The lasting impression has remained that the Acts and the appurtenant legal instruments have really served only the purpose of a venal administration, at the Centre and the States, to meet rent-seeking propensity at all levels. This impression has been further strengthened by waves of large scale 'clearances', coupled with major delays in approvals in individual cases'.[17]

With a preference for present growth and with unequal entities coming together as decision-makers, the governance of laws will leave much to be desired. With the best legislation on environment, and the most adaptive learning processes in place, the state of the environment would continue to deteriorate. It is a question of ensuring that laws put in place are followed. As Jairam Ramesh puts it, 'When closure notices are served to distilleries or paper mills illegally discharging wastes into India's most holy Ganga river, it is not a question of 'environment versus development' but again one of whether standards mandated by law are to be enforced effectively or not'.[18]

In looking for solutions to these dilemmas, we need new and reformed institutions for facilitating a change in human behaviour, to increase local appreciation of shared global concerns and to correct collective action failures that cause global-scale problems. However, this change in behaviour assumes acceptance of common norms, both nationally and internationally. Such norms are more likely to emerge with decreases in inequalities in distribution of income and power and more interactions across the globe which facilitate emergence of international institutions (Walker et al. in Science 2009).

This brings us back, full circle, to the issue of distributional justice and shared norms. In conclusion, it is true that shared values with regard to the linkages between economy, society and nature need to inform policy-making at both macro and project levels. It is these that we need to move towards, as we simultaneously strengthen the information and data bases which enable us to do so.

References

Brock WA, Carpenter SR (2007) Panaceas and diversification of environmental policy. Proc Natl Acad Sci 104(39):15206–15211

Chopra K (2016) Nature, economy and society: of values, valuation and policy-making in an unequal world. In: Ghosh N, Mukhopadhyaya P et al (eds) Nature, economy and society, understanding the linkages. Springer, New Delhi

Chopra K, Leemans R, Kumar P, Simons H (2005) Ecosystems and human well-being: policy responses (Findings of the responses working group of the Millennium Assessment). Island Press, Washington, DC

[17] See the Government of India (2014).

[18] While also arguing for pragmatic laws, he gives several other examples as well. See J. Ramesh (2015)

Colander D, Kupers R (2014) Complexity and the art of public policy: solving society's problems from the bottom up. Princeton University Press, Princeton/Oxford

Dayal V (2007) Social diversity and ecological complexity: how an invasive tree could affect diverse agents in the land of the tiger. Environ Dev Econ 12:1–19

Government of India (2014) Report of high level committee to review various acts administered by ministry of environment, forest & climate change

Guha R (2006) How much should a person consume, Thinking through the environment. Permanent Black/Black Kite, New Delhi

Kashwan P (2013) Greening a Machiavellian state? Insights for international environmental governance. J Polit Sci Public Aff 1:e106. doi:10.4172/jpspa.1000e106

Norgaard RB (2008) Finding hope in the millennium assessment. Conserv Biol 22(4):862–869

Ostrom E (2009) Beyond markets and states: polycentric governance of complex economic systems, Nobel lecture, Stockholm

Ostrom V, Charles M, Bout T, Warren R (1961) The organization of government in metropolitan areas: a theoretical inquiry. Am Polit Sci Rev 55(4):831–842

Ramesh J (2015) Green signals: ecology, growth and democracy in India. Oxford University Press, New Delhi

Walker B, Barrett S et al (2009) Looming global scale failures and missing institutions. Science 325(5946):1345–1346

MIX
Papier | Fördert gute Waldnutzung
FSC® C083411

Kolibri 360 GmbH
Ferdinand-Jühlke-Straße 7
99095 Erfurt, Deutschland
produktsicherheit@kolibri360.de

Maciej Serowaniec / Agnieszka Laskowska-Hulisz / Marcin Drewek (eds.)

What will the future bring?

Green energy transition and new technologies as current challenges of public and private law

With 3 figures

V&R unipress

MIX
Papier aus verantwortungsvollen Quellen
FSC www.fsc.org FSC® C083411

Bibliographic information published by the Deutsche Nationalbibliothek
The Deutsche Nationalbibliothek lists this publication in the Deutsche Nationalbibliografie; detailed bibliographic data are available online: https://dnb.de.

Cover image: Adobe Stock: #377799322
Printed and bound by CPI books GmbH, Birkstraße 10, 25917 Leck, Germany
Printed in the EU.

Vandenhoeck & Ruprecht Verlage | www.vandenhoeck-ruprecht-verlage.com

ISSN 3052-9042 (print) | ISSN 3052-9050 (digital)
ISBN 978-3-8471-1900-5 (print)
ISBN 978-3-7370-1900-2 (open access)

V&R unipress

Law – Society – Democracy

Volume 1

Edited by Maciej Serowaniec

Nicolaus Copernicus University in Toruń
(Faculty of Law and Administration)

Uniwersytet Mikołaja Kopernika w Toruniu
(Wydział Prawa i Administracji)

The volumes of this series are peer-reviewed.

Contents

Maciej Serowaniec / Agnieszka Lawskowska-Hulisz /
Marcin Drewek

Introduction

What does the future hold? Energy transition and new technologies as current challenges for public and private law bring together a diverse collection of legal analyses that address two of the most pressing challenges of our time: the global energy transition and the rapid development of new technologies, particularly artificial intelligence. As legal systems worldwide respond to environmental threats and technological disruptions, both public and private law must evolve to meet these new realities. This book explores how law can support sustainable development while safeguarding democratic values, individual rights, and the rule of law.

The climate crisis, paired with the urgent need to transition away from fossil fuels, is not merely a matter of science or policy but also a profound legal challenge. Energy law, environmental protection, taxation, land use, and administrative regulation intersect in complex ways that demand interdisciplinary and forward-looking legal frameworks (Faure & Peeters, 2011). Simultaneously, technological advancements such as artificial intelligence are redefining fundamental legal concepts—liability, personhood, decision-making authority—and prompting us to revisit established doctrines in criminal, civil, and medical law (Calo, 2015).

Today, legal frameworks are being tested by the scale and speed of the transformations underway. On one hand, legal institutions are expected to enable the shift to sustainable and resilient energy systems. On the other, they are tasked with confronting the ethical and operational challenges posed by artificial intelligence and other forms of automation. The interplay between these two spheres—energy and technology—is not coincidental. The digitalization of energy systems, for example, raises new issues of data protection, cybersecurity, and transparency, demanding responses that are as nuanced as they are robust (Ponce del Castillo, 2021).

This volume begins by grounding the discussion in one of the most ethically compelling questions facing modern societies: what responsibilities do we bear towards future generations? Aleksandra Kustra-Rogatka examines the rights of those not yet born and the legal theories that might support more substantial intergenerational justice. She probes the moral and legal obligations that should guide today's lawmakers as they shape long-term environmental and technological policy. This chapter provides a foundational lens through which the rest of the volume can be understood by bringing philosophical and jurisprudential perspectives into dialogue with environmental law.

The book moves into the practical terrain of regulatory and financial mechanisms related to the energy sector from this philosophical foundation. Chapter by Kinga Janowska, Aleksandra Kościelak, and Marcin Drewek analyze the regulation of energy sales prices in Poland within the context of European Union legal standards, highlighting the tension between energy affordability and energy security. The authors explore how energy law must mediate between short-term social needs and long-term sustainability goals, revealing the complex, often conflicting values.

Małgorzata Cilak and Martyna Wilmanowicz-Słupczewska further explore the legal basis for state aid mechanisms to support renewable energy sources, a cornerstone of the EU's climate policy. Their chapter investigates the compatibility of such aid with EU competition law and the broader environmental protection objectives. It provides an in-depth look at how law can serve as a constraint and a tool for policy innovation and economic transformation (Sadeleer, 2020).

The financial dimension of renewable energy development is explored through local taxation. Paweł Majka and Jacek Wantoch-Rekowski offer insights into how property and agricultural tax instruments can be leveraged to promote sustainable energy production. Their analysis underscores the importance of local-level legal instruments in achieving national and supranational energy goals. Meanwhile, Tomasz Kuczyński and Piotr Rączka address a vital environmental consideration: balancing renewable energy investments with preserving biologically active areas, underscoring the need for integrated legal approaches to land management. Their contribution highlights the tension between the green energy imperative and the equally crucial commitment to biodiversity conservation.

The ecological focus continues with Karolina Karpus's discussion of the precautionary principle in public law. She addresses how legal systems can and should respond to scientific uncertainty in the face of environmental threats, reflecting on how law can become more adaptive without sacrificing predictability and accountability. In a world of accelerating ecological risks, her analysis calls for a legal culture as anticipatory as responsive (Fisher et al., 2006).

The second half of the book shifts focus to legal questions emerging from the rise of artificial intelligence. Can AI be criminally liable? Jerzy Lachowski and Natalia Dańko tackle this question by exploring the boundaries of criminal law and how non-human actors challenge them. As AI systems become more autonomous, questions arise about mens rea, culpability, and punishment—core concepts that may no longer fit neatly within traditional legal frameworks.

Kinga Bączyk-Rozwadowska and Damian Kaczan examine the profound implications of AI in the medical field, where algorithmic decision-making raises new questions about professional responsibility, informed consent, and patient rights. Their chapter draws attention to the unique vulnerabilities of patients and the high-stakes nature of medical decision-making, arguing for safeguards that preserve human dignity and ethical accountability.

Agnieszka Laskowska-Hulisz explores how AI is already reshaping civil proceedings, examining issues ranging from automated decision-making in courts to the evidentiary value of AI-generated data. Her chapter reflects the growing need to ensure that technological efficiency does not come at the cost of procedural fairness or human oversight. It also raises broader concerns about access to justice and the democratization of legal processes.

Finally, Maciej Serowaniec considers the macro-level governance of energy and technology policy through the lens of the European Semester. He evaluates how this annual cycle of economic policy coordination can serve as a platform for promoting green energy and technological innovation across EU Member States, reinforcing the Union's broader sustainability goals. His chapter positions the European Semester as a vital mechanism for driving structural reform, though often overlooked.

Taken together, the chapters in this book provide a rich, multidimensional view of how contemporary legal thought grapples with the twin challenges of environmental and technological change. They reflect scholarly insight and a commitment to shaping a more just, sustainable, and resilient legal order. The volume speaks to lawyers, policymakers, academics, and all those thinking critically about how law should respond to the defining challenges of our century.

This publication results from collaborative research conducted by members of the Centre for Democracy, Accountability and Representation (CEDAR) at Nicolaus Copernicus University in Toruń. It was made possible through funding provided by the "Excellence Initiative – Research University" programme, which supports cutting-edge interdisciplinary work to address the complex challenges of the future.

We invite readers to engage critically with the ideas presented here and to join the broader conversation on how law must evolve to meet the demands of a changing world.

References

Calo, R. (2015). Robotics and the lessons of cyberlaw. *California Law Review, 103*(3), 513–563.

Faure, M., & Peeters, M. (Eds.). (2011). *Climate change liability.* Edward Elgar Publishing.

Fisher, E., Jones, J., & von Schomberg, R. (2006). *Implementing the precautionary principle: Perspectives and prospects.* Edward Elgar Publishing.

Ponce del Castillo, A. (Ed.) (2024). *Artificial intelligence, labour and society.* ETUI.

Sadeleer, N. de. (2020). *Environmental principles: From political slogans to legal rules* (2nd ed.). Oxford University Press.

Aleksandra Kustra-Rogatka

What do we owe our grand-grandchildren? The rights of future generations, environmental protection, and theories of intergenerational justice

1. Introduction

With the emergence of the first voices in the 1970s warning of the environmental catastrophe awaiting humankind if it did not reduce the negative impact of human activity on the environment, the concept of sustainable development emerged. It aims to ensure that human needs are met while limiting environmental damage. In 1972, the Club of Rome's report *The Limits to Growth* recognised for the first time that environmental problems are global in scope and that the cooperation of the entire Earth community is needed to solve them (Meadows et al., 1972). The same year, the United Nations Conference on Human Development in Stockholm placed environmental protection at the top of the issues urgently needing international negotiation (Thant, 1969).

Fifteen years later, the Brundtland Commission Report Our Common Future defined sustainable development as "development that meets the needs of the present without compromising the ability of future generations to meet their own needs" (World Commission on Environment and Development, 1987). Sustainable development has since become an essential element of public policies shaped both internationally and nationally. Its importance is also reflected in many international and constitutional legal instruments.

The spread of sustainable development has been accompanied by two phenomena central to contemporary narratives in public law. The first is the rise of international and constitutional protection of future generations. The second, complementary to the first, is the growing interest in theories of intergenerational justice in philosophical and legal debates concerning the rights of future generations. This growing interest in intergenerational justice signifies an evolving legal discourse and the increasing importance of considering future generations in legal frameworks.

This chapter aims to analyse the legal protections of future generations and the importance of so-called *posterity provisions* in an environmental context from the perspective of intergenerational justice theory. It is structured as follows. After this brief introduction, the chapter will delve into the significance of the protection of the rights of future generations in contemporary international and constitutional law, a topic of utmost importance. Attention will be paid to the multiplicity of types of posterity provisions and their varying relevance in environmental law application. The section will focus on the concept of intergenerational justice both as an element of contemporary public policies and an essential theory in modern ethics and political philosophy. The fourth section will examine emerging trends in the protection of the rights of future generations and implementing intergenerational justice in environmental contexts. The chapter concludes by identifying key challenges facing the development of international and constitutional protection of future generations' rights and the accompanying rise of intergenerational justice theory.

2. The rights of future generations – the complex genesis of posterity provisions

The rights of future generations must be considered in the broader context of *posterity provisions*, i. e., legal regulations referring directly or indirectly to future generations. The origins of such provisions are complex and have been present in constitutional law theory since its earliest stages. This evolution is tied to enduring tensions between constitutional authority and democratic principles. Two opposing views exemplify these dilemmas: Thomas Jefferson advocated for regular constitutional revision by each generation, famously declaring that "the dead have no right to rule over the living" (Jefferson, 1789). In contrast, Edmund Burke envisioned constitutions as intergenerational compacts binding past, present, and future generations in a shared political community (Burke, 1909–1914). These competing visions remain central to modern debates in public law (Chatziathanasiou, 2017).

Despite these tensions, developing legal protections for future generations—internationally and constitutionally—shows that future-oriented constitutionalism has gained ground. These provisions are no longer rare symbolic references but are increasingly embedded in substantive legal frameworks.

2.1. Posterity provisions on an international level

At the international level, references to the rights of future generations appear in foundational instruments such as the *Charter of the United Nations* and the *Universal Declaration of Human Rights.* The UN Charter's preamble invokes future generations as beneficiaries of peace and security, while the Universal Declaration suggests a broader intergenerational human community. UNESCO has played a significant role in developing this concept further. In 1997, it adopted the *Declaration on the Responsibilities of the Present Generations Towards Future Generations*, which explicitly addresses environmental protection alongside social and political dimensions.

According to Nyka (2016), binding and non-binding international legal instruments now include references to protecting future generations. Among binding treaties, the *Convention on Biological Diversity*, *CITES*, the *UN Framework Convention on Climate Change*, and the *Aarhus Convention* all recognise long-term environmental obligations. Non-binding instruments, such as *Agenda 21*, the *Rio Declaration*, the *Millennium Declaration*, and the *European Green Deal*, also incorporate intergenerational language and principles (Nyka, 2014).

The Maastricht Principles on the Human Rights of Future Generations are of particular note, a document resulting from six years of expert consultation. Though not legally binding, these principles seek to clarify and consolidate existing international obligations regarding future generations' rights. They offer a progressive interpretation of international and human rights law to strengthen the global normative framework.

The international legal landscape reflects a growing concern for intergenerational justice. References to future generations are found in both preambles and operative clauses of legal texts, with varying degrees of legal force and precision (Nyka, 2016). The Maastricht Principles represent an emerging consensus around future generations' legal personality and rights, reinforcing this dimension's legitimacy in global governance.

2.2. Posterity provisions on the constitutional level

Constitutional protection of future generations has seen dynamic development. Araújo and Koessler (2021) observe that while references to future generations existed in early constitutional preambles as early as 1789, it is only since the 1990s that constitutions have begun to include binding obligations toward them—especially in the environmental and economic domains. This trend reflects a broader shift toward universalist, values-based constitutional language. Modern constitutions include a variety of *posterity provisions*, ranging from general principles and state duties to enforceable rights and institutional mechanisms (e.g., ombudspersons for future generations). As Araújo and Koessler (2021) note, the normative strength of these provisions can be ranked from lowest to highest as principle, civic duty, state duty, and right. There has also been a linguistic shift toward more prescriptive and rights-oriented constitutional language (Tremmel, 2006). Some constitutions now establish duties to preserve environmental quality or economic resources explicitly for future generations. Others create oversight institutions charged with representing their interests.

According to González-Ricoy (in González-Ricoy & Gosseries, 2016), the constitutionalisation of intergenerational provisions serves several purposes: (1) it brings longer-term thinking into constitutional discourse, (2) it stabilises expectations about future policy commitments, and (3) it signals societal support for intergenerational fairness. However, measuring the impact of these provisions remains challenging. Comparative research shows that strong de jure protection does not necessarily translate into vigorous *de facto* enforcement (Araújo & Koessler, 2021).

3. Intergenerational Justice

Intergenerational justice is a central component of contemporary public law discourse, especially in the context of sustainable development. While the term may occasionally refer to the redress of historical injustices, its predominant use in political and academic literature is prospective and distributive. It concerns the relationship between present and future generations and the obligation to ensure that the latter have equal opportunities to fulfil their aspirations (Papuziński, 2014).

This prospective focus aligns with the concept of *longtermism*—the ethical view that positively influencing the distant future is a key moral priority (Macaskill, 2022). As Tremmel (2006) argues, this differentiates intergenerational justice from intragenerational justice. The latter typically focuses on the distribution of resources and opportunities within the current generation, whereas intergenerational justice compares the average well-being of individuals across non-overlapping generations.

A major theoretical challenge to intergenerational justice is the *non-identity problem*, formulated by Derek Parfit. This philosophical dilemma questions how moral obligations can apply to individuals who do not yet exist and whose identities depend on current actions (Roberts, n.d.; Parfit, 2017). Critics of Parfit's reductionist stance highlight the neglect of psychological and experiential continuity in identity formation (Matuszewska, 2013). For instance, Christine Korsgaard (1989), drawing on neo-Kantian thought, proposes that moral agency is tied to self-identification over time, regardless of metaphysical identity. Similarly, Michael Johnston (1987) maintains that concern for a person's future does not require a metaphysical grounding but stems from habits and practical considerations.

Narrative identity theory also contributes to this debate. Rather than relying on metaphysical unity, it defines personhood through coherence in one's autobiographical narrative (Filutowska, 2018).

A crucial dimension of intergenerational justice involves the concept of rights based on *interest theory.* This theory holds that if future people will have interests, those interests can already be represented in legal terms today (Feinberg, 1980). Joel Feinberg's "interest principle" claims that rights-holders must have interests that can be represented and that the ability to benefit or be harmed defines the scope of rights (Ekeli, 2006). According to Feinberg, current generations are responsible for preserving the world so future generations can pursue their interests.

Building on interest theory, Edith Brown Weiss (1988, 1990) introduced the concept of *intergenerational environmental equity.* She proposed that the planet is held in trust for past, present, and future generations, and that future generations hold *group rights,* which proxies can enforce. These rights are not individual, but generational, and require mechanisms for representation to be meaningful and actionable.

A complementary ethical perspective is found in Hans Jonas's *ethics of responsibility.* Jonas (1984) argues that modern technological civilisation demands a revised ethical framework for long-term survival. His imperative—"Act so that the effects of your action are compatible with the permanence of genuine human life"—shifts ethical responsibility from the individual to societal structures (Jonas, 1984; Chyrowicz, 2006). Jonas connects this responsibility to virtues such as temperance and moderation, countering the excesses of industrial production (Jonas, 1985).

Dieter Birnbacher echoes Jonas in asserting a moral imperative toward species survival. However, he adds that such responsibility can be grounded in existing ethical frameworks without entirely new ethical systems (Birnbacher, 1999.).

From a political-philosophical angle, intergenerational justice has been explored through Rawlsian contractualism, Gauthier's contractarianism, and the principle of indirect reciprocity. John Rawls offers the most developed framework, particularly through the *just savings principle* outlined in section 44 of *A Theory of Justice* (Rawls, 1971). This principle requires that each generation saves resources to maintain just institutions for future generations.

As Picchio (2024) and Meyer (2003) point out, Rawls integrates the just savings principle into the second of his two principles of justice. It is not a standalone rule but part of a broader difference principle aimed at fairness across generations. Gosseries (2008) notes that Rawls's model envisions two stages: an accumulation phase (to ensure economic and institutional stability) and a steady-state phase (where generations pass on at least what they received). Critics like Giannaccari (2024) observe that the rights-based framework struggles with the fact that future individuals are not yet identifiable rightsholders. This challenge continues to provoke debate in legal theory.

4. Significant trends in the protection of the rights of future generations and the implementation of intergenerational equity in the environmental context

The contemporary legal and political landscape for protecting the rights of future generations is highly diverse and dynamic. One of the key trends in recent decades has been the quantitative expansion of posterity provisions concerning environmental protection, both at the international and constitutional levels. However, their practical implementation remains uneven and dependent on several structural factors.

One of the most significant challenges in international law is the lack of effective enforcement mechanisms. Although multilateral environmental agreements and declarations have proliferated, systemic instruments for enforcing globally agreed standards are still underdeveloped. As noted in a 2024 report by the Parliamentary Assembly of the Council of Europe, "halfway to 2030, the world is woefully off track to achieve the UN Sustainable Development Goals" (Council of Europe, 2024, p. 5).

In contrast, constitutional protections often demonstrate a strong normative commitment to intergenerational justice. As highlighted earlier (see section 2.2), many national constitutions now include provisions explicitly referencing future generations. Nevertheless, as Araújo and Koessler (2021) observe, this strong de jure protection frequently fails to translate into de facto legal enforcement, and comparative studies show regional disparities in implementing such rights. Notably, courts in the Global South have often been more progressive than those in the Global North in applying intergenerational legal arguments, relying on strong constitutional guarantees and human rights jurisprudence (Setzer & Benjamin, 2019).

A second major trend is the rise of strategic litigation enforcing intergenerational and environmental rights. This includes climate litigation that frames climate inaction as violating future generations' rights. Steinkamp (2023) points out that litigation strategies based on intergenerational principles are gaining momentum, especially when they resonate with broader cultural and ethical values surrounding justice, sustainability, and responsibility.

One of the pivotal cases in this area was the Dutch Supreme Court's decision in the *Urgenda* case (2019), which required the Dutch government to reduce greenhouse gas emissions by at least 25% by 2020, based on Articles 2 and 8 of the

ECHR (Urgenda, 2019). While the judgment was framed primarily around the rights of the current population, it introduced a long-term perspective into the interpretation of fundamental rights.

The German Federal Constitutional Court established a more explicit recognition of intergenerational rights in its *Klimabeschluss* of 24 March 2021. The Court affirmed that insufficient climate action imposes disproportionate burdens on future generations and violates their constitutional right to a sustainable future (German FCC, 2021).

The EctHR judgment in *KlimaSeniorinnen* v. Switzerland (2024) marked a turning point at the European level. The Court acknowledged the intergenerational implications of climate change and held that disproportionate harm to future generations could violate the ECHR (EctHR, 2024). As Pedersen and Sulyok (2024) emphasise, this ruling reflects a growing awareness in international courts of intergenerational burden-sharing and the need to protect vulnerable groups in the face of long-term environmental threats. As Sulyok (2024) notes, recent jurisprudence from both domestic and international courts increasingly aligns around shared rule of law standards, including respect for human rights, legal clarity, the prohibition of arbitrariness, and access to justice. These rulings are helping to institutionalise intergenerational justice within broader legal frameworks.

5. Summary

The past few decades have witnessed a notable quantitative growth in posterity provisions—legal norms referring to future generations—at national and international levels. This development reflects a growing global awareness of the importance of protecting the rights of future generations and advancing the principles of intergenerational justice. However, the picture remains legally and politically complex. The mere constitutional or international codification of posterity provisions does not automatically result in more effective or enforceable protections for future generations.

In practice, the effectiveness of these provisions is shaped by a range of political, social, institutional, and cultural factors. National contexts vary considerably in terms of how strongly courts and policymakers implement or uphold legal guarantees for future generations. Despite these challenges, a parallel trend has emerged: the increasing relevance of strategic litigation in environmental and climate protection. This form of litigation plays a transformative role in reinforcing intergenerational justice and generating legal precedents that bind present-day institutions to long-term obligations.

Significantly, many influential court rulings—both at the domestic and international level—are not always based on explicit posterity provisions. Instead, courts have often invoked general constitutional or human rights norms—such as the right to privacy, life, or dignity—to articulate a jurisprudential framework that embeds the principles of intergenerational equity. Through these rulings, courts help to construct legal standards that extend the scope of state responsibility beyond the immediate present and toward future generations.

This evolution illustrates how intergenerational justice is increasingly being implemented through judicial interpretation, even without express legal mandates. As such, legal practice contributes to the realisation of intergenerational equity by aligning contemporary public law with long-term environmental and social imperatives.

References

Araújo, R., & Koessler, L. (2021). *The Rise of the Constitutional Protection of Future Generations.* LPP Working Paper Series No. 7-2021. https://verfassungsblog.de/the-rise-of-the-constitutional-protection-of-future-generations/.

Araújo, R., & Koessler, L. (2021). *The rise of the constitutional protection of future generations.* LPP Working Paper Series No. 7-2021, pp. 33 et seq.

Birnbarcher, D. (1999). Odpowiedzialność za przyszłe pokolenia, Warszawa: Oficyna Naukowa

Burke, E. (1909-1914). *Reflections on the Revolution in France.* New York: P. F. Collier & Son. (Bartleby.com, 2001).

Chatziathanasiou, K. (2017). Constitutions as Chains? On the Intergenerational Challenges of Constitution-Making. *Intergenerational Justice Review, 3*(1), 32-41.

Chyrowicz, B. (2006) Problem argumentacji z odpowiedzialności za przyszłe pokolenia, *Diametros, 9*, 7.

Council of Europe. (2024). *Safeguarding human rights for future generations.* Report of the Committee on Social Affairs, Health and Sustainable Development, Doc. 15999, 07 June 2024, p. 5.

EctHR. (2024). *Verein KlimaSeniorinnen Schweiz and Others v. Switzerland* [GC], 53600/20, para. 410.

Ekeli, K.S. (2006). The principle of liberty and legal representation of posterity, *Res Publica, 12*, 399.

Feinberg, J. (1980). The Rights of Animals and Unborn Generations. In J. Feiberg, Rights, Justice and the Bounds of Liberty, Princeton: Princeton University Press, pp. 159-185.

Filutowska, K. (2018). Tożsamość narracyjna jako empiryczna podmiotowość. MacIntyre, Taylor, Ricoeur Warszawa: Wydawnictwa Uniwersytetu Warszawskiego, p. 333.

German Federal Constitutional Court (FCC). (2021). *Klimabeschluss*, 1 BvR 2656/18, NJW 2021, 1723. https://www.gesetze-im-internet.de/englisch_ksg/index.html.

González-Ricoy, I. (2016). Constitutionalising Intergenerational Justice. In I. González-Ricoy & A. Gosseries (Eds.), *Institutions for Future Generations* (pp. 170–194). Oxford: Oxford University Press.

Gosseries, A. (2008). Theories of intergenerational justice: a synopsis, *S.A.P.I.E.N.S. Surveys and Perspectives Integrating Environment and Society* 1(1), 67.

Giannaccarri, C. (2024). Intergenerational justice and climate litigation. Some considerations about law and the deal with contemporary economic, social, and political issues, *Diritto Publico Comparato ed Europeo* 3, 1691.

Jefferson, T. (1789). *To James Madison, 6 September 1789.* Founders Online, National Archives. https://founders.archives.gov/documents/Madison/01-12-02-0248.

Johnston, M. (1987). Human Beings, *Journal of Philosophy, 84*, 59.

Jonas, H. (1984). The Imperative of Responsibility: In Search of Ethics for the Technological Age, Chicago: University of Chicago Press.

Jonas, H. (1985).Technik, Medizin und Ethik, Zur Praxis des Prinzips Verantwortung. Frankfurt am Main: Insel Verlag.

Korsgaard, Ch. (1989) Personal Identity and the Unity of Agency: A Kantian Response to Parfit, *Philosophy & Public Affairs 18*, 101.

Macaskill, M. (2022). What we owe the future: One-million year view, Basic Books, Oneworld Publications. https://cepcuyo.com/wp-content/uploads/2022/10/What-We-Owe-the-Future-William-MacAskill-1.pdf.

Meadows, D. H., Meadows, L., Randers, J., & Behrens, W. (1972). *The Limits to Growth: A Report for the Club of Rome's Project on the Predicament of Mankind.* New York: Universe Books.

Matuszewska, E. (2013) O racjach, osobach i teoriach w czasie, *Etyka* 46, 148.

Meyer, L. (2003), *Intergenerational Justice.* Stanford Encyclopedia of Philosophy. https://plato.stanford.edu/entries/justice-intergenerational/#RawlJustSaviPrin.

Nyka, M. (2014). Future Generations' Rights to Natural Resources. In M. Nyka & E. Scheider (Eds.), *Enacting Environmental Justice through Global Citizenship* (pp. 42–43). Oxford.

Nyka, M. (2016). Sprawiedliwość międzypokoleniowa w międzynarodowym prawie środowiska. *Gdańskie Studia Prawnicze, 35*, 359.

Papuziński, A. (2014). Zrównoważony rozwój w kontekście teorii sprawiedliwości międzygeneracyjnej. Próba konkretyzacji problem. *Studies in Global Ethics and Global Education, 2*, 14.

Parfit, D. (2017). Future People, the Non-Identity Problem, and Person-Affecting Principles, *Philosophy and Public* Affairs, 45, 83–194.

Picchio, M. (2024). Rawls on Just Savings and Economic Growth, *Journal of Ethics and Social Philosophy, 27(2)*, 342–343.

Pedersen, O. W., & Sulyok, K. (2024). Future generations litigation and transformative changes in environmental governance. *Transnational Environmental Law, 13*(4), 466.

Roberts, M.A. *The Nonidentity Problem*, Stanford Encyclopedia of Philosophy; https://plato.stanford.edu/entries/nonidentity-problem.

Setzer, J., & Benjamin, L. (2019). Climate litigation in the Global South: Constraints and innovations. *Transnational Environmental Law*, 1–25.

Steinkamp, T. (2023). Intergenerational justice as a lever to impact climate policies: Lessons from the complainants' perspective on Germany's 2021 climate constitutional ruling. *European Journal of Risk Regulation, 14*, 731.

Sulyok, K. (2024). Transforming the rule of law in environmental and climate litigation: Prohibiting the arbitrary treatment of future generations. *Transnational Environmental Law, 13*(3), 475.

Thant, U. (1969). *Man and His Environment.* Report by the UN Secretary-General.

Tremmel, J. C. (2006). Establishing Intergenerational Justice in National Constitutions. In J. C. Tremmel (Ed.), *Handbook of Intergenerational Justice* (p. 190). Cheltenham: Edward Elgar.

Urgenda Foundation v. State of the Netherlands. (2019). Supreme Court of the Netherlands, ECLI:NL:HR:2019:2006.

Weiss, E.B. (1988). In Fairness to Future Generations. Tokyo/New York: UN University/ Transnational Publishers.

Weiss, E.B. (1990). Our Rights and Obligations towards Future generations towards Environment, *The American Journal of International Law, 84*, 198.

World Commission on Environment and Development. (1987). *Our Common Future.* Retrieved from https://sustainabledevelopment.un.org/content/documents/5987our-common-future.pdf.

Kinga Janowska / Aleksandra Kościelak / Marcin Drewek

Regulation regarding energy sale prices and the issue of energy security – remarks in the light of current EU legal standards implementation on the example of the Polish legal system

1. Introduction

One of the central challenges in the contemporary regulation of renewable energy law, particularly in conjunction with emerging technological innovations, is the assurance of energy security. This concept encompasses the continuous availability of electricity in adequate quantities and its affordability for end users. Achieving this balance requires careful consideration of multiple economic dimensions, notably energy production, transmission, and sale costs.

The issue becomes even more complex when situated within the broader context of the ongoing energy transition, aimed at shifting away from fossil fuels toward renewable energy sources. This shift demands a regulatory framework that can reconcile two fundamental goals: maintaining affordable and stable electricity supply, and at the same time, facilitating a sustainable and timely transformation of the energy sector.

To respond to these challenges, the European Union has introduced several legal instruments, designed to shape a common approach among Member States. These include mechanisms for price regulation, support schemes for renewables, and legal provisions to enhance energy market integration and flexibility. However, the effectiveness and adequacy of these regulations remain the subject of intensive academic and policy debate.

This paper examines the implementation of current EU legal standards related to energy pricing and security, focusing specifically on their application within the Polish legal system. By analysing the practical aspects of transposing EU directives and regulations into domestic law, the study will offer insight into the Polish model's strengths and deficiencies in securing a reliable, fair, and sustainable energy system.

2. The current challenge of energy sale price shaping in Poland in terms of legal and economic analysis

As will be discussed in greater detail later in this article, an energy system must inherently guarantee safety in terms of uninterrupted supply and affordability. Within this framework, it is essential to consider whether allowing electricity prices to be determined purely by market mechanisms is a viable approach to meeting the broader objective of energy security.

A significant segment of economic theory is devoted to analyzing risk and uncertainty, with forecasting playing an important role. When applied to the energy sector, forecasting attempts to account for a broad spectrum of unpredictable variables, including price volatility, infrastructure performance, and external shocks (Thlon, Brożek & Thlon, 2024; Mun, 2006).

Crucially, energy policy must balance both supply-side and demand-side interests. Producers seek to maximize profit, while consumers aim to minimize costs. If one were to consider only the pure laws of economics, the price would be set by market equilibrium, where supply meets demand. However, the actual functioning of the energy sector is far more complex, especially in light of the intermittent nature of renewable energy sources, varying energy demand patterns, and technical constraints of the transmission network.

The integration of renewable energy sources (RES) introduces particular challenges. Their production is weather-dependent, making it less predictable and more challenging to manage within the framework of existing energy infrastructure (Marchel & Paska, 2015). Moreover, the daily and seasonal fluctuations in demand—compounded by RES volatility—create conditions of uncertainty that are not easily addressed using traditional economic odelling tools such as linear forecasting or deterministic optimization (Kamińska, Kubska-Maciejewicz & Laudańska-Trynka, 1998; von Mises, 2011).

Other layers of complexity stem from the current state of Poland's transmission infrastructure, which relies heavily on conventional sources such as coal-fired power plants, especially in periods of increased demand (Stawiany, 2017). Moreover, Poland's energy transition process, aimed at meeting EU climate goals and national energy security objectives, requires flexible regulatory tools that respond to short-term disruptions while maintaining a long-term investment trajectory (Pronińska, 2017).

The experience of blackouts and energy shortages, such as those observed in August 2015, underline the system's fragility when not properly balanced or diversified (Sobik, 2018). In such contexts, classical economic theories—centered on stable supply and demand curves—may fall short. What is needed is a multidimensional legal-economic framework that incorporates risk modelling, infrastructure resilience, regulatory flexibility, and strategic energy reserve planning (Bartosik et al., 2016).

Although in March 2024, a new record peak in instantaneous generation from renewable energy sources (RES) was reached—15,969 MW, covering approximately 80% of the national electricity demand—the Polish energy market continues to rely primarily on conventional generation sources, such as coal and gas-fired power plants. Nevertheless, a clear structural shift is occurring, driven by both EU policy and external geopolitical pressures, especially those related to the war in Ukraine, which have accelerated Poland's energy diversification efforts.

Data from Polskie Sieci Elektroenergetyczne (PSE) clearly illustrate this transformation. The year 2023 alone saw a surge of nearly 5 GW in photovoltaic (PV) capacity, with prosumer installations (households and small businesses) accounting for approximately 60% of this growth. In August 2024, a new record of 12,288 MW of instantaneous PV generation was recorded, highlighting the unprecedented pace of development. Although wind power growth has been more gradual—growing by 3 GW over the past four years—it remains a crucial stabilizing component in the RES portfolio.

However, this explosive growth of solar power has introduced new system-level challenges, notably the emergence of the so-called "duck curve" (Chart 1). This phenomenon, well-documented in jurisdictions with high PV penetration, describes a sharp drop in net electricity demand during midday hours, when solar generation peaks, followed by a steep ramp-up in the evening, when solar production falls and electricity demand rises.

The economic implications of this phenomenon are increasingly evident. Electricity prices turn negative during peak midday solar production, primarily due to oversupply and low demand. Conversely, the evening peak period—when the demand increases and solar production ceases—tends to produce the highest daily spot prices per MWh. This volatility poses a significant challenge for grid operators tasked with maintaining balance and market regulators and policy-makers, who must ensure that the energy pricing system remains rational, stable, and investment-friendly.

This also brings attention to the growing importance of energy storage systems, demand-side response programs, and more dynamic pricing models. Without these supporting mechanisms, high RES penetration may paradoxically lead to reduced system reliability, increased curtailment, and inefficient price signaling, thereby undermining long-term decarbonization goals (Schmalensee, 2020).

The increasing saturation of the energy mix with renewable energy sources (RES) in Poland has led to the emergence of two interconnected phenomena with significant economic implications: curtailment and profile costs.

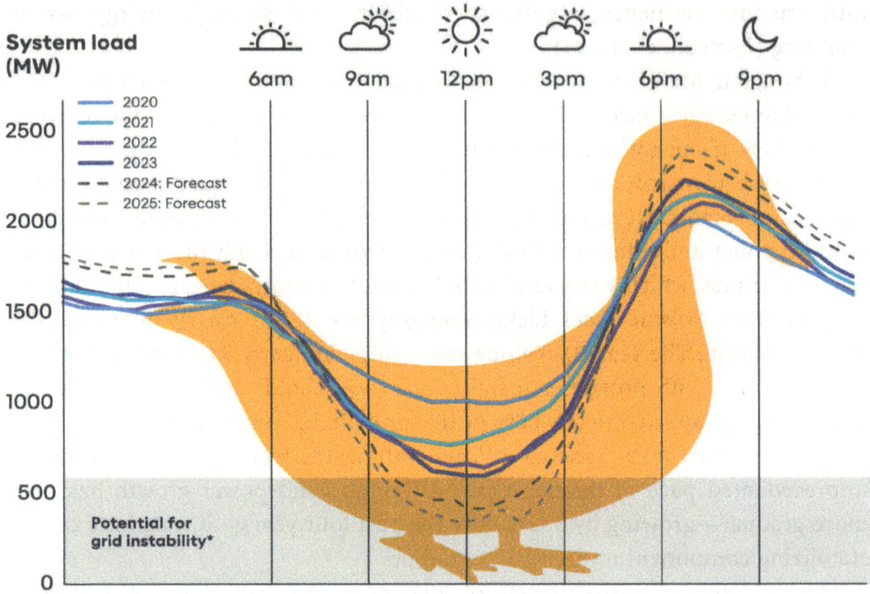

Chart 1. A graphical representation of the "Duck Curve". Source: Synergy (2021). https://www.synergy.net.au/Blog/2021/10/Everything-you-need-to-know-about-the-Duck-Curve.

Curtailment refers to the forced reduction or complete suspension of energy generation, particularly from RES, due to system limitations or excess supply. As the Cambridge Dictionary defines, curtailment as *"the action of reducing or limiting something, or of stopping something before it is"*. In the energy context, it typically involves the "loss" of potential clean energy that could not be injected into the grid. While this directly affects producers—who remain uncompensated or only partially compensated—it also reflects systemic inefficiencies that ultimately impact the national economy and long-term energy security (Cambridge Dictionary, 2024).

In Poland, curtailment is becoming increasingly common. The Transmission System Operator (TSO), Polskie Sieci Elektroenergetyczne (PSE), regularly issues orders for RES curtailment as part of its effort to balance electricity supply and demand. The scale of this curtailment depends on the grid's real-time operational conditions (PSE, 2024).

Alongside curtailment, producers also face profile costs—the economic penalty resulting from selling electricity at lower average prices than the daily market mean. This is particularly prevalent in photovoltaic energy, which is typically produced during midday hours when market prices are lowest due to oversupply. The profile cost is defined as the difference between the average daily market price and the average selling price of PV energy, which often leads to lower revenues for solar producers even when generation levels are high.

Recognizing the complexity of energy price formation and the challenges faced by RES operators, the Polish legislator has taken steps to reform the Balancing Market (Rynek Bilansujący). In June 2024, the second phase of the Balancing Market reform was implemented, aiming to enhance market-based mechanisms and limit non-market interventions. These interventions often trigger the obligation to compensate RES operators who are technically ready to deliver electricity but are denied access to the grid due to system constraints (URE, 2024).

The Balancing Market is a technical market managed by the TSO, where unscheduled production or consumption deviations outside the wholesale market are settled. Every system user (producers, suppliers, large consumers) must maintain energy balance within a designated time period. If balancing cannot be achieved through commercial transactions, the TSO intervenes and reallocates supply and demand to maintain grid stability.

According to the Energy Regulatory Office (URE), these reforms aim to introduce more accurate price signals, incentivising participants to act flexibly, adjusting their energy consumption or production in real-time in response to system needs. Theoretically, this creates a more responsive and resilient market structure, essential for an energy mix with growing shares of intermittent RES (Urbanek et al., 2018).

A central element of the second stage of Poland's Balancing Market reform, implemented on June 14, 2024, is the introduction of near-real-time pricing mechanisms. The reform has reduced settlement periods for balancing and imbalance energy to 15 minutes, bringing the Polish energy market closer to European and global standards. This technical update improves the temporal accuracy of price signals, better reflecting the actual operational status of the power system at any given moment (PSE, 2023).

Another important aspect of the reform is incorporating new cost components into the energy price, particularly the valuation of operational reserve and system-stabilizing services. These elements are intended to reflect better the real costs of ensuring system security and flexibility, especially in the context of increasing PV penetration and weather-dependent production patterns (Ciesielka et al., 2024).

Despite these improvements, the Transmission System Operator (TSO) reported significant irregularities in October 2024, stemming from algorithmic errors in the settlement process. As a result, the prices of balancing energy (CEB), imbalance prices (CEN), and operational reserve costs (COR) were either overestimated or underestimated, depending on the optimization data errors (PSE, 2024). These incidents underscore the technical and operational complexity of implementing high-frequency pricing models, and the critical importance of robust IT infrastructure and transparent correction mechanisms.

For market participants, the evolving system presents a new operational paradigm. Simply generating electricity is no longer sufficient for economic viability. Participants must understand market mechanics, forecast system behavior, and respond to price signals to avoid losses—primarily when negative pricing occurs, a risk notably higher for RES producers (Olszewski & Wrocławski, 2016).

A persistent technical challenge is balancing the National Power System (KSE) amid rapid RES integration. One major issue is the misalignment between PV generation profiles and peak electricity demand: solar production peaks at midday, when demand is low, while demand peaks in the evening, when PV output is negligible. This creates the need to rapidly ramp up dispatchable generation to fill the supply gap, which strains conventional power sources and complicates system operations (Mielczarski, 2021).

To mitigate these problems, the system must evolve toward greater dispatchable green generation, supported by proper market price coordination, and strengthened by frequency and non-frequency ancillary services. Market participants should be incentivized to provide flexibility, and the system should reward accurate forecasting, storage participation, and demand-side response.

Poland could benefit from studying more mature energy markets, such as CAISO in the United States, where granular price signals tied to real-time system status serve as effective tools for resource optimization. Such markets highlight the role of flexible capacity, real-time monitoring, and market transparency in enabling high RES shares without compromising security (Pach-Gurgul, 2011; Popczyk, 2023).

3. The issue of energy security from the perspective of the Polish legal system

3.1. The legal concept of energy security

In an era of dynamic transformation of energy markets and political instability in Europe, energy security is emerging as one of the foundational pillars of both national and EU energy policy. Like other EU Member States, Poland aims to combine market mechanisms with regulatory safeguards to ensure an uninterrupted energy supply, resilience to global energy crises, and reduced dependence on politically unstable regions.

The notion of energy security is deeply rooted in the Polish legal system, starting with Article 5 of the Constitution of the Republic of Poland, which obliges the state to "ensure the independence and inviolability of its territory and safeguard the freedoms and rights of its citizens, and ensure the security of the citizens". According to legal scholars, this article forms a constitutional basis for viewing energy security as a key element of the state's obligations (Florczak-Wątor, 2016).

The definition of energy security is further clarified in Article 3(16) of the Energy Law Act of 10 April 1997, which describes it as "the state of the economy that makes it possible to meet the current and prospective demand of consumers for fuel and energy in a technically and economically reasonable manner, while maintaining the requirements of environmental protection". This definition places the energy consumer at the center of concern, highlighting that security should be defined not only by supply continuity but also by affordability and environmental sustainability.

The Polish judiciary has also recognized energy security as an important economic and social interest. In its jurisprudence, the Supreme Administrative Court has emphasized that energy security transcends narrow sectoral interests and touches upon constitutional values relating to the public good (NSA, 2019, I OSK 2096/17).

In recent years, energy security has increasingly been associated with the need for independence from foreign energy supplies, especially from countries characterized by political or economic instability. This broader understanding of security includes legal and economic components and technological, environmental, and geopolitical dimensions (Ruszel & Podmiotko, 2019). The growing importance of this multidimensional approach is evident in EU-level initiatives, particularly the European Green Deal and the EU Energy Strategy 2024, which integrate climate objectives with the reduction of energy dependency.

As a member of the European Union, Poland's energy security policy is strongly influenced by EU directives and targets, especially those concerning greenhouse gas emission reductions, renewable energy deployment, and energy efficiency improvements. While ambitious, EU climate and energy goals are binding and require Member States to adopt mechanisms that may include reducing fossil fuel reliance, improving infrastructure, and diversifying energy sources (Mielczarski, 2021).

Thus, the current Polish legal framework for energy security rests on a foundation of constitutional obligations, statutory definitions, judicial interpretations, and supranational commitments. It reflects a gradual transition from traditional notions of supply continuity to modern, holistic concepts of resilience, sustainability, and long-term energy sovereignty.

3.2. Factors affecting energy security

One of the crucial elements in enhancing Poland's energy security is increasing public awareness of the role that various stakeholders—government institutions, energy companies, and citizens—play in ensuring the country's energy resilience. The state must act as the main coordinator, with both political and economic actors taking responsibility for shaping and executing energy strategies that are long-term, coherent, and adaptable to changing geopolitical and market conditions.

Public institutions are tasked with setting clear priorities in energy policy, identifying which sectors—production, transmission, distribution, or consumption—require regulatory intervention or targeted support to prevent future energy crises. Beyond legislative efforts, the state must actively implement its policies, engaging with private sector entities and local communities, coordinating strategic investments, negotiating international energy agreements, expanding critical infrastructure, and creating support systems for renewable energy and innovative technologies.

Furthermore, the state's role is to ensure regulatory compliance and align national development directions with global trends and EU law, enabling Poland to respond effectively to global energy challenges.

A fundamental and widely recognized factor in achieving energy security is the diversification of energy sources. Due to domestic resource availability, Poland's energy system has historically been based on hard coal and lignite. While this provided economic and strategic benefits for decades, it also led to a dependency on a single energy source. This model is no longer sustainable regarding the energy transition and the EU's climate policy.

The war in Ukraine has intensified the urgency of diversification, highlighting Poland's strategic vulnerability to external energy suppliers, especially Russian gas. As a result, Poland has accelerated its efforts to replace coal and Russian fossil fuels with a diverse energy mix including:

1) Renewable energy sources (RES) such as wind and solar power;
2) Liquefied Natural Gas (LNG) imports via terminals (notably in Świnoujście);
3) Expanded gas infrastructure connected to EU markets;
4) Cross-border interconnectors enhancing regional energy integration;
5) Support for nuclear energy as a long-term, zero-emission baseload option.

This approach aims to decrease reliance on politically unstable regions and increase system resilience. At the same time, it enhances Poland's ability to fulfill EU obligations, including targets set by the European Green Deal and the EU Fit for 55 package.

Poland's national strategy reflects these shifts. The Energy Policy of Poland until 2040 (PEP2040) and its subsequent updates place energy diversification, independence, and technological innovation at the heart of the country's security agenda. These policies recognize not only the strategic and economic dimensions of energy, but also the environmental and social aspects of the transition.

A central legal instrument for guaranteeing energy security in Poland is diversification, not only through the development of RES but also by investing in nuclear energy, which is seen as a strategic pillar for long-term energy stability. Unlike solar and wind power, nuclear energy is independent of weather conditions, offering a stable baseload supply and playing a complementary role to fluctuating renewable sources.

According to government plans, the first nuclear power plants are expected to become operational by 2033, reducing Poland's dependence on fossil fuels and ensuring compliance with the EU's climate targets. Nuclear power is crucial to future energy security despite the long and complex licensing process, which requires numerous permits, environmental approvals, safety audits, and international cooperation.

One notable advantage of nuclear investment in Poland lies in geological stability: the country is not exposed to high risks of natural disasters such as earthquakes, making it a favorable location for nuclear facilities. Research by Olech and Matiaszczyk (2022) indicates that nuclear diplomacy—especially partnerships with countries like France and the United States—has enhanced Poland's access to cutting-edge technologies and strengthened its position in global energy negotiations.

Nevertheless, over-reliance on a single foreign partner could pose risks, including political dependencies and reduced negotiating power. Therefore, a balanced and diversified portfolio of international agreements is recommended to preserve national sovereignty in energy policy.

The experience of the COVID-19 pandemic further highlighted the importance of resilient supply chains. Like many countries, Poland experienced delays in accessing energy-related equipment due to disruptions in global logistics and dependence on Asian and US markets. This has triggered discussions on increasing domestic production capacity and revising legal frameworks to ensure strategic energy supplies, particularly in the case of future crises.

In the legal domain, the Constitution of the Republic of Poland and the Energy Law of April 10, 1997, lay the foundation for safeguarding energy security. Article 5 of the Constitution mandates the state to ensure security and public order, including in the energy sector. The Energy Law defines energy security as the state of the economy that ensures "the possibility to satisfy current and future energy needs in a technically and economically justified manner, with respect for environmental requirements."

Moreover, Articles 16 and 16a EP stipulate the responsibilities of transmission and distribution system operators, requiring them to maintain supply continuity even during emergencies. Article 10 EP grants the President of the Energy Regulatory Office (ERO) powers to impose financial penalties for violations, such as insufficient supply provision, failure to meet energy efficiency requirements, or noncompliance with obligations related to crisis preparedness.

These regulations introduce preventive and repressive legal mechanisms, ensuring that energy companies and operators act in the public interest and comply with national strategic priorities. However, given evolving geopolitical realities—such as the war in Ukraine, global energy price fluctuations, and the strategic use of energy as a political tool—there is a growing consensus that Polish energy law requires further refinement. New legal provisions should address technical stability and market regulation, cybersecurity, strategic stockpiling, and supply chain localization in line with EU resilience goals.

The Constitution of the Republic of Poland obliges public authorities to act in the interest of national security, which by contemporary standards includes energy security. However, practice has shown that constitutional and statutory provisions, while foundational, may prove insufficient in the face of rapidly changing technological and geopolitical circumstances. This is especially relevant with regard to freedom of contract, enforcement of claims in the event of supply disruptions, and the scope of public intervention.

The Energy Law of April 10, 1997, while comprehensive in its duties assigned to public authorities—including preventive and repressive powers—may not adequately reflect the flexibility required to respond to current market challenges, such as technological dependence and supply chain disruptions. As J. Robel notes, the complexity of the "energy security" concept demands continuous legal reinterpretation and adaptation to evolving realities.

From the perspective of freedom of contract, it becomes necessary to evaluate whether the existing safeguards are sufficient to protect domestic consumers against market abuses, such as the monopolization of energy supply by a single foreign actor. The COVID-19 pandemic, the war in Ukraine, and disruptions in global logistics chains have all illustrated the need for more agile legal instruments, capable of enabling rapid, coordinated responses by national institutions.

There is also growing concern about the control of imported technologies, particularly those originating from outside the EU. Without legal oversight, the proliferation of technologically dependent energy infrastructure—such as systems controlled via foreign-built digital platforms—could threaten energy independence and critical infrastructure resilience. As such, there is a strong case for introducing clear legal mechanisms for certifying and vetting imported energy technologies.

Existing frameworks, such as the National Program for the Protection of Critical Infrastructure and the Cybersecurity Strategy of the Republic of Poland for 2019–2024, form an important basis for such efforts. Nevertheless, operationalizing these strategies within the energy sector would require precise legislative instruments that define obligations, procedures, and sanctions related to cyber incidents, sabotage, or physical threats to the energy grid.

Equally important is the need to align national legislation with EU standards, particularly in the context of energy solidarity, nuclear energy, digital infrastructure, and advanced RES technologies. Strengthening cooperation with EU agencies and international regulatory bodies could accelerate the implementation of shared technical standards, while also providing Poland with greater political leverage in shaping the future of the European energy security architecture.

De lege ferenda, it is proposed to:

1) Introduce explicit legal definitions and operational procedures for managing technological risks in energy infrastructure.
2) Strengthen the contractual protection of energy consumers in the event of market instability or politically motivated supply disruptions.
3) Enhance the emergency powers of national regulatory authorities to intervene swiftly in critical situations.
4) Create a legal framework for technology sovereignty in the energy sector, including mechanisms for vetting foreign-origin technologies.
5) Institutionalize legal provisions enabling rapid harmonization of Polish law with new EU regulations and directives.

Adopting these measures would not only strengthen the energy security of Poland but also ensure that the country remains resilient to geopolitical shocks, technological dependencies, and market fluctuations, while simultaneously building public trust in the reliability and safety of the energy system.

4. A review of the most significant legal regulations implemented into the Polish legal system

4.1. Outline of current legislative changes related to the implementation of EU law affecting energy prices and energy security

It is necessary to provide a dual perspective to assess the accuracy and completeness of EU legal standards implementation into the Polish legal system. First, this requires a general overview of the applicable and forthcoming EU legislative framework governing the energy market—particularly in renewable energy sources (RES). Second, one must examine the key normative measures introduced by the Polish legislator to align national law with EU requirements.

Although a detailed legal comparison exceeds the framework of this study, even a synthetic overview enables the identification of principal trends, strategic legislative choices, and areas of convergence or divergence between EU and Polish energy law.

One of the key developments in Polish energy law in recent years has been the amendment of two fundamental acts:

1) The Energy Law of April 10, 1997 (*Prawo energetyczne*, hereinafter: EP) as amended by the Act of July 28, 2023, Dz.U. 2023 poz. 1681;
2) The Renewable Energy Sources Act of February 20, 2015 (*Ustawa o odnawialnych źródłach energii*, hereinafter: RES Act), as amended by the Act of August 17, 2023, Dz.U. 2023 poz. 1762.

Complementary to these long-term reforms, the Act of May 23, 2024 on the energy voucher and the temporary freezing of electricity, gas and heat prices (Dz.U. 2024 poz. 859)was adopted. Although primarily temporary and reactive, this act nonetheless significantly impacts consumer protection and the practical implementation of Poland's EU energy transition policy.

These three legal acts form the core legislative foundation for Polish energy security and market reform. Other supporting laws exist, but their impact is typically transitory, sector-specific, or technical; thus, they fall outside the primary scope of this analysis.

The amendment to the Energy Law was explicitly aimed at harmonizing Polish law with EU legal standards, as stated in the preamble of the Act. It implements key provisions from:

1) Directive (EU) 2018/2001 on the promotion of the use of energy from renewable sources (RED II)EU OJ L 328, 21.12.2018;
2) Directive (EU) 2019/944 on common rules for the internal market in electricity, EU OJ L 158, 14.06.2019;
3) Regulation (EU) 2017/2195 establishing guidelines for electricity balancing, EU OJ L 312, 28.11.2017;
4) Regulation (EU) 2019/943 on the internal market for electricity, EU OJ L 158, 14.06.2019.

Among the major objectives of these reforms is to promote a market-based approach to electricity pricing, enhance consumer empowerment, and ensure system balancing in a flexible and technologically neutral manner. The implementation also supports mechanisms like active prosumer participation, energy communities, and the integration of digital technologies in the management of energy flows.

Similarly, the amendment to the RES Act also serves the purpose of implementing RED II, which includes:

1) Revised national RES targets;
2) Simplification of administrative procedures for installing RES;
3) New support mechanisms for small-scale producers and prosumers;
4) Provisions promoting innovation and new technologies, such as hydrogen and offshore wind.

These amendments show that Poland's regulatory landscape is increasingly converging with EU directives, though challenges remain regarding practical enforcement, market responsiveness, and regulatory transparency.

4.2. Regulatory changes directly affecting the price of energy

When analyzing in the scope of regulatory changes introduced into the Polish legal order in the context of adaptation to EU law through the aforementioned EL amendments and RES amendments, it should be noted at the outset that a very significant part of the introduced regulations affects the issue of electricity price relations and its impact on energy security. However, these regulations can directly and indirectly affect prices and energy security.

Among the major changes introduced by the amendment to the EL regarding the direct impact on the issue of electricity prices, one should first mention the new types of electricity sales contract. In addition to the existing typical agreement for the sale of electricity (Article 5(1) of the aforementioned Energy Law Act) introduced an agreement with a dynamic price of electricity (*umowa z ceną dynamiczną energii*). According to the wording of Article 1(1)(2)(b) of the amended EL, this is a contract for the sale of electricity or a comprehensive agreement, concluded between an electricity seller and an end-user, which reflects price fluctuations in the electricity markets, in particular in the day-ahead and intraday markets, at intervals at least equal to the imbalance settlement period within the meaning of Article 2(10) of Commission Regulation (EU) 2017/2195 of November 23, 2017 establishing balancing guidelines. In other words, such a contract allows customers to buy electricity at the most favorable price. However, it simultaneously passes him the risk of price changes over time. In addition, an additional protective mechanism has been introduced in the form of a standby sale of electricity to the end customer if information on the conclusion of a sales contract is not communicated to the central energy market information system (in which a standby seller sells case energy – Article 1(1)(2)(b) of the EL amendment).

Related to the issue of contracts for the sale of electricity is the second of the regulations created by the EP amendment, which creates an entitlement on the customer's part to change the seller in 24 hours. In fact, according to the wording of the disposition of Article 1(1)(6)(d) of the EL amendment, the energy market information operator, the electricity transmission system operator and the electricity distribution system operator are obliged to enable the electricity recipient to change the seller of electricity within 24 hours from the moment the new seller notifies the energy market information operator of the conclusion of an electricity sales contract or a comprehensive agreement. This power is intended to allow full freedom of contracting and create an effective legal mechanism for market price formation. However, consumers need to obtain relevant information from this point of view.

Related to this is another institution that directly affects the price of electricity, namely the comparison of offers (porównywarka ofert). It is regulated in the text of Article 1(1)(56) of the EL amendment. According to this provision, household and micro-enterprise electricity consumers are provided with access to a tool for comparing energy sales offers (offer comparison engine). Access to the comparator is free of charge. It takes place through a dedicated website maintained by the President of the Polish Energy Regulatory Office (hereinafter referred to as ERO). Importantly, the offer comparison engine includes several conveniences, in particular the posting of information on all current offers, the ability to report errors in offers, wording created in clear and simple language, adaptation to the needs of people with disabilities, and the posting of offers of other services offered by electricity sellers alongside electricity sales offers.

Other regulations that seem directly affecting the energy pricing sphere are those creating new elements in information obligations. Regarding information obligations, it is worth emphasizing that an electricity seller applying a tariff approved by the President of ERO is obliged to inform the household end-user at least quarterly about: the possibilities for that customer to purchase electricity from the electricity seller of his choice, savings on the competitive electricity market, as well as the conclusion of a contract with a dynamic electricity price, and, in addition, the availability of offers for the sale of electricity in the offer comparison engine (Article 1(1)(7)(m) of the EL amendment). Moreover, the electricity seller is required to notify household customers who are not party to contracts with a dynamic price for electricity, transparently and understandably, of the change in electricity prices or rates and the reasons and conditions for the change, within one month before the effective date of the change (Article 1(1)(7)(k) of the EL amendment).

Finally, in the group of regulations directly affecting energy prices on the market, one should mention the newly introduced and modified regulations concerning control and supervision of the electricity market by the ERO President. It should be noted that according to the content of Article 1(47)(c) of the EL amendment, the ERO President, at least once a year, publishes recommendations in the ERO Bulletin on ensuring compliance of electricity sales prices with the requirements of a competitive energy market and communicates these recommendations, if he deems it necessary, to the President of the Polish Office of Competition and Consumer Protection. In addition, the tasks of the ERO President, according to the wording of Article 1(1)(47)(a)(indent 10) of the EP amendment, will also include monitoring, in particular: the level and effectiveness of market opening and competition at the wholesale and retail levels, including on electricity exchanges, prices for household electricity consumers, the conclusion and application of contracts with dynamic electricity prices, bids of electricity sellers, the impact of these contracts and bids on prices and tariffs for household consumers, the ratio of prices applied by electricity sellers for household electricity consumers to wholesale electricity prices, as well as the development of tariffs and fees for distribution services.

4.3. Regulatory changes indirectly affecting the price of energy

Other regulations introduced by the EL amendment also significantly impact energy prices and the formation of the level of energy security. However, their impact seems somewhat more indirect (but this does not mean it is less significant). In this regard, it seems that three groups of regulations should be mentioned. Firstly, norms relating to the functioning and stability of the electricity market (balancing in particular), secondly, regulations in the field of distributed energy (including prosumer energy in particular), and thirdly, expanding the definition of renewable energy to include new sources.

Significant indirect effects on energy pricing and security issues may come from changes in energy market stability. A sizable part of the regulation addresses the issue of adequate market balancing. In particular, the provisions of the amendment define the balancing market for electricity (*rynek bilansując energii elektrycznej*), taking into account the requirements of Commission Regulation (EU) 2017/2195 of November 23, 2017 establishing balancing guidelines (Article 1(1)(2)(p) of the EL amendment). The concept of system balancing as an activity in the sphere of balancing demand for specific types of energy has also been defined, again ensuring compliance with EU regulations in the form of Regulation (EU) 2019/943 of the European Parliament and of the Council of June 5, 2019 on the internal market in electricity and Commission

Regulation (EU) No. 312/2014 of March 26, 2014 establishing a network code for gas balancing in transmission networks (Article 1(1)(2)(k) of the EL amendment).

Furthermore, in the scope of ensuring the stability of the energy market, there are regulations concerning the so-called flexibility of the power market, i. e. the rapid consumption or storage of excess energy in power grids, which is particularly important for the further development of renewable energy and the application of new technologies in the power industry. Thus, one can find regulations relating to the definition and indication of a rather wide range of flexibility services (usługi elastyczności), as services provided to the electricity distribution system operator by an aggregator or by system users who are active consumers, generators, holders of electricity storage to ensure security and increase the efficiency of the development of the distribution system, including the management of network congestion in the electricity distribution network (Article 1(1)(2)(g) of the EL amendment). The concept of aggregation services (usługi agregacji) has also been introduced, as the activity of combining the volume of capacity or electricity offered by customers, electricity generators or electricity storage holders, taking into account the technical capacity of the network to which they are connected, to sell electricity, provide system services or flexibility services in electricity markets (Article 1(1)(2)(b) of the EL amendment).

It should be noted that existing legal constructs regarding energy market players have been introduced or expanded, so it will be possible to counteract better the phenomenon of overloading the grid with new RES generation capacity. At the same time, this applies in particular to RES prosumers. It would therefore be worthwhile to pay attention to the construction of an active consumer (dbiorca aktywny). Under this term, the legislator has defined a final customer acting individually or in a group, who consumes, stores or sells electricity generated on its own, as well as who carries out projects to improve energy efficiency, provides system services or flexibility services. It is important, however, that this activity is not its primary business activity (Article 1(1)(2)(i) of the EL amendment).

Besides, the concept of a citizen energy community (obywatelskia społeczność energetyczna) has been introduced. This entity with legal capacity brings together individuals, local government units and micro or small entrepreneurs for whom activities in the energy sector are not their primary business under certain rules. At the same time, the primary objective here is the generation, consumption, distribution, sale, trading, aggregation, or storage of electricity, or implementing projects to improve energy efficiency. In addition, the purpose of the business may include the provision of electric vehicle charging services, relevant biogas, agricultural biogas, biomass and biomass activities, as well as partnership trading in energy from renewable energy sources (Article 1(1)(2)(i) of the EL amendment). What is more, the concept of an energy cluster (klaster energii) has also been significantly redefined, broadening its scope to include, in particular, elements precisely referring to increasing energy market flexibility (Article 1(3)(g) of the RES amendment).

As mentioned at the beginning of this section, several vital legislative changes have also been introduced to improve the applicability of new activities for more comprehensive and long-term development of renewable energy, including in particular the introduction of the concept of energy (Article 1(3)(d) of the RES amendment), hybrid renewable energy installation – Article 1(3)(e) of the RES amendment). and renewable hydrogen (Article 1(3)(s) of the RES amendment). Renewable energy source (Article 1(3)(k) of the RES amendment) and renewable energy source installation (Article 1(3)(f) of the RES amendment) were also aptly expanded. More extensive presentation of any changes, though, would exceed the scope of this paper.

5. An attempt at legal evaluation of the implemented regulations and *de lege ferenda* conclusions

As mentioned in the previous chapters of this paper, the main purpose of the regulations currently being introduced in the context of the current needs of legal trading should be, first of all, from the economic side, to ensure an adequate level of energy prices and its proper distribution in the event of an oversupply of production (and therefore adequate balancing of the power market), and from the energy security side, to ensure stability of access to electricity (and therefore diversification of supply, price stability, ensuring access to adequate market information, as well as providing mechanisms for the state authorities to respond adequately quickly to rapid changes on the electricity market).

In this context, it should be pointed out that the fundamental direction of the changes introduced into the Polish legal system by the presented regulations amending the Energy Law and the Law on Renewable Energy Sources is correct. This is because the basic problem in the sphere of the current challenges of developing renewable energy and new technologies concerning it, which is the issue of grid instability, has been broadly addressed. This is because provisions have been introduced relating specifically to such problems as balancing, flexibility and energy storage. In the context of optimizing production and ensuring security of supply, regulations were strengthened and improved in distributed energy, particularly social and prosumer energy (Petelski, 2023; Kostecka-Jurczyk & Marak, 2024).

Moreover, the possibility of cooperation between large state-owned entities and consumers in shaping the electricity market and prices has been increased, moving away from significant monopolization toward a more free-market model. The regulations on dynamic pricing, comparison of offers, and seller switching are worth mentioning, among others. More supervision by the President of the Energy Regulatory Authority over the market and energy prices has also been introduced, which certainly increases security, prevents excessive price increases and reduces energy oversupply. Finally, the need for a broader understanding of renewable energy into emerging technologies has been recognized, particularly in the use of hydrogen (Marzec, 2023; Filipiak, 2023).

Conversely, while the general direction of the changes is very pertinent, these changes do not touch the essence of the issues facing the electricity market. For all the time, the problem of the inadequacy of the number of networks and transmission capacities (leaving aside the issue of quality and the need to modify the currently existing ones) remains very relevant and unresolved. Additionally, challenges persist in sustainably implementing a long-term model for the energy transition—such as delays in the construction of wind farms in the Baltic Sea, incomplete use of the potential of geothermal, hydroelectric and pumped storage energy, or the cessation of investment in nuclear power plants and SMRs (Handzel & Gajer, 2023; Krawczyk & Wysocka, 2023). Also problematic is the reduction in funding for large energy entities in favor of short-term subsidies for unstable photovoltaics, rather than comprehensive and long-term development of social and prosumer entities.

Without these structural changes, current regulations—however right—will only be leveling the effects without removing the causes. In conclusion, it should additionally be noted that this is precisely the direction in which the current efforts of EU legislative bodies seem to be heading, particularly concerning price stability, long-term planning, cooperation between different energy markets, and prevention of energy poverty (Council of the EU, 2024a; Council of the EU, 2024b; European Parliament, 2024a).

To summarize, while the direction of the legal changes in the Polish legal system regarding energy sale prices and the issue of energy security in context of the current EU legal standards implementation is the appropriate one, a great deal remains to be done (Sokołowski & Taylor, 2023; Marhold, 2023; Mauger, 2023).

References

Bartosik, M., Kamrat, W., Kaźmierowski, M., Lewandowski, W., Pawlik, M., Peryt, T., Skoczkowski, T., Strupczewski, A., & Szeląg, A. (2016). *Wytwarzanie energii elektrycznej – diagnoza i terapia. Przegląd Elektrotechniczny*, 279–289.

Bojarski, W. (2004). *Bezpieczeństwo energetyczne. Wokół Energetyki*, 7(3), 1.

Cambridge Dictionary. (2024). *Definition of "curtailment"*. Retrieved from https://dictionary.cambridge.org/dictionary/english/curtailment.

Chadam, J. (2022, September 7). *Episode 30. Energy security of Poland – opportunities and challenges* [Interview by M. Cichocka].

Ciesielka, E., Dybowski, P., & Wójcik, J. (2024). *Zmiany struktury rynku energii i ich wpływ na kształtowanie taryf sprzedaży energii elektrycznej i usług dystrybucyjnych. Optymalizacja kosztów zakupu. Przegląd Elektrotechniczny*, 8, 26–29.

Filipiak, B. Z. (2023). Polityka energetyczna jednostek samorządu terytorialnego szczebla gminnego w świetle ryzyka finansowego i niefinansowego. W: D. Rynio & A. Zakrzewska-Półtorak (red.), *Przestrzeń i regiony w nowoczesnej gospodarce. Księga jubileuszowa dedykowana Profesorowi Stanisławowi Korenikowi* (s. 231–232). Wrocław.

Florczak-Wątor, M. (2016). Artykuł 5. In M. Safjan & L. Bosek (Eds.), *Konstytucja RP. Tom I. Komentarz do art. 1–86.* Warszawa: C.H. Beck.

Handzel, Z., & Gajer, M. (2023). Energetyka wiatrowa jako główna konkurencja dla fotowoltaiki i wynikające stąd problemy związane z koniecznością zbilansowania mocy w systemie elektroenergetycznym. *Zeszyty Naukowe Wyższej Szkoły Ekonomii i Informatyki w Krakowie, 19*, 135–161.

Kamińska, T., Kubska-Maciejewicz, B., & Laudańska-Trynka, J. (1998). *Teoria podejmowania decyzji przez podmioty rynkowe.* Gdańsk.

Kostecka-Jurczyk, D., & Marak, K. (2024). Spółdzielnie energetyczne i klastry energii jako formy energetyki obywatelskiej w Polsce. *Studia Prawnoustrojowe, 63*, 157–170.

Kowalczuk, K. (2023). Wdrożenie "Smart Metering" w kontekście cyberzagrożeń. *Nowa Energia, 4*, 4.

Koziński, M. (2014). *Bezpieczeństwo energetyczne Polski.* Gdańsk.

Krawczyk, M., & Wysocka, P. (2023). Nowelizacja pakietu legislacyjnego dedykowanego offshore wind w Polsce. *Nowa Energia, 1*, 86–89.

Marchel, P., & Paska, J. (2015). *Niezawodność wytwarzania energii elektrycznej w systemie elektroenergetycznym przy uwzględnieniu odnawialnych źródeł energii.* Jastrzębia Góra.

Marhhold, A.-A. (2023). Towards a 'security-centred' energy transition: Balancing the European Union's ambitions and geopolitical realities. *Journal of International Economic Law, 26*(4), 756–769.

Marzec, T. (2023). Rozwój energetyki obywatelskiej na obszarach wiejskich w Polsce. *Przegląd Prawa Rolnego, 1*, 61–80.

Mauger, R. (2023). Finding a needle in a haystack? Identifying degrowth-compatible provisions in EU energy law for a just transition to net-zero by 2050. *Journal of Energy & Natural Resources Law, 41*(2), 175–193.

Mielczarski, W. (2021). *Odnawialne źródła energii jako element nowego zielonego ładu. Magazyn Polskiej Akademii Nauk*, 1, 84–87.

Mun, J. (2006). *Modeling Risk: Applying Monte Carlo Simulation, Real Options Analysis, Stochastic Forecasting, and Optimization.* California.

Olech, A., & Matiaszczyk, N. (2022). *Atomic Diplomacy. Report.* Warsaw.

Olszewski, A., & Wrocławski, M. (2016). *Bilansowanie mocy w systemie dystrybucyjnym czynnikiem wspierającym rozwój usług systemowych. Energia Elektryczna*, 3, 1–4.

Pach-Gurgul, A. (2011). *Jednolity Rynek Energii Elektrycznej w Unii Europejskiej a bezpieczeństwo energetyczne Polski.* Kraków, p. 28.

Petelski, Ł. (2023). Generacja rozproszona. Czy nowe regulacje wyjdą naprzeciw oczekiwaniom inwestorów? *Nowa Energia*, 4, 74–77.

Popczyk, J. (2023). *Druga ustrojowa reforma elektroenergetyki – główny filar transformacji TETIP do elektroprosumeryzmu.* p. 25.

Pronińska, K. (2017). *Rozwój odnawialnych źródeł energii a wymiar geostrategiczny bezpieczeństwa energetycznego Unii Europejskiej* (Vol. 53). Warszawa.

PSE. (2023). *Projekt nowych Warunków Dotyczących Bilansowania (WDB).* Retrieved from https://www.pse.pl/documents/20182/20962655/Projekt_nowych_WDB-prezentacja_na_spotkanie_informacyjne_20230329.pdf.

PSE. (2024). Raporty miesięczne z funkcjonowania Krajowego Systemu Elektroenergetycznego i Rynku Bilansującego. Retrieved from https://www.pse.pl/dane-systemowe/funkcjonowanie-kse/raporty-miesieczne.

Robel, J. (2015). *The complexity of the concept of "energy security" and its basis in the Polish Constitution.* UJK in Kielce, pp. 135–137.

Ruszel, M., & Podmiotko, S. (2019). *Bezpieczeństwo energetyczne Polski i Europy. Uwarunkowania – wyzwania – innowacje.* Rzeszów: Wydawnictwo UR.

Schmalensee, R. (2020). Competitive Energy Storage and the Duck Curve. The Energy Journal, 2–14.

Sobik, B. (2018). *Analiza przyczyn wystąpienia zagrożenia bezpieczeństwa dostaw energii elektrycznej w sierpniu 2015 roku i sposoby zapobiegania takim zdarzeniom.* Kraków, 193–208.

Sokołowski, M. M., & Taylor, M. (2023). Just energy business needed! How to achieve a just energy transition by engaging energy companies in reaching climate neutrality: (Re)conceptualising energy law for energy corporations. *Journal of Energy & Natural Resources Law, 41*(2), 157–174.

Stawiany, W. (2017). *Ogólnopolski system wsparcia doradczego dla sektora publicznego, mieszkaniowego oraz przedsiębiorstw w zakresie efektywności energetycznej oraz OZE.* Gdańsk.

Synergy. (2021). Everything you need to know about the Duck Curve. Retrieved from https://www.synergy.net.au/Blog/2021/10/Everything-you-need-to-know-about-the-Duck-Curve.

Thlon, M., Brożek, A., & Thlon, J. (2024). *Rynek energii elektrycznej w Polsce: perspektywa ryzyka i niepewności. Horyzonty Polityki*, 15, 301–322.

Urbanek, D., Paska, J., Pawlak, K., Terlikowski, P., & Kaliński, J. (2018). *Analiza działania rynku bilansującego.* In Z. Połecki & P. Pijarski (Eds.), *Rynek energii elektrycznej – rozwój, polityka, ekonomia* (pp. 121–133). Warszawa.

URE. (2024). *Notice on the second phase of the reform of the Balancing Market.* Retrieved from https://www.ure.gov.pl/pl/urzad/informacje-ogolne/aktualnosci/12002,Dzis-wchodzi-w-zycie-drugi-etap-reformy-Rynku-Bilansujacego.html.

von Mises, L. (2011). *Ludzkie działanie. Traktat o ekonomii.* (Human Action: A Treatise on Economics).

Małgorzata Cilak / Martyna Wilmanowicz-Słupczewska

Legal basis of state aid for energy from renewable sources

1. EU climate and environment policies – introductory remarks

As an introduction to the legal basis of state aid for renewable energy, it is worth briefly referring to the historical outline of the European Union's climate and environmental policy. The literature highlights that "European environmental policies over the last 30 years have always been very sensitive to wider economic and political cycles" (Hey, 2007). The European Union is the competent authority for environmental policy, and international declarations that have impacted environmental issues are an indispensable part of the analysis.

The first UN Conference on the Human Environment took place in 1972 in Stockholm, where the Stockholm Declaration and the Action Plan on the Human Environment were adopted. The 1992 'Earth Summit' in Rio de Janeiro led to adopting Agenda 21, the Rio Declaration, the United Nations Framework Convention on Climate Change (UNFCCC) and the Convention on Biological Diversity (Kurrer & Petit, 2024).

Adopting the European Treaties significantly strengthened the EU's position as a decisive actor in environmental policy. In 1972, the European Council announced the need for a Community environmental policy. The Single European Act of 1987 introduced the first legal basis for a common environmental policy (the "Environmental Title"). With the Maastricht Treaty of 1992, the environment was recognised as an official EU policy area. Later, the Amsterdam Treaty (1999) integrated environmental protection into all EU sectoral policies through Article 3c, and the Lisbon Treaty (2007) made climate change and sustainable development core elements of the EU's agenda (Kurrer & Petit, 2024).

In today's environmental challenges, particular attention should be paid to the European Green Deal (EGD). This strategy aims to transform the EU into a fair and prosperous society living in a modern, resource-efficient and competitive economy, with net-zero greenhouse gas emissions by 2050 and economic growth decoupled from resource use (European Commission, 2019). It forms the basis of the European Green Deal Strategic Framework (EGDSF), intended to guide the

EU's green transition. However, the implementation of this plan has been affected by unexpected global events, notably the COVID-19 pandemic, Russia's invasion of Ukraine, and the resulting energy crisis (Paleari, 2024).

2. State aid and renewable energy sources

Following Article 2(22) of the Renewable Energy Sources Act, a renewable energy source is defined as "renewable, non-fossil energy sources including wind energy, solar energy, aerothermal energy, geothermal energy, hydrothermal energy, hydropower, wave, current and tidal energy, ambient energy, energy obtained from biomass, biogas, agricultural biogas, biomethane, bioliquids and renewable hydrogen" (Długosz, 2024). This statutory definition aligns with the one found in Article 2(1) of the RED II Directive.

The formal legal definition of state aid is derived from Article 107(1) of the Treaty on the Functioning of the European Union (TFEU), which defines it as aid granted by a Member State or through state resources, in any form, which distorts or threatens to distort competition by favouring certain undertakings or the production of certain goods, insofar as it affects trade between Member States.

In Poland, the President of the Office of Competition and Consumer Protection is responsible for monitoring public aid. This authority ensures that state aid schemes comply with EU regulations. Based on reports and collected data, the President prepares and submits to the Council of Ministers an annual report on public aid, including the volume, forms and purposes of the granted aid, along with an assessment of its effects on competition (Journal of Laws, 2023, Art. 31 (2)).

The data used for the report is also submitted to the European Commission under Commission Regulation (EC) No. 794/2004 of 21 April 2004, which implements Council Regulation (EU) 2015/1589 and lays down detailed rules for applying Article 108 TFEU (Official Journal of the EU, 2004). This information feeds into the State Aid Scoreboard, a tool introduced by the European Commission in 2001 to promote transparency and comparability of state aid across the EU (European Commission, 2024a).

The State Aid Scoreboard 2023 reports that by the end of 2022 and 2023, the European Commission had approved 14 decisions relating to 12 state aid measures notified by 10 Member States, including Finland, France, Germany, Hungary, Italy, Ireland, Lithuania, Portugal, Slovakia, and Slovenia. These approvals were granted under Section 2.5 of the Temporary Crisis and Transition Framework to accelerate the deployment of renewable energy and energy storage aligned with the REPowerEU Plan. The total value of the aid approved amounted to approximately EUR 19.36 billion (European Commission, 2024b).

Through these instruments, EU state aid policy fosters investment in renewable energy while aiming to limit distortions of competition—highlighting how such legal frameworks are essential for the green transition.

3. Treaty on the Functioning of the European Union

When identifying the legal basis in the Treaty on the Functioning of the European Union (TFEU) for state aid supporting renewable energy, two articles are key: Article 191, which provides the framework for EU environmental policy, and Article 107, which lays down the rules governing the permissibility of state aid.

Article 191 TFEU is closely linked with other EU policy areas such as energy and competition policy. EU energy policy must balance the need for energy security with environmental protection, particularly given the environmental impact of electricity generation. According to Article 191(1), third indent, Member States must pursue an environmental policy that supports the prudent and rational utilisation of natural resources, including primary energy sources such as coal or natural gas (Nowacki & Przyborowska-Klimczak, 2012). From this, renewable energy is integral to EU energy and environmental policy.

Article 107(1) TFEU states that aid granted by Member States through public funds is incompatible with the internal market, as it affects trade between Member States. The European Commission's Notice on the concept of State aid under this provision provides that a measure constitutes state aid if it (1) benefits an undertaking engaged in economic activity, and (2) provides an advantage unavailable under normal market conditions (European Commission, 2016). This implies that not all public support for renewables qualifies as state aid—only that which targets specific undertakings and exceeds normal market benefits.

State aid is considered a form of public intervention and, in EU law, is viewed as an exception to the principle of free competition. As Gurba (2009) points out, EU environmental law is grounded in the "polluter pays" principle from Article 191 TFEU, under which polluters should bear the cost of environmental protection. State aid, funded through public taxes, is allowed only in cases of market failure, where environmental goals cannot be achieved by market forces alone. In these situations, the high cost of compliance might make green production economically unviable, justifying public support (Nowacki, Przyborowska-Klimczak, 2012).

Article 107(3)(c) TFEU provides an exception, allowing state aid to be considered compatible with the internal market when it facilitates the development of certain economic activities or areas, as long as it does not harm trade to an extent contrary to the common interest. The Commission considers environmental protection and green energy development to fall under this provision (Nowacki & Przyborowska-Klimczak, 2012).

Typically, the state aid procedure requires Member States to notify the Commission of their intent to provide aid and to wait for approval. This aid can be ad hoc measures or aid schemes targeting multiple beneficiaries over time. However, Articles 108 and 109 TFEU, in conjunction with Regulation 651/2014, provide for automatic approval in specific cases, including certain renewable energy aid types (Official Journal of the EU, 2014).

Additionally, de minimis aid—which does not exceed a certain threshold—is not considered state aid under Article 107(1) and is therefore exempt from Commission assessment. The current threshold under Regulation 2023/2831 is EUR 300,000 per undertaking over three years (European Commission, 2023). This type of aid can also support renewable energy, provided it stays within the quantitative limits.

4. Guidelines on State aid for climate and environmental protection and energy-related objectives 2022

Based on Article 107(3)(c) of the TFEU, the European Commission issued the *Guidelines on State aid for climate, environmental protection and energy 2022* (hereinafter: the Guidelines), which define the criteria for assessing the compatibility of state aid, including aid for renewable energy, with the internal market (European Commission, 2022).

According to the Guidelines, aid based on Article 107(3)(c) TFEU may be considered compatible with the internal market if it meets two key conditions: a positive condition and a negative condition (para. 8). The positive condition requires that the aid facilitates the development of an economic activity. The negative condition means that the aid must not distort competition and trade in a manner contrary to the common interest.

The European Commission explains that environmental costs are often not reflected in market prices, as companies typically do not internalise them and consumers are not inclined to pay more for environmentally responsible products (paras. 9–10). Therefore, market mechanisms alone are insufficient to drive green transformation. The Guidelines recognise that public aid may be necessary to meet the EU's 2030 and 2050 climate goals, as established in the European Climate Law. In this context, aid for renewable energy is explicitly acknowledged as a form of support contributing to reducing or removing greenhouse gas emissions (section 2.2, point 16(a)).

Chapter 3 of the Guidelines elaborates on the positive condition, which includes:

1) Identification of the economic activity promoted by the aid and its positive societal and policy relevance;
2) Incentive effect, showing that aid is necessary to trigger behaviour that would not occur without it;
3) Compliance with applicable provisions of EU law.

The negative condition, described in Chapters 3 and 4, includes criteria to minimise distortions of competition and trade, focusing on:

1) The need for aid, i. e. the existence of market failures;
2) The appropriateness of the aid instrument selected;
3) Clear eligibility criteria;
4) Proportionality, ensuring that the aid is limited to the minimum necessary;
5) Transparency, through accessible and published information about the aid measure.

Moreover, the Guidelines call for balancing the positive effects of aid with any undue negative effects on competition and trade, thereby ensuring alignment with the common interest.

When notifying a state aid measure, the Member State is required to identify the specific economic activities that will be facilitated by the aid and explain how their development will be supported. It must also describe how the measure contributes to achieving the EU's climate, environmental and energy objectives, particularly highlighting the expected material benefits of the aid in supporting those objectives (European Commission, 2022, paras. 23–25).

A crucial element in the assessment of compatibility is the incentive effect. Aid has an incentive effect when it induces the beneficiary to undertake an action that it would not have taken without the aid, or would have taken to a lesser or different extent. The aid must enable the beneficiary to act. Suppose a project starts before the beneficiary has submitted a formal aid application to the competent national authority. In that case, the incentive effect is deemed absent, and the aid is considered ineffective and potentially distortive (European Commission, 2022, paras. 26–27).

This requirement ensures that public funds are used efficiently and do not finance actions that would have occurred regardless. As Wojtaczka (2014) notes, aid without an incentive effect constitutes a misallocation of public resources and can distort competition by benefiting certain undertakings without contributing to additional value.

There are three exceptions to the general rule requiring ex-ante application. According to paragraph 30 of the Guidelines, two of these exceptions apply when the beneficiary can reasonably expect the aid to be granted. The third exception refers to operating aid granted to support the ongoing activities of environmentally friendly production installations. In this case, the incentive effect may be demonstrated through a change in operation toward a greener alternative, compared to a cheaper, more polluting option (European Commission, 2022, para. 30).

However, not all measures can demonstrate an incentive effect. This applies particularly to:

1) aid that merely covers the cost of complying with existing EU standards;
2) aid compensating for normal business risks;
3) aid covering the costs of activities the beneficiary would undertake anyway.

In such cases, the incentive effect is not considered proven. The European Commission examines two scenarios to determine the existence of an incentive effect: the real plan of action with aid and a counterfactual scenario where the aid is absent.

Another element of the positive compatibility condition is that the aid measure must not breach other EU laws. For instance, a condition that obliges the beneficiary to use domestically produced goods may violate internal market principles and be incompatible with EU law (European Commission, 2022, para. 33).

The elements comprising the negative condition for renewable energy aid are discussed in detail in Chapters 3 and 4 of the Guidelines (European Commission, 2022). This condition ensures that aid does not distort competition or trade to an extent contrary to the common interest.

Regarding the necessity of aid for measures aimed at reducing greenhouse gas (GHG) emissions, including renewable energy aid, the Guidelines require the Member State to identify existing policy instruments addressing emissions and demonstrate the need for aid in light of a counterfactual scenario. The analysis must also consider associated revenues and costs. If a residual market failure remains—i. e., one that cannot be corrected without state aid—this is sufficient for the Commission to recognise the need for public intervention (European Commission, 2022, Chapter 4).

For the appropriateness criterion, the Commission generally presumes that state aid is a suitable instrument to support decarbonisation goals. It even allows the use of potentially distortive forms of aid such as direct subsidies, where warranted by the policy objective (European Commission, 2022, para. 93).

The principle of proportionality requires that the aid amount does not exceed what is necessary for the project or activity to proceed. For aid to renewable energy in particular, the Commission typically expects that support will be allocated through competitive tendering procedures, which help ensure that only the most cost-effective projects are selected. These procedures are described in paragraphs 103–106 of the Guidelines.

Member States may also apply alternative mechanisms for determining aid amounts and allocation, such as certificate systems or supplier obligation schemes, as provided in paragraph 108 of the Guidelines.

Under the eligibility criterion, if the aid measure targets only specific activities competing with others, the Member State must justify this selective approach, particularly if it could lead to greater distortions.

In the context of avoiding undue negative effects and balancing, the Commission stresses that aid for renewable energy must result in a real and overall reduction in GHG emissions—not simply a shift of emissions to other sectors. Aid that supports highly polluting energy sources over less polluting ones is considered incompatible. Furthermore, concerns are raised about some biofuels, especially when their production leads to land use changes that negatively impact food production or forest preservation. For this reason, the Commission limits the admissibility of aid for biofuels beyond the thresholds set in Directive (EU) 2018/2001.

5. Regulation declaring certain categories of aid compatible with the internal market in application of Articles 107 and 108 of the Treaty

According to Article 108(4) in conjunction with Article 109 TFEU, the Council of the European Union and the European Commission may adopt regulations that exempt certain categories of state aid from the obligation of prior notification. Acting on this mandate, the Commission adopted Regulation No. 651/2014, which declares selected types of aid compatible with the internal market, provided they are granted in line with the requirements of the regulation (European Commission, 2014).

As Kurcz (2015) notes, the regulation concerns categories of aid for which the Commission already has extensive experience and is confident that the result of the balancing test—weighing the positive effects of aid against potential distortions—will be favourable. Among the categories of aid covered are:

1) Investment and operating aid for the production of energy from renewable sources (Article 4(1)(v) in conjunction with Articles 41 and 42),
2) Aid for the promotion of renewable energy in small-scale installations (Article 43),
3) Investment aid for energy infrastructure (Article 48) (A. Sikora, 2015).

The Regulation introduces notification thresholds, i.e. upper limits beyond which state aid must be notified. This threshold is EUR 15 million per undertaking and project for operating and promotional aid for renewables. For aid granted via tendering procedures (Article 42), the annual threshold is EUR 150 million across all covered schemes. Additionally, Article 1(2)(a) and Article 4 set maximum threshold levels for other forms of aid (European Commission, 2014).

Only transparent aid is covered by the Regulation. Transparency means the aid value (gross grant equivalent) can be calculated without risk assessment. As Kaznowski & Stasiak (2023) explains, grants and interest rate subsidies are inherently transparent. Loans and guarantees can also be considered transparent if their aid value is calculated following standard methods. Similarly, tax benefits are deemed transparent under certain conditions (Sikora, 2015).

The Regulation generally requires that aid demonstrate an incentive effect. However, Article 6(5)(o) introduces an exception for renewable energy aid: if the aid is granted automatically, based on objective and non-discriminatory criteria, and the relevant measure was adopted and implemented before the start of the project, then the requirement for a separate incentive effect does not apply.

Finally, aid covered by the Regulation must not infringe any provision of EU law, including rules on public procurement, environmental protection, or the internal market.

Aid for environmental protection, including renewable energy, can be investment or operating aid. Investment aid is regulated in Article 41 of the Regulation. It is granted for newly installed or renewed capacity and its amount is independent of capacity. The eligible costs are considered to be the total investment cost. The aid intensity must not exceed 45% of the eligible costs for investments in the production of renewable energy sources or 30% of the eligible costs for any other investment falling under Article 41. The aid intensity may be increased by 20% for aid for small enterprises and by 10% for aid for medium-sized enterprises. Where aid is granted following a tender procedure in accordance with Article 41(10) of the Regulation, the aid intensity may amount to 100% of the eligible costs.

Operating aid is regulated in Article 42 of the Regulation. It stipulates that it should only be granted through a tendering procedure, the rules of which are set out in Article 2(38) and Article 42 of the Regulation. The aid is granted in the form of a surcharge on the market price or the form of a contract for difference transactions. In principle, generators and aid beneficiaries should sell their energy directly on the market. From this requirement, the regulation exempts small-scale renewable electricity generation installations which, per Article 4(3) of Directive (EU) 2018/2001, may benefit from direct price support covering the full operation costs.

Following Article 43 of the Regulation, it is possible to grant operating aid for promoting energy from renewable sources in small projects and renewable energy communities under the conditions set out in this provision.

It is important to note that Articles 41–43 are not the only regulations setting out the conditions for the permissibility of renewable energy aid. Other provisions of the Regulation may govern such aid, e.g. when it is provided as part of the financial products supported by the InvestEU Fund (Article 56e(4)). Aid for renewable energy may be cumulated with certain types of aid covered by the Regulation, under the rules set out in that act.

6. State aid for renewable energy in Poland in 2018–2022 using selected examples

The EU concepts of *"energy from renewable sources"* and *"renewable energy"* are defined in Article 2(1) of Directive (EU) 2018/2001. The term covers renewable, non-fossil energy sources such as wind, solar, geothermal, hydropower, biomass, biogas and other forms of ambient or ocean energy (Directive 2018/2001, 2018).

The provisions of the directive have been implemented into Polish law through the Act of 20 February 2015 on Renewable Energy Sources (*ustawa o odnawialnych źródłach energii*, hereinafter: RES Act) (Journal of Laws, 2024). According to the Explanatory Memorandum to the draft law, the purpose of adopting this act was to align Poland's legal framework with the legislative standards in other EU countries, such as Austria (2002), Sweden (2003), and Cyprus (2003) (Sejm RP, 2024).

Before it entered into force, Poland had no comprehensive statutory act regulating renewable energy. The act introduced a dual system of support instruments, namely certificates of origin and an auction-based mechanism—a system expected to evolve in the coming years (Piotrowska, 2024). Certificates of origin were implemented as early as 2005 to fulfil obligations stemming from Directives 2001/77/EC and 2009/28/EC, and are still regulated under Article 44(1) of the RES Act.

From a legal-institutional perspective, state aid for renewable energy in Poland is granted through aid schemes, which may be designed and implemented by public bodies or authorised entities. Under Council Regulation (EU) 2015/1589, such a scheme refers to any act enabling the automatic granting of aid to multiple beneficiaries over time, without requiring case-by-case implementation (Council Regulation 2015/1589, Art. 1(d)).

Practical examples of this include decisions approved by the European Commission. One notable example is Decision C(2016) 4944, in which the

Commission approved Poland's support scheme for renewable energy auctions, recognising that it complied with EU state aid rules (European Commission, 2016).

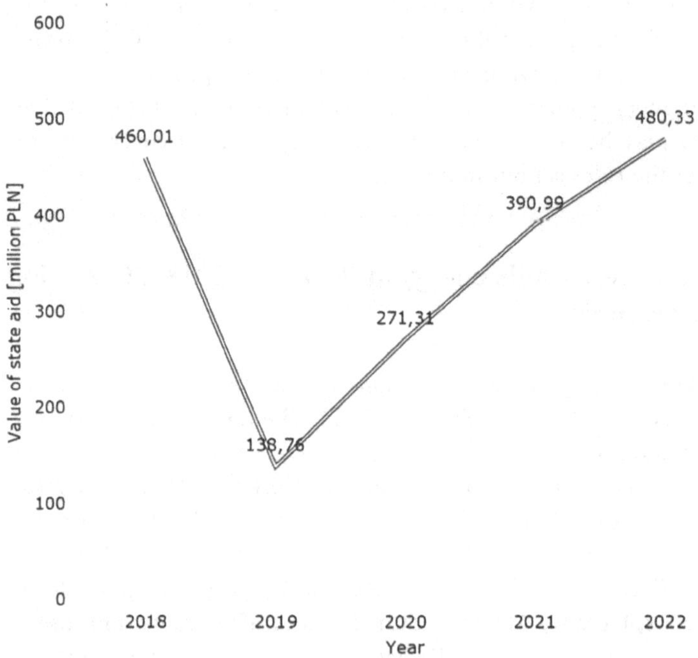

Chart 1. Value of state aid in million PLN granted under the aid programme "Polish system of certificates of origin to support renewable energy sources and reduce the burden of RES for energy-intensive consumers" in 2018–2022. Own graph based on data from the UOKiK Report on State Aid in Poland Granted to Entrepreneurs in 2022, pp. 119–120. Source: https://uokik.gov.pl/bip/raporty-pomoc-publiczna.

Chart 1 shows the value of state aid granted under the aid programme "Polish system of certificates of origin to support renewable energy sources and reduce the burden of RES for energy-intensive consumers" from 2018 to 2022. From 2019 to 2022, an upward trend in the value of state aid under the aid programme under analysis can be observed. Between 2018 and 2022, it was in 2022 that the value of aid reached the highest amount, i.e. PLN 480.33 million. The aid was granted by the President of the Energy Regulatory Office, which granted aid with a total value of PLN 1,402.3 million under aid schemes in 2022.

Chart 2 shows the value of state aid, including: horizontal aid and support for the aid programme "Aid for high-efficiency cogeneration systems and the promotion of energy from renewable sources under the regional operational programmes 2014–2020" granted by the provincial marshals between 2018 and 2022. The data analysis from 2018 to 2022 generally shows a decrease in the amounts

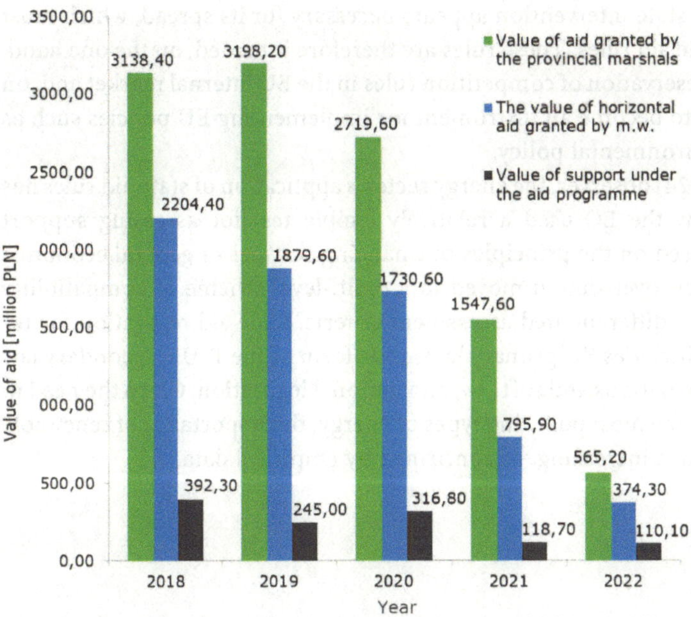

Chart 2. The value of state aid, including: horizontal aid and support for the aid programme "Aid for high-efficiency cogeneration systems and the promotion of energy from renewable sources under the regional operational programmes 2014–2020". Own chart based on data from the OCCP Reports on State Aid in Poland granted to entrepreneurs in 2018, 2019, 2020, 2021 and 2022. Source: https://uokik.gov.pl/bip/raporty-pomoc-publiczna.

granted under state aid. The value of aid granted by the provincial marshals decreased by 82% in 2022 compared to 2018. The value of horizontal aid granted by the provincial marshals decreased by 97.4% in 2022 compared to 2018, while the value of support under the aid programme "Aid for high-efficiency cogeneration systems and for the promotion of energy from renewable sources under the regional operational programmes 2014–2020" decreased by 71.9% in 2022 compared to 2018.

7. Summary

The EU has set ambitious climate and environmental targets for Member States through significant reductions in greenhouse gas emissions by 2030 and 2050. As part of this policy, EU law promotes renewable energy, recognising it as reducing greenhouse gas emissions. In order to achieve the required levels of greenhouse gas emissions, Member States are encouraged to make greater use of renewable energy. Given the high costs of producing and putting renewable energy into the economic cycle, state intervention appears necessary for its spread, which must consider EU state aid rules. These rules are therefore intended, on the one hand, to ensure the preservation of competition rules in the EU internal market and, on the other hand, to become an instrument for implementing EU policies such as climate and environmental policy.

As Olczak (2024) observes, the energy sector's application of state aid rules has evolved. Initially, the EC used a relatively simple test for assessing support mechanisms, based on the principles of financing services of general economic interest. However, over time it moved to a multi-level scheme of compatibility analysis based on differentiated assessment criteria. State aid regulation for renewable energy includes EU primary law in the form of the TfUE, secondary law in the form of regulations and soft law, and national legislation. Given the need to move away from the most polluting types of energy, the importance of renewable energy in Poland is increasing, as confirmed by empirical data.

References

Council Regulation (EU) 2015/1589 of 13 July 2015 laying down detailed rules for the application of Article 108 of the Treaty on the Functioning of the European Union. Official Journal of the EU, L 248, 9–29.

Directive (EU) 2018/2001 of the European Parliament and of the Council of 11 December 2018 on the promotion of the use of energy from renewable sources. Official Journal of the EU, L 328, 82–209.

Directive 2001/77/EC of the European Parliament and of the Council of 27 September 2001 on the promotion of electricity produced from renewable energy sources in the internal electricity market. Official Journal of the EU, L 282, 33–40.

Directive 2009/28/EC of the European Parliament and of the Council of 23 April 2009 on the promotion of the use of energy from renewable sources. Official Journal of the EU, L 140, 16–62.

Długosz, T. (2024). Article 2. In A. Mituś & A. Piotrowska (Eds.), Odnawialne źródła energii. Komentarz [Renewable energy sources. Commentary]. Warsaw: LEX.

European Commission. (2014). Commission Regulation (EU) No 651/2014 of 17 June 2014 declaring certain categories of aid compatible with the internal market in application of Articles 107 and 108 of the Treaty. Official Journal of the EU, L 187, 1–78.

European Commission. (2016). Notice on the notion of State aid as referred to in Article 107(1) of the Treaty on the Functioning of the European Union. Official Journal of the EU, C 262, 1–50.

European Commission. (2016). State aid SA.43697 (2015/N) – Poland – Auction-based support for renewable electricity. C(2016) 4944 final. Retrieved from https://ec.europa.eu/competition/state_aid/cases/261395/261395_1832262_134_2.pdf.

European Commission. (2019). The European Green Deal. Communication from the Commission to the European Parliament, the European Council, the Council, the European Economic and Social Committee and the Committee of the Regions (COM/2019/640 final). Brussels.

European Commission. (2022). Communication from the Commission: Guidelines on State aid for climate, environmental protection and energy 2022. Official Journal of the EU, C 80, 1–56.

European Commission. (2023). Regulation (EU) No 2023/2831 of 13 December 2023 on the application of Articles 107 and 108 of the Treaty on the Functioning of the European Union to de minimis aid. Official Journal of the EU, L Series of 15 December 2023.

European Commission. (2024a). Publications on State aid. Retrieved October 26, 2024, from https://competition-policy.ec.europa.eu/state-aid/publications_en.

European Commission. (2024b). State Aid Scoreboard 2023: Competition Policy and Strategy – State Aid Case Support and Policy. Retrieved October 27, 2024, from https://competition-policy.ec.europa.eu/document/download/0b2037c5-c43f-4917-b654-f48f74444015_en?filename=state_aid_scoreboard_note_2023.pdf.

European Council. (2015). Council Regulation (EU) No 1588/2015 of 13 July 2015 on the application of Articles 107 and 108 of the Treaty to certain categories of horizontal State aid. Official Journal of the EU, L 248, 1–8.

Gurba, B. (2009). Chapter VII. We thank the polluter. State aid to finance low CO_2 energy. In B. Kurcz (Ed.), Pomoc państwa. Wybrane zagadnienia [State aid. Selected issues] (pp. 192–194). Warsaw: C.H. Beck.

Hey, C. (2007). EU Environmental Policies: A short history of the policy strategies. In EU Environmental Policy Handbook (p. 4 et seq.). Retrieved from https://aei.pitt.edu/98675/1/environ_policies...pdf.

Journal of Laws. (2024). Act of 20 February 2015 on Renewable Energy Sources (consolidated text), item 1361, as amended.

Kaznowski, A., & Stasiak, M. (2023). Commentary to Article 5. In A. Kaznowski & M. Stasiak, Commentary to Regulation No 651/2014 declaring certain categories of aid compatible with the internal market in application of Articles 107 and 108 of the Treaty (3rd ed.). LEX/el.

Kurcz, B. (2015). Commentary to Article 109. In Treaty on the Functioning of the European Union. Commentary.

Kurrer, C., & Petit, A. (2024). Environment policy: general principles and basic framework. European Parliament Factsheets.

Nowacki, M., & Przyborowska-Klimczak, A. (2012). Commentary to Article 191. In K. Kowalik-Bańczyk, M. Szwarc-Kuczer, & A. Wróbel (Eds.), Treaty on the Functioning of the European Union. Commentary. Volume II (Articles 90–222). Warsaw: WKP.

Official Journal of the European Union. (2014). Commission Regulation (EU) No 651/2014 of 17 June 2014 declaring certain categories of aid compatible with the internal market. L 187.

Olczak, K. O. (2024). Problematyka prawna instrumentów finansowych na rynku odnawialnych źródeł energii [Legal issues of financial instruments in the renewable energy sources market]. Warsaw: Instytut De Republica.

Paleari, S. (2024). The Role of Strategic Autonomy in the EU Green Transition. Sustainability, 16(2597). https://doi.org/10.3390/su16062597.

Piotrowska, A. (2024). Article 44. In A. Mituś (Ed.), Odnawialne źródła energii. Komentarz [Renewable Energy Sources. Commentary]. Warsaw: LEX.

Sejm Rzeczypospolitej Polskiej. (2024). Explanatory Memorandum to the Draft Law on Renewable Energy Sources - Draft No. 2604. Retrieved from https://www.sejm.gov.pl/Sejm7.nsf/druk.xsp?nr=2604.

Sikora, A. (2015). Selected aspects of public financing of renewable energy in light of state aid rules. European Judicial Review, (3), 30.

Wojtaczka, B. (2014). On the incentive effect in state aid law. Internet Kwartalnik Antymonopolowy i Regulacyjny, (9), 63.

Pawel Majka / Jacek Wantoch-Rekowski

Property tax and agricultural tax as tools to support renewable energy production – selected issues

1. Introduction

One of the current challenges facing modern tax legislators is the need to design legal frameworks that incorporate environmental protection objectives, including support for the so-called green transition. Within the field of tax law, scholars identify a category of "environmental taxes", which includes emission-based charges, indirect taxes, and tax-like levies aimed at stimulating pro-environmental behaviour. These instruments are increasingly recognised as effective tools for influencing environmental outcomes through economic mechanisms (Głuchowski, 2002). The article considers the legal status as of 31 December 2024.

In this context, the objective of resource conservation can be pursued by introducing new "green taxes" and embedding environmental incentives into existing tax structures. This strategy enables a gradual yet impactful shift toward environmentally friendly policy implementation using familiar fiscal tools (Ogonowska , 2016).

In the Polish legal system, this issue arises particularly concerning property taxes, most notably the real estate tax (*podatek od nieruchomości*) and the agricultural tax (*podatek rolny*), especially concerning land and installations used for energy production. These taxes appear to be promising instruments for implementing sustainability objectives, not only due to their potential environmental impact but also because of their structural simplicity, stable tax base, and the absence of significant legislative changes in recent years.

However, growing doubts persist about whether these areas' current and proposed legal regulations meet their stated environmental and developmental objectives. For this reason, it is essential to analyse disputed legal norms, relevant doctrinal interpretations, and court rulings concerning real estate and agricultural taxation in the context of the green transformation. Such an analysis should also evaluate planned legislative changes to determine their effectiveness in supporting Poland's energy transition goals.

2. Taxation of structures related to "clean energy" production

The real estate tax is characterised by a relatively simple structure, which ostensibly should make it easy to identify taxed objects of energy production and resolve related interpretation problems. According to Article 2(1)(1–3) of the Act of 12 January 1991 on Local Taxes and Charges Act, land, buildings or parts thereof and structures or parts related to business activities are subject to property tax. According to Article 3(1)(1)-(3) of the Local Taxes and Charges Act, real estate tax payers are natural persons, legal persons, organisational units, including companies without legal personality, who are owners of real estate or structures, self-owners of real estate or structures, and perpetual usufructuaries of land. Under Article 3(1)(4) of the Local Taxes and Charges Act, taxpayers of real estate tax are also natural persons, legal persons, organisational units, including companies without legal personality, who are owners of real estate or parts thereof or of buildings or parts thereof which are the property of the State Treasury or a local government unit, if the possession results from an agreement concluded with the owner.

Under Article 4(1)(1)-(3) of the Local Taxes and Fees Act, the basis for taxation is: for land – the surface area; for buildings or parts thereof – the usable surface area; for structures – the value referred to in the provisions on income taxes, determined as at 1 January of the tax year, constituting the basis for calculating depreciation in that year, not reduced by depreciation write-offs, and in the case of fully depreciated structures – their value as at 1 January of the year in which the last depreciation write-off was made.

The municipal council determines tax rates in the real estate tax annually through a resolution, with the proviso that the rates may not exceed the amount specified in the Local Taxes and Charges Act annually. Under Article 5(1)(1) and (2) of the Local Taxes and Charges Act, the amount of tax rates is determined by the municipal councils and depends, inter alia, on the type of property and its purpose. According to Article 5(1)(3) of the said Act, for structures the maximum rate is 2% of their value.

The key legal issue in the taxation of facilities used for energy production is whether such facilities qualify as structures (*budowle*) within the meaning of the Local Taxes and Charges Act. This classification is decisive for determining the existence and amount of the tax obligation.

According to Article 1a(1)(2) of the Local Taxes and Charges Act (valid until 1 January 2025), a structure is defined as a construction object within the meaning of the Construction Law, excluding buildings and small architectural objects, as well as construction equipment related to a construction object, provided it ensures the object's use under its purpose (Journal of Laws, 2023a).

Under Article 3(1) of the Construction Law (which was applied directly to Local Taxes and Charges Act until 31 December 2024), a construction object is defined as a building, a structure (*budowla*) or a small architectural object (*mała architektura*), together with technical installations that enable the object's intended use, provided they are built using construction products (Journal of Laws, 2023b). Therefore, classifying a facility as a "structure" for tax purposes hinges on its inclusion within the scope of this construction law definition.

Further clarification is provided by Article 3(3) of the Construction Law, which offers an illustrative, though non-exhaustive, list of examples considered structures. This includes, among others: roads, antenna masts, technical networks, freestanding industrial installations, sewage treatment plants, waste disposal sites, wind power stations, and the construction parts of technical equipment such as foundations of machines or boilers, provided they constitute technically distinct parts of a functional utility whole. Importantly, wind power stations (*elektrownie wiatrowe*) are explicitly mentioned in this enumeration.

Article 3(9) of the Construction Law defines construction equipment (*urządzenia budowlane*) as technical devices that ensure the construction object's operability, such as connections, fences, parking areas or waste bins. This provision can also influence tax classification, as certain devices may qualify as construction-related elements subject to taxation as part of a structure.

This legal framework has been interpreted and upheld by the Polish Constitutional Tribunal, which in its judgment of 13 September 2011 (P 33/09) confirmed the link between the Construction Law and tax law definitions, asserting that tax obligations must be based on precise and constitutionally defined criteria (Constitutional Tribunal, 2011). Therefore, classification of energy installations, such as photovoltaic panels or wind turbines, depends on whether they fulfill the characteristics of structures within the meaning of construction law, and whether they perform an economic function, as required by tax regulations.

The current statutory provisions defining structures are drafted in a complicated and imprecise manner, which gives rise to numerous legal uncertainties —particularly concerning the classification of specific facilities as taxable structures. These doubts extend to the legislator's rationale for selecting certain energy-related facilities, including those that serve environmental protection purposes, for real estate taxation under the guise of being "structures" (Koślicki, 2022, p. 272; Kałążny, 2020, p. 315).

A common criticism in legal doctrine concerns the lack of consistency and rationality in how similar facilities are taxed depending on their industry sector. For instance, similar objects may or may not be taxed as structures depending on whether they relate to power generation, gas transmission, or mineral extraction. This inconsistent treatment undermines the principle of equality before the law and contributes to a growing body of litigation.

In the realm of environmental protection, interpretative doubts persist regarding the real estate taxation of hydro-technical infrastructure, such as that associated with hydroelectric power plants and biogas facilities, or even electrostatic precipitators used in coal-fired power plants.

The Act on Local Taxes and Charges currently prescribes a uniform taxation model for various types of renewable energy facilities—such as hydroelectric, photovoltaic, and wind power plants—under which only structural components (e.g., foundations, support towers) are subject to taxation. On the surface, this approach satisfies the principle of equality (Journal of Laws, 2023a).

However, hydroelectric power plants pose a specific challenge: their construction components typically comprise a significantly larger proportion of the facility than in other types of renewable energy installations. As a result, these plants are subject to disproportionately higher tax burdens. This imbalance has been widely criticised, particularly concerning the EU and national goals of promoting clean energy.

The classification of hydroelectric infrastructure as a structure is reinforced by Article 3(3) of the Construction Law, which explicitly lists hydro-technical facilities, and by Annex XXVII to the same law, which includes dams, water sills, weirs, sluices, and flood protection embankments. Annex XXIV lists water management facilities, including retention reservoirs and canals, which commonly form part of hydroelectric systems (Journal of Laws, 2023b).

Administrative courts have confirmed this position, consistently treating hydroelectric power plants as hydrotechnical structures subject to taxation under the real estate tax framework. For example, in its judgment of 22 September 2020 (I SA/Gd 364/20), the Voivodship Administrative Court in Gdańsk upheld the classification of a hydroelectric facility as a taxable structure (WSA Gdańsk, 2020).

Given the increasing policy emphasis on renewable energy, such tax treatment penalises hydroelectric energy despite its sustainability. This discrepancy has led to calls for preferential treatment or at least more equitable solutions in the tax system to ensure that hydropower is not unduly disadvantaged compared to other clean energy sources.

The biomass power plant (also called a *biogas plant* or *agricultural biogas plant*) is another renewable energy facility facing significant taxation burdens under the current legal framework until 31 December 2024. The majority of its infrastructure components are classified as structures within the meaning of the Act on Local Taxes and Fees, making them subject to the maximum tax rate applicable to such facilities.

Although case law points out that in biomass power plants certain components—such as cooling towers or flue installations for desulphurisation and dust removal—do not directly serve the energy production process and thus do not increase the taxable base, the core elements of such plants (e.g., boilers, generators) are taxed similarly to coal-fired power stations. Biomass-based energy production involves additional storage and processing infrastructure due to the greater volume of raw material required than fossil fuels (Supreme Administrative Court [NSA], 2023a).

These plants often include numerous technical facilities such as silage silos, digestate tanks, digestion chambers, biogas treatment units, and technical containers, which fall under the category of structures or buildings and are taxed accordingly. The result is a significant financial burden on producers of renewable energy, despite the environmental benefits of this form of generation.

Notably, the interpretation of the relevant legal provisions is not contested in this area. However, the absence of tax preferences for biomass-based energy facilities raises similar concerns as those discussed in relation to hydroelectric power plants. In both cases, a lack of tailored fiscal support results in renewable energy being treated less favourably than traditional energy sources. This outcome seems inconsistent with national and EU climate policy objectives.

In contrast, the taxation of coal-fired power plants generally raises fewer interpretative issues, as they consist of clearly identifiable land, buildings, and structures. However, electrostatic precipitators that filter pollutants from exhaust gases have recently emerged as a grey area in judicial interpretations.

Until 2021, administrative courts consistently treated electrostatic precipitators as technical equipment attached to a construction object, thus qualifying them as construction devices under Article 3(9) of the Construction Law, and thereby subject to real estate tax (WSA Poznań, 2021; WSA Poznań, 2022). However, more recent case law no longer accepts this automatic qualification, instead requiring an individualised assessment of whether:

1) The precipitator is connected to a specific construction object; and
2) That object qualifies as a structure or building under the Act on Local Taxes and Fees (NSA, 2023b; WSA Gdańsk, 2023).

Wojciech Morawski (2013, 2016) explains that no legal grounds exist to treat an entire power plant as a single taxable structure. Rather, each component must be assessed separately—yet inconsistencies persist. While most rulings accept taxation of foundation-based elements, the treatment of air cleaning systems such as electrofilters remains inconsistent, indicating the need for a clearer regulatory framework.

In conclusion, it must be stated that the real estate tax legislation does not adequately reflect the specificity of energy-producing installations, especially those associated with environmental protection. While the law currently provides clarified rules for wind and solar power plants, it lacks systemic preferences for other clean energy facilities such as biogas, hydroelectric power plants, and electrostatic precipitators for reducing atmospheric pollution. As a postulate de lege ferenda, it is appropriate to recommend explicitly excluding these facilities from taxation as "structures" under the Act on Local Taxes and Fees.

Such an exclusion would constitute a legitimate and desirable form of preferential treatment for entities investing in clean energy technologies, contributing to the broader goals of the EU Green Deal and Poland's national energy strategy.

This issue is particularly relevant in light of the judgment of the Constitutional Tribunal of 4 July 2023 (ref. SK 14/21), which declared Article 1a(1)(2) of the Act on Local Taxes and Fees inconsistent with Articles 84 and 217 of the Polish Constitution. The Tribunal held that defining key tax elements outside of tax legislation, such as the subject of taxation, was unconstitutional. As a result, the existing provision will cease to be in force on 1 January 2025, allowing the legislator to introduce a new and more transparent definition of a "structure" (Constitutional Tribunal, 2023).

According to the draft act of 15 October 2024 amending the Local Taxes and Fees Act (Amendment Bill, 2024), the new Article 2(1)(a) proposes a redefinition of taxable structures. Notably, it limits taxation of facilities such as photovoltaic, wind, nuclear, and agricultural biogas plants to their construction parts, thereby aligning their tax treatment. Such a solution reflects long-awaited recognition of the structural differences among clean energy sources and deserves legislative support.

However, the draft still fails to resolve two important issues:

1. Electrostatic precipitators remain undefined regarding their taxable status, and the law does not provide clear guidance on whether or not these pollution-control devices should be taxed.
2. The taxation of hydrotechnical infrastructure—critical in hydroelectric power plants—remains unchanged, meaning these facilities will continue to be taxed as fully taxable structures, even when they account for a disproportionate share of construction value compared to other RES facilities.

Therefore, while the planned reform introduces a more equitable framework for some sectors, it also reveals gaps and inconsistencies that must be addressed if real estate tax is to serve as a tool for promoting rather than penalising renewable energy development.

3. Taxation of land on which a photovoltaic power plant is located

The operation of a photovoltaic power plant may generate a tax obligation not only in the scope of structures, but also in terms of the land on which the installation is located. This taxation may occur under either the real estate or agricultural tax regime, depending on the land's legal classification and actual use.

When the land is not classified as agricultural or forestry land in the land and buildings register, there is no doubt that it is subject to real estate tax. In such cases, the nature of the land is automatically associated with business activity, and the origin of the energy (whether renewable or conventional) does not alter this outcome.

However, legal uncertainty arises in cases where a photovoltaic power plant is built on land formally classified as agricultural land. The question then becomes whether such land should be taxed under the Agricultural Tax Act or the Act on Local Taxes and Fees.

Under Article 1 of the Agricultural Tax Act, land recorded in the land and building register as agricultural land is subject to agricultural tax unless used for non-agricultural business purposes (Journal of Laws, 2024). This principle is mirrored in Article 2(2) of the Local Taxes and Fees Act, which excludes agricultural land from property taxation, except where such land is occupied for business activities (Journal of Laws, 2023).

Determining whether the land is "occupied" for business activity is crucial. Suppose the physical placement of photovoltaic panels and accompanying infrastructure effectively prevents or significantly limits the agricultural use of the land. In that case, it is generally accepted—also in the jurisprudence—that such land becomes subject to real estate tax. This is true regardless of whether the land continues to be designated as agricultural in the register.

As specified in Article 3(1) of the Agricultural Tax Act, taxpayers include natural persons, legal entities, and organisational units, including those in possession of land owned by the State Treasury or local governments, provided such possession results from an agreement or other legal title (Journal of Laws, 2019).

The tax base under the agricultural tax system depends on the status of the land:

1) The base is the number of converted hectares for land within an agricultural holding, determined by land area, type, and class.
2) The base is the number of actual hectares listed in the land register for land outside an agricultural holding.

Consequently, the key to determining the applicable taxation lies in both the formal classification in the land register and the actual use of the land in practice. A photovoltaic farm located on agricultural land but incompatible with agricultural use due to installing panels and other fixed infrastructure will likely trigger real estate tax liability, regardless of formal entries in the cadastre.

In light of the legal framework outlined above, a significant issue arises regarding the proper qualification of agricultural land partially or wholly occupied by photovoltaic installations. The core of the controversy stems from the interaction between Article 1 of the Agricultural Tax Act and Article 2(2) of the Local Taxes and Fees Act, which together state that land registered as agricultural is subject to agricultural tax unless it is "occupied for business activity" (Journal of Laws, 2024; Journal of Laws, 2023).

This problem is compounded in situations where only a portion of the agricultural parcel is developed with photovoltaic structures (e.g., foundations and support systems for solar panels), while the remaining land remains suitable for agriculture, such as grazing or crop cultivation. It is not uncommon for such land to be fenced off and used simultaneously for energy production and limited agricultural activity.

The case law has generally held that actual use of the land for energy-related business purposes, even if partial or indirect, suffices to disqualify the land from agricultural tax. The key criterion is not whether agricultural activities continue, but whether the land is functionally and physically needed for operating the photovoltaic farm (Supreme Administrative Court [NSA], 2023; WSA Warsaw, 2019).

This principle has led to the position that all land located within the fenced perimeter of a photovoltaic installation—including land not directly occupied by infrastructure—is treated as occupied for business activity. Even partial agricultural use does not requalify such land for agricultural taxation, and property tax applies in its place (Etel, Pahl & Popławski, 2021). This can result in tax burdens significantly exceeding the rental value of the land, especially since property tax rates for business-related land are substantially higher than those applied to agricultural use.

A broader systemic issue is revealed when comparing this situation to the taxation of protective zones of industrial plants or land used for mineral extraction, which also raise similar classification difficulties and inconsistencies in interpretation (Majka, 2017).

In summary, the entire land of a photovoltaic power plant should be considered to be occupied to carry out a business activity other than farming and is subject to property tax at the same rate as for business property. Suppose one considers the necessity of occupying large plots of land to place photovoltaic panels on them and applying the highest property tax rate. In that case, this solution constitutes a significant burden for producers of energy from solar panels. Without questioning *the ratio legis of* the introduced solutions in the construction of the real estate tax, indicating the intention to tax with this tax also the income that these properties bring (Brzeziński, 2017; Borszowski, 2010; Litwińczuk, 1985), one can of course justify the very rule of taxing agricultural properties occupied for economic activity with the highest rates. However, concerning entrepreneurs producing energy from renewable sources, who additionally carry out limited agricultural activity on the area of the power plant, it is reasonable to propose the introduction of a statutory preference in the treatment of the land occupied by them by taxing with agricultural tax the land located outside the foundations of the panels or applying reduced rates of real estate tax.

4. Investment tax credit in agricultural tax: construction, limitations and inconsistencies

A specific legal instrument that supports the green transformation in agriculture is the investment tax credit provided for in Article 13(1)(2)(c) of the Agricultural Tax Act. Under this provision, agricultural taxpayers may deduct 25% of investment expenditure related to the purchase and installation of equipment using natural energy sources (e.g. wind, biogas, sun, water) for production purposes, provided that the expenditure was not covered in full or in part by public funds (Journal of Laws, 2024).

This investment tax credit (ulga inwestycyjna) applies only after completion of the investment and only concerning land located in the municipality where the investment was made. It may be applied over 15 years, and the deduction must be documented with receipts. According to the prevailing interpretation, the relief also covers photovoltaic installations used to supply energy to residential buildings on the farm occupied by the taxpayer and their family members (Etel, Pahl & Popławski, 2021).

From a legislative drafting perspective, the construction of this relief is clear and coherent, as evidenced by the low number of administrative disputes concerning its application (Burzec, 2018). This sets it apart from the numerous controversies surrounding the taxation of land and structures related to renewable energy.

Nonetheless, the practical value of the relief is limited in terms of its fiscal impact and motivational strength. Agricultural tax is generally low in value, especially compared to property tax rates applicable to land used for business purposes. Moreover, limiting the benefit to 25% of eligible expenses and 15 years undermines its capacity to act as an effective financial incentive (Etel, 2005).

From the perspective of financial law theory, incentives are most effective when the monetary benefit is significant, predictable and timely. According to Renigier (1982), the "strength" of the incentive—i. e. the scale of the advantage—is the most important element determining its effectiveness. If the benefit is marginal and distributed over many years, as in the current model, its psychological and financial effect is diminished (Renigier, 1982; Małecki, 1981).

Therefore, legislative reform is warranted. Two primary *de lege ferenda* recommendations are:

1) Increasing the percentage of deductible expenditure (e. g. from 25% to 50% or more),
2) Removing or extending the 15-year limit, especially in the case of large-scale investments in green technologies.

A further systemic inconsistency arises from the asymmetry between agricultural and property tax. As the doctrine points out, a taxpayer may benefit from the agricultural tax investment relief for expenditures on renewable energy infrastructure, while simultaneously being subject to property tax at the highest business rate on the same parcel of land, if it is deemed occupied for economic purposes (Etel, 2005). This situation creates a legal contradiction that discourages investment and undermines the pro-environmental objective of the relief.

5. Summary

The doctrine has rightly argued that constitutional values such as environmental protection and sustainable development are implemented, among other ways, through the proper design of tax instruments in the energy sector (Lewandowski, 2024). Property tax remains a significant financial burden for entrepreneurs engaged in electricity generation, primarily due to the extensive use of structures that qualify as taxable assets. In this light, the property tax could be an effective regulatory tool for promoting environmental goals. However, like other real estate-related taxes, this tax was not originally designed with environmental incentives.

Currently, the existing environmental preferences within the real estate tax system are limited to a few exemptions, which do not apply to energy sector entrepreneurs. Legislative gaps and ambiguous legal formulations have also resulted in interpretative disputes, particularly concerning the classification and taxation of energy-related infrastructure, such as electrostatic precipitators, hydropower plants, or biogas facilities. These disputes are typically resolved only in administrative court proceedings, underscoring the law's reactive—rather than proactive—nature in this area.

The comprehensive analysis presented in this study shows that neither the real estate tax system nor the agricultural tax regime currently provides clear and consistent incentives for investments in renewable energy infrastructure. This absence of targeted fiscal tools fails to support the EU and national goals for green transformation and creates systemic barriers for environmentally conscious investors. Similarly, the lack of unambiguous provisions concerning the taxation of structures in property tax causes doubts regarding, inter alia, the taxation of electrostatic precipitators. The scope of the investment tax credit in agricultural tax for renewable energy producers should also be extended. At the same time, as an example of proper legislative action, one should cite the legislative changes about taxation of biogas plants, which will lead to taxation only of the construction parts of these plants.

References

Borszowski, P. (2010). Działalność gospodarcza w konstrukcji prawnej podatku. Warsaw: Wolters Kluwer.

Brzeziński, B. (2017). Prawo podatkowe. Zagadnienia teorii i praktyki. Toruń: TNOiK.

Burzec, M. (2018). Podatek rolny. In P. Smoleń (Ed.), Opodatkowanie rolnictwa w Polsce. Weryfikacja założeń – perspektywa zmiany (p. 404). Warsaw: Instytut Wydawniczy EuroPrawo.

Constitutional Tribunal. (2011). Judgment of 13 September 2011, case P 33/09. Retrieved from https://trybunal.gov.pl.

Constitutional Tribunal. (2023). Judgment of 4 July 2023, SK 14/21. Retrieved from https://trybunal.gov.pl.

Etel, L. (2005). Podatek od nieruchomości, rolny, leśny. Warsaw: LexisNexis.

Etel, L., Pahl, B., & Popławski, M. (2021). Commentary to Article 2. In Podatek rolny. Komentarz. LEX/el.

Etel, L., Pahl, B., & Popławski, M. (2021). Commentary to Article 13. In Podatek rolny. Komentarz. LEX/el.

Głuchowski, J. (2002). Podatki ekologiczne. Warsaw: Wydawnictwo Naukowe PWN.

Jankowska, D., & Kałążny, A. (2022). Taxation of photovoltaic power plants – the further into the forest, the more trees. Tax Review, 4, 42.

Journal of Laws. (2024). Act of 15 November 1984 on Agricultural Tax (consolidated text), item 1176.

Journal of Laws. (2023a). Act of 12 January 1991 on Local Taxes and Charges (consolidated text), item 70, as amended.

Journal of Laws. (2023b). Construction Law – Act of 7 July 1994 (consolidated text), item 682.

Journal of Laws. (2024). Act of 20 July 2017 on the National Real Estate Resource, item 1026.

Kałążny, A. (2020). Opodatkowanie infrastruktury podatkiem od nieruchomości. Warsaw: Wolters Kluwer.

Koślicki, K. (2022). Opodatkowanie budowli podatkiem od nieruchomości. Warsaw: Wolters Kluwer.

Litwińczuk, H. (1985). Podatki majątkowe. In M. Weralski (Ed.), System instytucji prawno-finansowych PRL, Vol. III, Ossolineum, pp. 340–342.

Majka, P. (2017). Taxation of agricultural land used for conducting business activity. In P. Burzec & P. Smoleń (Eds.), Essential problems with taxation of agriculture (pp. 140–147). Lublin: Wydawnictwo KUL.

Małecki, J. (1981). Legal and financial incentives and sanctions. Ruch Prawniczy, Ekonomiczny i Socjologiczny, 1, 188–189.

Morawski, W. (2013). Podatek od nieruchomości w orzecznictwie sądów administracyjnych. Komentarz. Linie interpretacyjne. Warsaw: Wolters Kluwer.

Morawski, W. (2016). Ustawa o podatkach i opłatach lokalnych. Komentarz. Gdańsk: C.H. Beck.

Ogonowska, A. (2016). Ecological aspects in the Polish tax system. In W. Bożek (Ed.), System podatkowy w Polsce. Jego rola i znaczenie w procesach gospodarczych (p. 263). Szczecin: Wydawnictwo Naukowe Uniwersytetu Szczecińskiego.

Renigier, H. (1982). Legal and financial incentives. In M. Weralski (Ed.), System instytucji prawno-finansowych PRL. Tom I: Instytucje ogólne (pp. 317, 333). Wrocław: Ossolineum.

Sejm Rzeczypospolitej Polskiej. (2024). Draft Act of 15 October 2024 on Amendments to the Act on Agricultural Tax, the Act on Local Taxes and Fees and the Act on Stamp Duty, Sejm Paper No. 10-020-238-2024. Retrieved from https://orka.sejm.gov.pl/Druki10ka.nsf/Projekty/10-020-238-2024/$file/10-020-238-2024.pdf.

Supreme Administrative Court [NSA]. (2023). Judgment of 9 August 2023, III FSK 385/23.

Supreme Administrative Court [NSA]. (2023a). Judgment of 4 November 2023, III FSK 4332/21.

Supreme Administrative Court [NSA]. (2023b). Judgment of 19 September 2023, III FSK 1257/22.

Supreme Administrative Court [NSA]. (2024). Judgment of 7 March 2024, III FSK 827/23.

Voivodship Administrative Court in Gdańsk [WSA Gdańsk]. (2020). Judgment of 22 September 2020, I SA/Gd 364/20.

Voivodship Administrative Court in Gdańsk [WSA Gdańsk]. (2023). Judgment of 7 February 2023, I SA/Gd 484/22.

Voivodship Administrative Court in Poznań [WSA Poznań]. (2021). Judgment of 22 April 2021, I SA/Po 853/20.

Voivodship Administrative Court in Poznań [WSA Poznań]. (2022). Judgment of 26 May 2022, I SA/Po 11/22.

Voivodship Administrative Court in Warsaw [WSA Warsaw]. (2019). Judgment of 7 May 2019, III SA/Wa 1932/18.

Tomasz Kuczyński / Piotr Rączka

Investment in renewable energy sources against the background of the problem of maintaining biologically active areas

1. Introduction

Renewable sources currently satisfy only a small share of the total energy demand in the Republic of Poland. Nevertheless, a gradual upward trend in its share of gross final energy consumption is noticeable. According to the Central Statistical Office (2022), the share of renewable energy in gross final energy consumption amounted to 16.9% in 2022. Although this figure may not appear impressive compared to countries such as Norway, it still reflects a continuous effort by the Polish legislator to stimulate the sector's growth.

A pivotal step in this direction was the adoption of the Act of 20 February 2015 on Renewable Energy Sources (*u.o.z.e.*), which transposed Directive 2009/28/EC of the European Parliament and of the Council into the Polish legal order (Długosz, 2024; Directive 2009/28/EC, 2009). The main goal of this legal act is to promote and develop renewable energy sources—forms of energy generation not reliant on fossil fuels but grounded in the sustainable use of natural resources.

Support for investments in renewable energy sources (RES) also manifests as administrative and legal facilitation, aimed at simplifying burdensome permitting procedures. A notable example is the Act of 17 August 2023, which amended the Renewable Energy Sources Act and other regulations, including the Construction Law of 7 July 1994 (*p.b.*). According to Article 3(2) of the amendment, the limit of installed capacity exempt from a building permit or notification under Article 30 *p.b.* has been raised from 50 kW to 150 kW for free-standing solar collectors, photovoltaic devices, and electric heat pumps (Journal of Laws, 2023). This legislative change aims to streamline the approval process for small-scale RES infrastructure.

However, such exemptions do not apply to large-scale investments like constructing photovoltaic farms. Even if such projects comply with all applicable legal norms, they must follow the standard, often complex, administrative procedure. Among the conditions to be fulfilled for obtaining a building permit is the requirement to maintain a biologically active area on the investment site. The required percentage of such an area may stem from various legal sources and often proves problematic due to inconsistencies in interpretation—particularly regarding whether the ground beneath photovoltaic panels qualifies as biologically active.

The article outlines and critically analyses the legal framework using the dogmatic-legal method. It highlights inconsistencies in interpreting and applying the concept of "biologically active area" by administrative bodies and considers their implications for investors undertaking RES projects.

2. Administrative-legal rationing of the investment process for photovoltaic farms

Although the main objective of this paper is not to present a comprehensive analysis of the investment process or its legal regulation, it is necessary—given the central focus on biologically active areas—to outline the administrative procedures associated with the localisation and realisation of photovoltaic (PV) farm investments. The necessity of maintaining biologically active land often intersects directly with these procedural stages.

The investment process for constructing a photovoltaic farm in Poland is multi-phased and procedurally complex, often prolonging the time required to obtain a building permit. In principle, the process involves three key stages: (1) obtaining a decision on environmental conditions, (2) determining the land development conditions, and (3) securing a building permit. However, the duration and complexity of these procedures may vary depending on the location and capacity of the planned installation.

The first stage involves obtaining a decision on environmental conditions, regulated primarily by the Act of 3 October 2008 on the provision of information on the environment and its protection, public participation in environmental protection, and environmental impact assessments (Journal of Laws, 2024, item 1112). Under Article 71 of this Act, a planned PV farm may be classified as a project potentially impacting the environment. As such, the competent local authority—typically a commune head, mayor, or city president—may require the investor to prepare an environmental impact report, which considerably extends the process.

The second stage is the assessment of spatial development compatibility. Following the Act of 27 March 2003 on Spatial Planning and Development (*u.p.z.p.*), municipalities are responsible for shaping and implementing local spatial policy (Journal of Laws, 2024, item 1130). Suppose a local spatial development plan exists for the area in question. In that case, the investment must comply with its provisions—including any requirements concerning the percentage of biologically active area, as specified in Article 15(2)(6) *u.p.z.p.*

In the absence of a local plan, the investor must obtain a decision on development conditions (WZ). While such decisions are normally subject to several preconditions, RES installations have been exempted from three of them—such as the need for neighbouring development continuity and access from a public road—according to Article 61(3)(3) of the amended Act. However, since 24 September 2023, the compatibility of development decisions with municipal master plans requires consideration of minimum biologically active area thresholds for the relevant planning zones.

The third and final stage involves applying for a building permit under the Construction Law (*p.b.*), a process governed by the Act of 7 July 1994 (Journal of Laws, 2024, item 1112). The investor initiates these proceedings before the competent architectural and construction administration authority, typically the county starost or the mayor in cities with county rights. The building permit must conform to the conditions established at the prior stages—whether defined by local plans or individual development decisions.

In conclusion, the administrative-legal rationing of PV farm construction in Poland remains procedurally demanding. The three main stages—environmental assessment, spatial planning compatibility, and construction permitting—may trigger considerations regarding biologically active area compliance, particularly concerning interpretive inconsistencies between local authorities. Ensuring clarity and legal certainty in this domain is critical for streamlining the development of renewable energy infrastructure.

3. RES investments and the problem of maintaining a biologically active area

As previously noted, for an investor to receive planning permission for a photovoltaic farm, one of the conditions is to maintain an appropriate percentage of biologically active area on the land where the installation is to be located. While this requirement may not pose a significant issue for smaller installations, it can become a serious planning challenge for large-scale projects, which often require extensive land use.

The concept of "biologically active area" is defined in § 3(22) of the Regulation of the Minister of Infrastructure of 12 April 2002 on the technical conditions to be met by buildings and their location (*r.w.t.*). According to this definition, a biologically active area includes land surfaces for natural vegetation and rainwater retention. Also, it includes 50% of terraces, flat roofs with plant growth surfaces (minimum 10 m²), and surface waters (Journal of Laws, 2022, item 1225).

Before 2023, the legal sources regulating the required share of biologically active area were limited primarily to provisions of the *r.w.t.* and local spatial development plans. For example, § 39(1) of the *r.w.t.* stipulated that on plots for multi-family housing, education, or healthcare (excluding clinics), at least 25% of the plot should remain biologically active—unless a local plan specifies otherwise. However, photovoltaic farms are not covered by these categories, so their biologically active requirements could only be enforced via the local spatial plan (Journal of Laws, 2022, item 1225).

The legal landscape changed following adopting the Act of 7 July 2023 amending the Spatial Planning and Development Act (*u.p.z.p.*), significantly expanding the range of legal instruments governing biologically active areas (Journal of Laws, 2023, item 1688). Two new sources have been introduced: the general plan and the decision on development conditions (WZ).

In the general plan context, Article 13e *u.p.z.p.* allows municipal authorities to define minimum shares of biologically active areas for designated planning zones. These values must comply with thresholds specified in executive regulations, such as the Minister of Development and Technology Ordinance of 8 December 2023, which defines biologically active area minimums for different planning zones (Journal of Laws, 2023, item 2758).

In parallel, decisions on development conditions must now comply with the standards defined in the general plan, including the biologically active area share applicable to the relevant planning zone. This framework closes a previously existing legal gap. It ensures that biologically active area requirements can be imposed even in areas not covered by local plans—as long as a general plan is in place.

Overall, this regulatory shift indicates a growing role of biologically active area preservation in spatial planning, including for RES investments. However, it also introduces new layers of complexity, especially for investors seeking to build photovoltaic farms on undeveloped land.

As indicated above, the amendment to the Act on Spatial Planning and Development (u.p.z.p.) also empowered authorities to define the required percentage of biologically active area in decisions on development conditions (WZ). This is based on Article 54(2)(1)(b) of the u.p.z.p., which refers to decisions concerning the location of public-purpose investments and, by analogy through Article 64(1), also applies to WZ decisions. These provisions ensure that the detailed development principles in WZs must align with the general plan, particularly regarding minimum biologically active area standards for a given planning zone. In the case of inner-city development, the minimum must not be less than two-thirds of the standard established in the applicable zone (Journal of Laws, 2023, item 1688).

Notably, even before this amendment, certain administrative bodies imposed requirements regarding biologically active areas in WZ decisions, although such practices were deemed by the courts to be without legal basis. For example, the Voivodship Administrative Court in Poznań, in a 2017 ruling, clearly stated that such provisions were unsupported under the then-current legal framework (WSA Poznań, 2017).

A complex and multilayered legal regime currently governs the biologically active area requirement. The applicable percentage may now derive from local spatial development plans, development conditions, or general plans, the latter of which must themselves comply with minimum thresholds established in the Ordinance of the Minister of Development and Technology of 8 December 2023 (Journal of Laws, 2023, item 2758). However, full legal applicability of these mechanisms hinges on the formal adoption of general plans by municipalities—a ongoing process.

When considering the situation of an investor wishing to develop a photovoltaic farm on previously undeveloped land, reference must again be made to § 3 (22) of the *r.w.t.*, which requires ensuring natural vegetation. Since this term is not legally defined, doctrinal interpretation becomes crucial. As noted by Mazurkiewicz (2024), drawing on dictionary definitions, "natural vegetation" refers to plant development under natural lighting, soil, and irrigation conditions—factors essential for plant life.

Modern photovoltaic farm construction techniques typically involve mounting panels on elevated metal structures, rather than placing them directly on the ground (Klimek, 2024). This raises a critical legal question: Can the land beneath such installations be classified as biologically active?

Jurisprudence suggests that a biologically active area should, by default, include land not subject to any interference. However, exceptions exist: a technically modified area may still be considered biologically active if it allows for natural plant growth and rainwater retention. A good example is land covered with eco-grid structures, which, although technically developed, still support vegetation (NSA, 2019).

Administrative courts have also clarified that space beneath overhanging elements of a building, such as balconies or bays, may qualify as biologically active, provided vegetation is feasible (WSA Warsaw, 2019). These interpretations widen the possible legal understanding of biologically active land—potentially including land beneath photovoltaic structures.

This interpretation is shared by professional bodies such as the Małopolska Regional Chamber of Architects. In an official opinion, its Team of Experts emphasized that land technically classified as built-up may still accommodate functions consistent with biologically active area requirements (ZR 255, 2023). The opinion also addresses solar exposure in Poland (latitude 50–51°), noting that sunlight is predominantly non-vertical and, therefore, plant growth under panels—especially grass—is viable due to horizontal and reflected light (ZR 255, 2023).

Some local authorities have followed this logic. For example, the Mayor of Skrzyszów, in a 2021 administrative decision, held that land beneath photovoltaic panels mounted at least 0.5 meters above the ground retains the status of biologically active area, given that it still allows for vegetation and natural processes (Skrzyszów, 2021).

However, not all municipalities share this position. The City of Gliwice, in its 2023 local zoning plan, explicitly excluded from the biologically active area the land beneath PV installations, as measured by the rectangular projection of the entire supporting structure and panels (Resolution No. XLIX/1006/2023). This approach directly contradicts the broader interpretation adopted by administrative courts and raises doubts about its compliance with statutory and constitutional planning limits (Małysa-Sulińska, 2021; Filipowicz & Plucińska-Filipowicz, 2024).

While municipalities enjoy broad planning autonomy, both doctrine and case law stress that this authority is not unlimited. The lack of explicit statutory grounding for such exclusions may lead to legal uncertainty and restrict investor rights (Filipowicz & Plucińska-Filipowicz, 2024).

These inconsistencies also complicate individual administrative procedures. Although Article 7a of the Code of Administrative Procedure (CAP) enshrines the principle of resolving doubts in favour of the party, it does not apply where the party applies for a discretionary right, such as a building permit (CAP, 2024; Wróbel, 2024). Nevertheless, strict exclusion of PV land from biologically active classification substantially limits the investor's freedom to develop their land—even in cases where ecological functions are maintained.

Further complications arise from technical legal regulations, especially determining construction and land-use parameters. One such regulation is the Regulation of the Minister of Development of 11 September 2020 on the detailed scope and form of the construction project, which mandates using PN-ISO 9836 standards during project assessment (Journal of Laws, 2022, item 1679).

The regulation requires the use of the latest Polish edition of the standard. This is PN-ISO 9836:2022-07, which defines "built-up area" as the surface of land occupied by a building in its final form. According to the standard, this area is determined by the horizontal projection of the building's structure on the ground surface. Importantly, the built-up area excludes any building components or parts that do not extend above the ground, such as exterior stairs, ramps, canopies, greenhouses, and auxiliary annexes.

This technical definition poses serious interpretative issues for photovoltaic farms. The standard does not explicitly cover PV panel installations, typically elevated and freestanding structures mounted on light steel frames. As a result, administrative authorities often lack a clear legal basis to determine whether such structures contribute to the built-up area, and if so, to what extent.

Therefore, the current legal framework leaves significant uncertainty regarding calculating the development footprint of photovoltaic farms. These ambiguities reinforce the broader legal doubts described earlier and complicate the decision-making process for both investors and permitting authorities.

4. Conclusions and requests *de lege ferenda*

An analysis of the binding legal framework for photovoltaic farm investments reveals the existence of a wide array of regulations, many of which directly influence the investor's legal position and limit their options for land use. Apart from the procedural burden—stemming from the complex multi-stage permitting process—investors face interpretative uncertainty, particularly concerning the definition and classification of biologically active areas.

Among these, one of the most pressing issues is the lack of clarity regarding biologically active land. As this study demonstrates, jurisprudence has developed a flexible approach, allowing for the recognition of technical interference (e.g., eco-grids or elevated structures) as compatible with maintaining biologically active character. In contrast, public administration authorities have taken more polarized positions—some applying restrictive interpretations via individual decisions or local laws, and others favoring broader criteria. Nevertheless, in both cases, no clear statutory basis would definitively resolve these inconsistencies.

Given the growing relevance of RES investments and their role in energy transition policies, it appears necessary to amend the legal framework to reduce the described uncertainties. A relevant example of such codification efforts is the recent introduction of Article 2(30) of the amended Spatial Planning Act, which defines the concept of *"height of development"*. This concept had long been a subject of interpretative disputes, particularly in the absence of harmonized definitions in older local plans. While courts occasionally referred to § 6 of the *r.w.t.*—which governs how building height is measured—this reference was problematic given that *"height of development"* and *"height of building"* are not legally equivalent (WSA Gdańsk, 2020; NSA, 2021; 2023).

The new statutory definition now applies only to spatial plans adopted after the amendment enters into force (24 September 2023), and its long-term effectiveness will depend on how it is implemented and interpreted over time. Nevertheless, it sets a precedent for legislative clarification of previously vague spatial planning concepts.

Similarly, we recommend legislative clarification of the notion of biologically active area—ideally by introducing a statutory definition or amendment to the *r.w.t.*, explicitly stating whether technically altered areas (such as land beneath PV installations) can retain biologically active status. While photovoltaic farms are central to achieving sustainability goals, current rules paradoxically risk classifying them as harmful to the environment, solely due to spatial planning definitions.

This legal contradiction—where an investment intended to improve the environment may be rejected for allegedly degrading it—demonstrates the need for systemic alignment of energy, construction, and environmental law. A clear and unified definition of biologically active area would ease administrative burden, reduce litigation, and provide predictability for investors and authorities—thus serving the dual objectives of environmental protection and sustainable energy development.

References

Central Statistical Office. (2022). *Energy from Renewable Sources in 2022.* Retrieved from https://stat.gov.pl/download/gfx/portalinformacyjny/pl/defaultaktualnosci/5485/3/17/1/energia_ze_zrodel_odnawialnych_w_2022_r.pdf [Accessed: 23.10.2024].

Directive 2009/28/EC of the European Parliament and of the Council of 23 April 2009 on the promotion of the use of energy from renewable sources. *Official Journal of the European Union*, L 140, p. 16.

Długosz, T. (2024). In A. Mituś & A. Piotrowska (Eds.), *Odnawialne źródła energii. Komentarz.* Warsaw: LEX.

Filipowicz, T., & Plucińska-Filipowicz, A. (2024). In M. Wierzbowski (Ed.), *Planowanie i zagospodarowanie przestrzenne. Komentarz* (4th ed.). Warsaw: LEX.

Journal of Laws. (2019). Regulation of the Council of Ministers of 10 September 2019 on projects likely to have a significant impact on the environment, item 1839, as amended.

Journal of Laws. (2022). Regulation of the Minister of Development of 11 September 2020 on the detailed scope and form of the construction project, item 1679, as amended.

Journal of Laws. (2022). *Regulation of the Minister of Infrastructure of 12 April 2002 on the technical conditions to be met by buildings and their location*, consolidated text, item 1225, as amended.

Journal of Laws. (2023). *Act of 17 August 2023 amending the Renewable Energy Sources Act and certain other acts*, item 1762.

Journal of Laws. (2023). *Act of 7 July 2023 amending the Act on Spatial Planning and Development*, item 1688.

Journal of Laws. (2023). *Act of 7 July 2023 amending the Spatial Planning and Development Act and certain other acts*, item 1688.

Journal of Laws. (2023). *Ordinance of the Minister of Development and Technology of 27 October 2023 amending the Ordinance on technical conditions to be met by buildings and their location*, item 2442.

Journal of Laws. (2023). *Ordinance of the Minister of Development and Technology of 8 December 2023 on the draft general plan of a municipality*, item 2758.

Journal of Laws. (2023). *Ordinance of the Minister of Development and Technology of 8 December 2023 on the draft general plan of a municipality*, item 2758.

Journal of Laws. (2024). Act of 27 March 2003 on spatial planning and development, consolidated text, item 1130.

Journal of Laws. (2024). Act of 3 October 2008 on providing information on the environment and its protection, public participation in environmental protection and environmental impact assessments, consolidated text, item 1112.

Journal of Laws. (2024). *Act on Renewable Energy Sources*, consolidated text, item 1361.

Journal of Laws. (2024). *Kodeks postępowania administracyjnego*, item 572.

Judgment of the Supreme Administrative Court [NSA] of 4.06.2019, II OSK 1436/18, LEX no. 2753964.

Judgment of the Voivodship Administrative Court [WSA] in Warsaw of 29.01.2019, VII SA/Wa 2616/18, LEX no. 2621780.

Judgment of the WSA in Poznań of 26.04.2017, II SA/Po 87/17, LEX no. 2291379.

Klimek, J. (2024). *Construction of a photovoltaic farm with a capacity of up to 26 MW....* Retrieved from http://archiwum.bip.margonin.pl/PDF/02_KIP_2.PDF.

Małysa-Sulińska, K. (2021). *Władztwo planistyczne gmin a określanie sposobów zagospodarowania i warunków zabudowy terenu. Acta Universitatis Wratislaviensis*, 4058, 328.

Mazurkiewicz, J. (2024). *Biologically active area – definition*. Retrieved from https://www.prawo.pl/biznes/teren-biologicznie-czynny-definicja,146267.html.

Municipal Council in Gliwice. (2023). *Resolution No. XLIX/1006/2023 on the local zoning plan for the landfill area. Dz.Urz.Woj.Sla*, item 7101.

Skrzyszów Municipality. (2021). *Decision GPŚiG.6220.2.9.2021*, https://bip.malopolska.pl/api/files/2652760.

Team of Experts, Małopolska Regional Chamber of Architects. (2023). *Opinion No. ZR 255*. Retrieved from https://www.mpoia.pl/index.php/wsparcie/opinie/2259-opinia-nr-255.

Wróbel, A. (2024). In M. Jaskowska, M. Wilbrandt-Gotowicz, & A. Wróbel (Eds.), *Kodeks postępowania administracyjnego. Komentarz aktualizowany*. LEX/el.

Karolina Karpus

Nature conservation and scientific uncertainty – the transformation of public law in the light of the precautionary principle

1. Introduction

The complexity and dynamics of social relations present public authorities with several challenges. Among them is the necessity to make decisions in conditions of lack of full scientific knowledge regarding the risks of human activity for protected goods, e.g., human life, health, and the environment. From an axiological perspective, the model of conduct of the public authority in such a case is determined by the precautionary principle. Its perception is changing over time, as illustrated, inter alia, by the discussion on its status as a general principle – no longer only environmental law, but a system-wide principle. It is now particularly evident at the level of EU law (Morag-Levine, 2014; Craig, 2012).

Deciding in situations of scientific uncertainty is an interdisciplinary, non-legal issue. A "prudent" proceeding is one in which the main emphasis is on the resulting risks to the environment and other assets, which must be minimised. In interdisciplinary terms, Beder (2007, p. 53) indicates that the process includes: "(i) The political decision whether to act, which requires: identification of potential adverse effects that threaten the desired level of protection now or in the future, when these adverse effects are caused or exacerbated by human activity, and scientific evaluation of such effects shows they are plausible and highly probable, and the exact risk cannot be determined because of scientific uncertainty, and postponing action will make effective action more difficult later on; (ii) the measures to be taken if action is decided upon."

The transposition of this model of conduct into law within the framework of the precautionary principle consists of allowing the public authority to take a decision (temporarily) prohibiting or limiting such environmentally risky human activity when the existing scientific uncertainty cannot be eliminated to the extent that it has a chance of safeguarding the protected good. This purpose is served by the so-called reversal of the burden of proof, the presumption in dubio pro natura and the modified perception of causation in the context of the degree of environmental risk.

The personal scope of the precautionary principle is two-tiered. It binds the legislative authority in the lawmaking process, since, under the rule of law, human and civil rights and freedoms may be limited only by a legislative act. Likewise, the judicial and executive authorities interpret positive law in the light of this value, as the precautionary principle binds them when making a final decision on a case. The executive is also responsible for organising a system of data collection showing the state of natural elements and human pressures (e.g. the scale of emissions introduced into them). On the other hand, obligations are imposed on individual entities as addressees of this principle, related to the consequent obligation to strive to eliminate existing gaps in knowledge regarding their activities and their effects on the environment, which also have a financial dimension (under the "polluter pays" principle) (Kreilhuber & Kariuki, 2020).

The transformation of the law resulting from the principle of sustainable development and the general principles of environmental law derived from it, such as the precautionary principle, is a reality. To the extent analysed, it follows the pattern characterised above. However, it is subject to additional factors, revealing further challenges. One is the lack of coherence in the multicentric legal system regarding the perception of the precautionary principle, which has, for example, serious implications for the assessment of the correctness of the implementation of a country's international obligations (especially if it has EU membership). Another factor is the specificity of the area where the risk is being analysed. It may result in a shifting emphasis on the burden of proof to reach the standard of the best scientific data within a particular case.

This state of affairs can be illustrated today by taking nature conservation law, particularly the Habitats Directive (in the context of the Natura 2000 impact assessment and the species protection) as a starting point. The Court of Justice of the EU (CJEU) has consistently developed the precautionary principle in this group of cases in its jurisprudence in a way that has resulted in a progressive transformation of the public law of the EU Member State, which also includes procedural administrative law or public economic law. In the first case, this is due to the consistent overcoming of the procedural autonomy of the Member State in areas of EU competence. In the second, inter alia, from the interdisciplinary nature of the legal instrument of environmental impact assessment. Therefore, the chapter aims to present the de lege lata status and current challenges in this respect, at the level of EU and Polish law.

2. The precautionary principle in the reality of a multicentric legal system

2.1. General remarks

Given the evolution of the precautionary principle, the characterisation of this value should be set in the reality of the multicentric legal system. As follows from Article 9 of the 1997 Constitution of the Republic of Poland, "the Republic of Poland shall observe international law binding upon it" (Constitution of the Republic of Poland, 1997). Against the background of this article, the Polish Constitutional Tribunal concluded in its judgment of 11 May 2005 that the system of law in force on the territory of the Republic of Poland is "multicomponent" since "next to the norms (provisions) established by the national legislator, there are regulations (provisions) created outside the system of national (Polish) legislative bodies; (...) on the territory of Poland, therefore, subsystems of legal regulations, originating from different legislative centres, are in force concurrently. They should coexist on mutually friendly interpretation and cooperative co-application" (Judgment of the Constitutional Tribunal, 2005).

This outlined external aspect of the analysed phenomenon (the so-called external multicentrism) is, according to Kalisz (2007), a situation "in which centres external to the state can, in a binding manner, make decisions that are effective on the territory of that state." At the same time, according to this author, such a situation occurs in the context of the jurisprudential activity of the CJEU and the European Court of Human Rights (ECtHR) in relation to the process of law application in Poland.

The multiplicity of "legislative centres" within the legal system is therefore a fact that has a wide-ranging impact on all of its components, i. e. besides the law application, also on its axiology and law making process. This is reflected in concepts such as the "internationalisation" or "Europeanisation" of law (Mik, 2021). The term "global legal pluralism," synonymous with the "internationalisation and regionalisation of the law," may also be cited. As Bergé (2011, p. 244) points out, this term "describes (...) a multiplicity of places of fabrication and application of law that appear outside of the state model. Law is no longer only constructed in the national sphere. (...) The national level, which is not a stranger to certain forms of legal pluralism, does not disappear. Rather, it coexists with models developed at the international and European contexts."

A parallel fact is the need to ensure vertical consistency in such complex realities of a "multi-component" law system. In a modern state, the formal sources of law and their hierarchy are usually defined at the constitutional level. The example of Polish law shows, however, that the solutions expressed expressis verbis in the text of the current Constitution do not fully reflect the dynamics taking place in this field between the "legislative centres." For example, it does not reflect the subtleties arising from the principle of primacy of EU law, binding national courts and public administration bodies in applying this law in Poland.

As Lierman (2014, p. 629) rightly points out, "law is also a complex adaptive system. The phenomenon of increased complexity gives rise to adapted learning methods and the equilibrium between the concurring legal systems is to a certain extent restored by convergence of methods of interpretation, of legal instruments and legal principles beyond the limits of separate branches of law and legal orders." The search for convergence understood in this way appears as the starting point for achieving coherence in the reality of a multicentric legal system, which primarily refers to its axiology (Wouters, 2019).

2.2. Precaution as an emanation of the principle of sustainable development

The precautionary principle is an example of a value recognised at each of the three levels – international, EU and national (Polish) law. At the same time, it can be an interesting subject of classical comparative studies, as a significant group of states now include it in their legal systems (OECD, 2023). Its essence can be expressed by recalling Principle 15 of the Rio Declaration: "in order to protect the environment, the precautionary approach shall be widely applied by States according to their capabilities. Where there are threats of serious or irreversible damage, lack of full scientific certainty shall not be used as a reason for postponing cost-effective measures to prevent environmental degradation" (UNGA, 1992).

The precautionary principle is considered to have originated from the German Vorsorgeprinzip formulated in the 1970s (Trindade, 2015, p. 404; de Sadeleer, 2020, p. 137). The role of the OECD in promoting it at the international level is also emphasised (Korzeniowski, 2010). This value has been included in several international environmental agreements (Fitzmaurice, Wong & Crampin, 2022, pp. 70–74). However, the nomenclature, positioning (preamble and/or main text), and scope of its characterisation (name alone or full description) are not uniform (Nyka, 2017).

For example, the term "precautionary measures" is used in the 1992 United Nations Framework Convention on Climate Change (UNFCCC, 1992, Art. 3(3)), while "precautionary approach" is used in the 1996 London Protocol to the 1972 Convention on the Prevention of Marine Pollution by Dumping of Wastes and Other Matters (London Protocol, 1996, Art. 3(1)). In turn, the "precautionary principle" is characterised, inter alia, in the 1992 Convention on the Protection and Use of Transboundary Watercourses and International Lakes (UNECE,

1992, Art. 2(2)(a)) and the 1992 Convention for the Protection of the Marine Environment of the North-East Atlantic (OSPAR, 1992, Art. 2(5)).

In addition to treaty law, the precautionary value has been the subject of analyses reflected in several soft law instruments. Two of those in which the precautionary principle is considered at the international level deserve special attention.

The first is the New Delhi Declaration of Principles of International Law Relating to Sustainable Development, adopted in 2002 by the International Law Association (ILA) (Schrijver, 2004, pp. 549–550). This declaration includes "the principle of the precautionary approach to human health, natural resources and ecosystems". It indicates, inter alia, that "sustainable development requires that a precautionary approach (...) should include (...) consideration in an environmental impact assessment of all possible means to achieve an objective (including, in certain instances, not proceeding with an envisaged activity); and (...) in respect of activities which may cause serious long-term or irreversible harm, establishing an appropriate burden of proof on the person or persons carrying out (or intending to carry out) the activity" (UN WSSD, 2002, p. 5).

The second is the 2016 IUCN World Declaration on the Environmental Rule of Law. Among the "principles aimed at promoting and achieving ecological justice through the environmental rule of law", a presumption is included as Principle 5 (In Dubio Pro Natura), under which: "in cases of doubt, all matters before courts, administrative agencies, and other decision-makers shall be resolved in a way most likely to favour the protection and conservation of the environment, with preference to be given to alternatives that are least harmful to the environment" (IUCN, 2016).

2.3. The precautionary principle and EU law

In EU law, the treaty basis for environmental policy and law was introduced into the Treaty of Rome through the Single European Act (Single European Act, 1987, Art. 25). The then Article 130r(2) covered the general principles of environmental law, among which, however, the precautionary principle was not yet included. The situation changed with the Treaty on European Union (Douma, 2000, pp. 132–133), which amended the Treaty establishing the European Economic Community (Treaty on European Union, 1992, Art. G(38)). Its current equivalent is Article 191(2), sentence I, TFEU, according to which "Union policy on the environment shall aim at a high level of protection taking into account the diversity of situations in the various regions of the Union. It shall be based on the precautionary principle and on the principles that preventive action should be taken, that environmental damage should as a priority be rectified at source and that the polluter should pay" (TFEU, 2016, Art. 191(2)).

Given the brief reference in the Treaties, the Commission's Communication on the precautionary principle provides valuable elaboration (European Commission, 2000a). Regarding scientific uncertainty, the Communication explains that recourse to the precautionary principle presupposes: (i) identification of potentially negative effects resulting from a phenomenon, product or procedure; and (ii) a scientific evaluation of the risk, which, due to insufficient or inconclusive data, makes it impossible to determine with certainty the level of risk involved (European Commission, 2000a, p. 14).

Regarding the reversal of the burden of proof, the Commission distinguished between two approaches: (1) the basic approach involving a prior approval procedure for placing certain products on the market (e.g., medicines, pesticides, food additives); and (2) an alternative involving a clause reversing the burden of proof in individual cases (European Commission, 2000a, pp. 20–21).

Notably, the Communication extends the scope of the precautionary principle beyond environmental protection. According to the Commission, it "is far wider and covers those specific circumstances where scientific evidence is insufficient, inconclusive or uncertain and there are indications through preliminary objective scientific evaluation that there are reasonable grounds for concern that the potentially dangerous effects on the environment, human, animal or plant health may be inconsistent with the chosen level of protection" (European Commission, 2000a, p. 9). As such, the principle influences broader areas of public economic law, particularly health and safety regulation.

The CJEU has affirmed the status of the precautionary principle in its case law, sparking debate as to whether it should be considered a general principle of EU law (de Sadeleer, 2020, p. 143). In Commission v Netherlands, the Court recognised the precautionary principle's applicability not only to environmental policy under Article 130r EC (now Article 191 TFEU), but also to public health policy under Article 129 EC (now Article 168 TFEU) (CJEU, 2004, paras. 45–46).

The Court held that "a Member State may, under the precautionary principle, take protective measures without having to wait until the existence and gravity of those risks become fully apparent. However, the risk assessment cannot be based on purely hypothetical considerations" (CJEU, 2004, para. 52). Furthermore, a "proper application" of the principle involves identifying potential health risks and conducting a comprehensive risk assessment based on the most reliable scientific data and recent international research. Restrictive measures are justified where uncertainty remains but the risk of real harm persists (CJEU, 2004, paras. 53–54).

This approach remains valid, as reaffirmed in Bayer CropScience AG, where the Court confirmed that under the precautionary principle, protective measures may be taken before risks are fully proven (CJEU, 2021, para. 80).

2.4. Preliminary summary

The precautionary principle as a value emanating from the principle of sustainable development emerged at all three levels of the multicentric legal system in the late 1980s and early 1990s. Developed at the supranational level, it was transplanted into the domestic law of many states within a relatively short period, often as a direct consequence of implementing their international obligations shaped in the light of the precautionary principle (Przybojewska, 2018, pp. 80–82). For EU Member States, in areas of exclusive and shared competences (such as the environment), applying the precautionary principle gained additional momentum through the jurisprudence of the CJEU and soft law instruments of the European Commission.

The example of the Polish state can illustrate this process. In 1976, environmental protection was introduced into the Constitution of the People's Republic of Poland (Constitution of the People's Republic of Poland, 1952, Art. 12(2), Art. 71). The Act of 31 January 1980 on the protection and management of the environment was the first normative act aiming at an integrated legal approach (Journal of Laws, 1980, No. 3, item 6). Although it introduced concepts akin to sustainable development, general principles of environmental law, such as precaution or prevention, were not yet articulated directly.

The breakthrough came in the 1997 Constitution, which included the principle of sustainable development (Art. 5), made environmental protection a public duty (Art. 74), and imposed environmental responsibility on individuals (Art. 86). Subsequently, the Act of 27 April 2001 on Environmental Protection Law included the precautionary principle explicitly in Article 6(2), stating: "Whoever undertakes an activity whose negative impact on the environment is not yet fully recognised is obliged, guided by prudence, to take all possible preventive measures" (Environmental Protection Law, 2001, Art. 6(2); see also: Gruszecki, 2022, pp. 87–91; Pchałek, 2019, Nb. 39; Rakoczy, 2013, p. 58).

This Act was drafted with Poland's EU accession in mind. Following accession in 2004, Polish courts and public administration became subject to the EU law principles, such as primacy, effectiveness, direct effect, and consistent interpretation (Karpus, 2017, pp. 147–156). This implies that the precautionary principle must be applied under its EU-level interpretation, which may differ from domestic understandings.

Nevertheless, the Polish legislator has not clearly defined the principle's material or subjective scope. The Constitution's Article 31(3) provides that limitations on rights may be introduced by statute when necessary to protect the environment but may not infringe the essence of freedoms. Given the potential tension with the freedom to conduct business, it would be justified to incorporate the precautionary principle explicitly into public economic law, such as the 2018 Entrepreneurs' Law (Entrepreneurs' Law, 2024). This act emphasises the in dubio pro libertate principle (Art. 8) without addressing environmental values.

This situation is mirrored in administrative law theory. Although scholars acknowledge the Europeanisation of administrative procedures (Wilbrandt-Gotowicz, 2020; Niedźwiedź, 2014), the intersection between procedural law and the precautionary principle remains insufficiently analysed—especially regarding evidentiary standards and legal decision-making model (Jennings, 2022, pp. 10–27).

In conclusion, the precautionary principle has been incorporated into Polish law, but not in a way that ensures theoretical consistency in a multicentric legal system. This impairs its application by public authorities and courts. In EU exclusive or shared competence areas, such inconsistencies may undermine the state's international obligations.

3. Scientific uncertainty in CJEU jurisprudence on the Habitats Directive: environmental impact assessment and species protection

3.1. Precautionary principle and nature conservation

The precautionary principle finds a prominent place in nature conservation law. The preamble of the Convention on Biological Diversity signed in 1992 states that "where there is a threat of significant reduction or loss of biological diversity, lack of full scientific certainty should not be used as a reason for postponing measures to avoid or minimise such a threat" (Convention on Biological Diversity, 1992). The EU and Poland are parties to this landmark international agreement, which promotes an ecosystem approach in legal nature conservation (Council Decision 93/626/EEC, 1993).

The same year, the EU adopted the Habitats Directive, whose objective, according to Article 2(1), is "to contribute towards ensuring bio-diversity through the conservation of natural habitats and of wild fauna and flora in the European territory of the Member States to which the Treaty applies" (Directive 92/43/EEC, 1992).

Scientific uncertainty is difficult to define clearly. Sharon Beder (2007, pp. 56–57) offers a typology of uncertainty that includes: (1) pragmatic uncertainty (lack of data or doubts about their accuracy and relevance); (2) theoretical uncertainty (disagreements over interpretation or scientific method); (3) complexity in open systems (ecological variability and indeterminacy); and (4) intangible damage (which may be hard to observe, monitor, or comprehend). All these challenges are present in nature conservation due to ecosystems' dynamic and complex nature.

In legal terms, scientific uncertainty under the precautionary principle can be analysed in external and internal dimensions. The external dimension relates to assessing potential environmental impacts of human activities. The internal dimension focuses on biodiversity conservation and the management of natural elements and ecosystems.

These dimensions correspond to different types of legal disputes. The external one arises when an individual is required to obtain prior consent for an activity (e. g., an infrastructure project) that may affect the environment. Environmental Impact Assessment (EIA) and Strategic Environmental Assessment (SEA) are tools used in this context (Yang, 2019, pp. 545, 570). The Rio Declaration affirms their importance, stating that "[e]nvironmental impact assessment, as a national instrument, shall be undertaken for proposed activities that are likely to have a significant adverse impact on the environment and are subject to a decision of a competent national authority" (UNGA, 1992).

Both types of assessments are also embedded in EU law and the Habitats Directive for Natura 2000 protection (Directive 2011/92/EU; Directive 2001/42/EC). Under EIA, the burden of proof lies with the applicant, who must also bear the financial cost (following the "polluter pays" principle). Public authorities, in turn, must decide based on the presumption in dubio pro natura.

SEA applies to state-level actions like adoption of development plans or programmes. Here, the authority must identify gaps in scientific knowledge. Legal disputes in this area often arise post-adoption through "private enforcement" of environmental law, where public members—motivated by environmental concerns—seek judicial review (Greve, 1991; Hay & Shleifer, 1998). The core of such litigation usually lies in the claim that environmental interests were not properly accounted for in the adopted act.

The internal dimension of precaution emerges in species protection. Legal regimes for nature conservation impose general prohibitions but also foresee derogations. The authority deciding on exemptions (e. g., for capturing protected species) carries the burden of proof. In such cases, the precautionary principle aligns with the objective truth principle found in inquisitorial administrative proceedings (Jacobs et al., 2011; Polish Code of Administrative Procedure, Art. 7).

The implications of this model include constraints on the types of admissible evidence, the manner of assessing it, and the limits of administrative discretion. As Moyle (2005, pp. 159–172) and Born & Schoukens (2023, pp. 293–329) argue, the precautionary principle must be interpreted in light of biodiversity objectives and scientific uncertainty, requiring high standards of proof when exceptions are granted.

Translating these insights into practice, implementing the Habitats Directive has proven difficult for Member States operating within a multicentric legal system. A lack of coherent understanding of the precautionary principle creates serious challenges for national authorities and courts. This can be illustrated by key judgments of the CJEU in Poland (relating to EIA/SEA and Natura 2000 sites) and Spain (relating to species protection).

3.2. Environmental Impact Assessment: Case C-441/17 (Białowieża Forest)

The case resolved by the CJEU in 2018 concerned nature conservation in Poland in the context of the Habitats Directive and the Birds Directive—in three forest districts: Białowieża, Browsk and Hajnówka (CJEU, 2018). The protection of this portion of the forest ecosystem, within which Natura 2000 sites had been designated, was related to the issue of the spread of the spruce bark beetle in managed forests located in these districts. The first is particularly relevant among the four allegations made by the European Commission against Poland. It concerned the Polish forestry administration's breach of Article 6(3) of the Habitats Directive by adopting an annex to the forest management plan (FMP) for the Białowieża Forest District without ensuring that it would not adversely affect the integrity of the Site of Community Importance (SCI) and Special Area of Conservation (SAC) PLC200004 Białowieża Forest.

The FMP was adopted in 2012, but to control the spruce bark beetle outbreak, an annex was added in 2016, increasing logging quotas. In 2017, for all three forest districts, the Director General of State Forests issued Decision No. 51, which authorised the removal of infested trees and the harvesting of trees that posed a threat to public safety and fire risk, in all age classes of stands (CJEU, 2018, para. 151).

Article 6(3) of the Habitats Directive provides that "any plan or project not directly connected with or necessary to the management of the site but likely to have a significant effect thereon, either individually or in combination with other plans or projects," must be subject to an appropriate assessment. Public authorities of Member States must verify through an Environmental Impact Assessment (EIA) or Strategic Environmental Assessment (SEA) that "the plan or project will not adversely affect the integrity of the site concerned." The original

2012 FMP was assessed through a SEA, as was the 2016 annex. However, Decision No. 51 was not assessed.

Scientific uncertainty surrounding the destruction of stands by the spruce bark beetle was multilayered. However, the main dispute centred on the choice of response measures, particularly the method of increased logging and removal of infected trees. The CJEU addressed this in its analysis of the first plea, linking the precautionary principle to the requirement for proper EIA/SEA implementation. Although Article 6(3) does not explicitly mention scientific uncertainty, it is inherent to the purpose and function of the EIA/SEA procedure. Additionally, EIA Directive 2011/92/EU (Annex IV, para. 6) specifies that EIA reports must describe "forecasting methods or evidence used to identify and assess the significant effects on the environment, including details of difficulties (for example technical deficiencies or lack of knowledge) encountered in compiling the required information and the main uncertainties involved."

Concerning the required quality standard for EIA/SEA under EU law, the CJEU held that "the appropriate assessment of the implications of the plan or project for the site concerned (...) requires that all the aspects of the plan or project which can, either by themselves or in combination with other plans or projects, affect the conservation objectives of that site must be identified in the light of the best scientific knowledge in the field" (CJEU, 2018, paras. 113–114). Such assessments "may not, therefore, have lacunae and must contain complete, precise and definitive findings and conclusions capable of removing all reasonable scientific doubt as to the effects of the proposed works on the protected site concerned." Therefore, consent for a plan or project may only be granted "if no reasonable scientific doubt remains as to the absence of such effects" (CJEU, 2018, paras. 117, 120).

Based on this reasoning—and having qualified the 2016 Annex and Decision No. 51 as subject to Article 6(3)—the CJEU concluded that the 2015 assessment of the annex contained several serious deficiencies. It therefore found that "the Polish authorities did not have all the data relevant for assessing the implications of the active forest management operations at issue for the integrity of the Puszcza Białowieska Natura 2000 site, they did not carry out an appropriate assessment of those implications before the 2016 appendix and Decision No. 51 were adopted and, therefore, failed to fulfil their obligation arising from the first sentence of Article 6(3) of the Habitats Directive" (CJEU, 2018, para. 151).

3.3. Species protection: Case C-436/22 (ASCEL)

In Case C-436/22 (ASCEL), the dispute before the referring Spanish court concerned the annulment of a 2019 decision approving a regional plan for the exploitation of wolves in hunting areas north of the Duero River in Castilla y León for the 2019/2020, 2020/2021, and 2021/2022 hunting seasons, as well as compensation for each wolf shot during those seasons (CJEU, 2024, para. 2). Under the Habitats Directive, the Canis lupus species is, in principle, strictly protected (Article 12 in conjunction with Annex IV), but some EU Member States have negotiated total or partial exemptions. In Spain's case, strict protection is provided for the wolf population south of the Duero River. In contrast, only partial protection (Article 14 in conjunction with Annex V) applies to the population north of the river. Exceptions to both regimes are permitted under Article 16 of the Habitats Directive.

A key condition for applying such exceptions is the requirement of maintaining a favourable conservation status in the species' natural range. According to Article 1(i) of the Habitats Directive, this status is achieved when (1) population dynamics indicate long-term viability, (2) the natural range is stable or expanding, and (3) a sufficiently large habitat exists to ensure long-term survival (Directive 92/43/EEC, 1992, Art. 1(i)).

Article 11 of the Directive obliges Member States to conduct systematic surveillance (monitoring), and Article 17 requires them to report results at six-year intervals. These mechanisms are critical for generating the scientific data that form the basis for determining whether the derogations permitted by Article 16 are justifiable.

The Iberian wolf case again raised the issue of how to interpret the concept of "favourable conservation status," a term which, in the case law of the CJEU, has both spatial (e. g., natural range) and temporal dimensions (CJEU, 2019; 2021). It also highlighted a broader conflict between species protection and competing interests such as livestock protection or public safety. At the heart of the legal discussion was scientific uncertainty surrounding population status and how it is monitored.

In practice, controversy often arises when public authorities allow hunting despite formally reporting the species' status as "Unfavourable-Inadequate" (U1) or "Unfavourable-Bad" (U2), or when no data are reported at all. For instance, under Article 17, EU Member States submit data on conservation status using codes: FV (Favourable), U1 (Unfavourable-Inadequate), U2 (Unfavourable-Bad), and XX (Unknown) (European Environment Agency, n.d.).

In this case, the CJEU ruled that proper surveillance is indispensable. It stressed: "That surveillance is essential in order to ensure compliance with the conditions laid down in Article 14 of that directive and to determine the need to adopt measures ensuring that the exploitation of that species is compatible with the maintenance at a favourable conservation status, and constitutes in itself one of the measures necessary to ensure the conservation of that species. Consequently, a species cannot be the subject of cynegetic exploitation and hunted if effective surveillance of its conservation status is not ensured" (CJEU, 2024, para. 59).

In addition to the lack of monitoring data, the failure of national authorities to use existing data when making species protection decisions was identified as a key problem. The Court stated: "Since the effect on the conservation status of the species concerned of the taking from the wild and exploitation of that species must be assessed 'in the light of the surveillance provided for in Article 11' of the Habitats Directive, Member States must, when taking decisions authorising the hunting of that species, according to Article 14(1) thereof, justify those decisions and provide the surveillance data on which the decisions are based" (CJEU, 2024, paras. 61–62).

The judgment thus clarified the limits of national procedural autonomy under EU nature conservation law. National decisions on derogations must consider not only population data at the local level but also at the biogeographical region level or, when relevant, cross-border impacts (CJEU, 2024, para. 64). In doing so, the Court once again invoked the "best scientific data available" standard that underpins both the Habitats Directive and previous judgments (CJEU, 2019, para. 51; CJEU, 2021a).

Moreover, the Court underscored that national authorities must update their factual findings by comparing the most recent surveillance data (e. g., post-2018 data) with the official Article 17 reporting period (2013–2018). This is necessary to maintain compliance with the obligation to rely on current and comprehensive data in species protection decisions.

Finally, the CJEU directly invoked the precautionary principle in confirming that Member States must refrain from authorising hunting in cases of scientific uncertainty regarding a species' conservation status. It concluded that: "If, after examining the best scientific data available, there remains uncertainty as to whether the exploitation of a species of Community interest is compatible with the maintenance of that species at a favourable conservation status, the Member State concerned must refrain from authorising such exploitation" (CJEU, 2024, para. 72).

4. Conclusions

The precautionary principle has been a significant factor in the transformation of the law of modern states over the last three decades. In the realities of a multi-centric legal system, this process has most often occurred under the influence of obligations assumed in the framework of international environmental cooperation. In the case of the EU, this occurred in connection with its Member States' implementation of treaty obligations. The spread of the use of the environmental instrument EIA/SEA directly confirms this. A further stage in this process has now been outlined, during which the precautionary principle is sometimes ascribed to a system-wide value because of its importance in ensuring public safety and health protection.

The precautionary principle was the basis for a model of decision-making by public authorities in circumstances of scientific uncertainty concerning the environment as a protected good. As originally conceived, this model referred to an arrangement in which the public authority was pushing the public interest (environmental protection), which in turn had to limit individual subjects' private interest. The precautionary principle was therefore intended to help ensure that scientific uncertainty did not, in such a case, block public authority action to safeguard the environment. This arrangement was reflected in Article 6(3) of the Habitats Directive, which provides the legal basis for the application of EIA/SEA in the protection of Natura 2000 sites designated in EU Member States. However, in the light of the first of the CJEU judgments cited above, it can be pointed out that the precautionary principle no less intensively affects the legal system in a modified version of this arrangement. The proceedings on the submission to EIA/SEA of an annex to a forest management plan covering a forest ecosystem with the status of a Natura 2000 site illustrate the action of a public authority in a situation of direct conflict of two public interests – environmental protection and public safety. In doing so, it can be argued that there was an additional aspect to this problem. For there were also two diverging interpretations of the environmental interest itself – on the one hand, cutting down and removing infected trees to protect the remaining stand, and on the other hand, not cutting down and looking for other methods to improve the situation. Similarly, a conflict of this kind comes to the fore in species protection when assessing the acceptability of a derogation under Article 16 of the Habitats Directive. The precautionary principle in such a case is intended to help ensure that scientific uncertainty is not ignored by the public authority, which not infrequently acts in such situations under strong pressure arising from non-legal circumstances. At the same time, this value successively contributes to highlighting the importance in the process of applying the law of actively seeking and acquiring knowledge by the public authority about the state of natural elements and the influence exerted on them by human activity. As a result, it is no coincidence that in the context of scientific uncertainty, the EIA/SEA standard of 'adequate quality' and the standard of 'the best scientific data available' are being developed.

Recognising the precautionary principle at all three legal system levels requires modern states' national environmental administrations to be familiar with its contexts and seek convergence and system-wide coherence. The cited examples of the definition of this value in positive law confirm that the "legislative centres" usually stop at generalising this value in the legal text. The fact that in certain areas of the specific part of environmental law the precautionary principle is already widely implemented through "prior consent procedures" (permits, authorisations) does not significantly change this state of affairs. At the same time, the degree of Europeanisation of environmental law is steadily increasing, as a result of the active role played by the CJEU. The essence of this principle and its consequences in terms of the organisational responsibilities of the public administration (such as ensuring effective nature monitoring) and the significant limitation of the procedural autonomy of the EU Member States (resulting, inter alia, in a modification of the rules of administrative jurisdictional proceedings) therefore call for an in-depth theoretical reflection. In turn, its results will provide valuable inspiration for the national legislator on consciously striving for the necessary system-wide coherence against this background.

References

Act of 3 October 2008 on the provision of information on the environment and its protection, public participation in environmental protection and environmental impact assessments (consolidated text 2024, item 1112).

Act of 31 January 1980 on the protection and management of the environment, Dz. U. 1980, No. 3, item 6.

Beder, S. (2007). Environmental principles and policies: An interdisciplinary introduction. Earthscan.

Bergé, J.-S. (2011). Implementation of the law, global legal pluralism and hierarchy of norms. European Journal of Legal Studies, 4(2), 222–244.

Born, C.-H., & Schoukens, H. (2023). Biodiversity litigation before the Court of Justice of the European Union. In G. Futhazar, S. Maljean-Dubois, & J. Razzaque (Eds.), Biodiversity litigation (pp. 293–329). Oxford University Press.

CJEU. (2004). Commission v Netherlands, Case C-41/02, EU:C:2004:762.

CJEU. (2021). Bayer CropScience AG, Case C-499/18 P, EU:C:2021:367.

Constitution of the People's Republic of Poland of 22 July 1952, unified text Dz. U. No. 7, item 36.

Constitution of the Republic of Poland of 2 April 1997, Journal of Laws No. 78, item 483 as amended.
Convention for the Protection of the Marine Environment of the North-East Atlantic. (1992). UNTS 2354, p. 67.
Convention on Biological Diversity. (1992). United Nations Treaty Series, 1760, 79.
Convention on the Protection and Use of Transboundary Watercourses and International Lakes. (1992). UNTS 1936, p. 269.
Council Decision 93/626/EEC of 25 October 1993 concerning the conclusion of the Convention on Biological Diversity, OJ L 309, 13.12.1993, p. 1–2.
Council Directive 92/43/EEC of 21 May 1992 on the conservation of natural habitats and of wild fauna and flora, OJ L 206, 22.7.1992, 7–50.
Court of Justice of the European Union (CJEU). (2018). Judgment of the Court (Grand Chamber) of 17 April 2018 — European Commission v Republic of Poland, Case C-441/17, ECLI:EU:C:2018:255.
Court of Justice of the European Union (CJEU). (2019). Judgment in Case C-674/17, Tapiola, ECLI:EU:C:2019:851.
Court of Justice of the European Union (CJEU). (2021). Judgment in Case C-357/20, Magistrat der Stadt Wien-II, ECLI:EU:C:2021:881.
Court of Justice of the European Union (CJEU). (2024). Judgment in Case C-436/22, ASCEL v Castilla y León, ECLI:EU:C:2024:656.
Craig, P. (2012). EU Administrative Law (2nd ed.). Oxford University Press.
de Sadeleer, N. (2020). Environmental Principles (2nd ed.). Oxford University Press.
Directive 2001/42/EC of the European Parliament and of the Council of 27 June 2001 on the assessment of the effects of certain plans and programmes on the environment, OJ L 197, 21.7.2001, p. 30–37.
Directive 2009/147/EC on the conservation of wild birds (Birds Directive), OJ L 20, 26.1.2010, p. 7–25.
Directive 2011/92/EU of the European Parliament and of the Council of 13 December 2011 on the assessment of the effects of certain public and private projects on the environment, OJ L 26, 28.1.2012, p. 1–21.
Directive 92/43/EEC on the conservation of natural habitats and of wild fauna and flora (Habitats Directive), OJ L 206, 22.7.1992, p. 7–50.
Douma, W. T. (2000). The precautionary principle in the European Union. Review of European, Comparative & International Environmental Law, 9(2), 132–143.
Entrepreneurs' Law. (2024). Unified text Dz. U. of 2024, item 236 as amended.
Environmental Protection Law. (2001). Unified text Dz. U. of 2024, item 54 as amended.
European Commission. (2000a). Communication from the Commission on the precautionary principle, COM(2000) 1 final. Retrieved from https://eur-lex.europa.eu.
European Environment Agency. (n.d.). Article 17 reporting tool. https://nature-art17.eionet.europa.eu/article17/.
Fitzmaurice, M., Wong, M. S., & Crampin, J. (2022). International Environmental Law: Text, Cases and Materials. Edward Elgar Publishing.
Greve, M. S. (1991). Private enforcement of environmental law. Tulane Law Review, 66(2), 339–394.
Gruszecki, K. (2022). Prawo ochrony środowiska. Komentarz. Warsaw: Wolters Kluwer.

Hay, J. R., & Shleifer, A. (1998). Private enforcement of public laws: A theory of legal reform. The American Economic Review, 88(2), 398–403.

IUCN. (2016). World Declaration on the Environmental Rule of Law. Retrieved from https://iucn.org/our-union/commissions/world-commission-environmental-law/our-work/history/foundational-documents-4.

Jacobs, L., et al. (2011). The nature of inquisitorial processes in administrative regimes: Global perspectives. Canadian Journal of Administrative Law and Practice, 24(2), 261–283.

Jennings, R. (2022). The use of scientific evidence in precautionary decision-making in EU environmental law. European Journal of Law Reform, 24(1), 10–27.

Judgment of the Constitutional Tribunal of 11 May 2005, K 18/04, OTK 49/5/A/2005.

Kalisz, A. (2007). Multicentrism of the Polish legal system and the jurisprudential activity of the European Court of Justice and the European Court of Human Rights. Ruch Prawniczy, Ekonomiczny i Socjologiczny, 69(4), 35–49.

Karpus, K. (2017). Rules of application of EU law in the activity of Polish public administration. Annales Universitatis Mariae Curie-Skłodowska – sectio G, (2), 147–156.

Korzeniowski, P. (2010). Zasady prawne ochrony środowiska. Łódź: Wydawnictwo Uniwersytetu Łódzkiego.

Kreilhuber, A., & Kariuki, A. (2020). Environmental rule of law in the context of sustainable development. Georgetown Environmental Law Review, 32(3), 591–598.

Lierman, S. (2014). Law as a complex adaptive system: The importance of convergence in a multi-layered legal order. Maastricht Journal of European and Comparative Law, 21(4), 629–652.

London Protocol. (1996). Protocol to the Convention on the Prevention of Marine Pollution by Dumping of Wastes and Other Matter, 1972. Art. 3(1).

Mik, C. (2021). The impact of internationalisation and integration on the classical paradigm of state and law (Vol. 1). Toruń: Wydawnictwo UMK.

Morag-Levine, N. (2014). The history of precaution. American Journal of Comparative Law, 62(4), 1095–1132.

Moyle, B. (2005). Making the precautionary principle work for biodiversity: Avoiding perverse outcomes in decision-making under uncertainty. In R. Cooney & B. Dickson (Eds.), Biodiversity and the precautionary principle: Risk and uncertainty in conservation and sustainable use (pp. 159–172). Routledge.

Niedźwiedź, M. (2014). Przekształcenia prawa o postępowaniu administracyjnym i postępowania egzekucyjnego. In R. Hauser, Z. Niewiadomski, & A. Wróbel (Eds.), Europeizacja prawa administracyjnego (pp. 745–784). Warsaw: Wolters Kluwer.

Nyka, M. (2017). Legal aspects of precaution in the international legal protection of the environment. Gdańskie Studia Prawnicze, 38, 501–512.

OECD. (2023). Understanding and Applying the Precautionary Principle in the Energy Transition (Annex A). Paris: OECD Publishing.

Pchałek, M. (2019). Komentarz do art. 6. In M. Górski et al. (Eds.), Prawo ochrony środowiska. Komentarz, Legalis/el.

Polish Code of Administrative Procedure. (1960). Ustawa z dnia 14 czerwca 1960 r. – Kodeks postępowania administracyjnego, Dz.U. 1960 Nr 30 poz. 168, tekst jednolity: Dz.U. z 2023 r. poz. 775.

Przybojewska, I. (2018). Extensional interpretation of environmental law as a special branch of law. Studia Prawnicze KUL, (2), 67–85.

Rakoczy, B. (2013). Komentarz do art. 6. In Z. Bukowski et al. (Eds.), Prawo ochrony środowiska. Komentarz (pp. 57–58). Warsaw: LexisNexis.

Schrijver, N. (2004). The New Delhi Declaration of Principles of International Law Relating To Sustainable Development. In M.-C. Cordonier Segger & C. G. Weeramantry (Eds.), Sustainable Justice (pp. 549–560). Brill.

Single European Act. (1987). Official Journal of the European Communities, L169, 1–28.

TFEU. (2012). Consolidated Version of the Treaty on the Functioning of the European Union. OJ C326, 26.10.2012, 47–390.

Treaty on European Union. (1992). OJ C 191, 29.7.1992, 1–112.

Trindade, A. A. C. (2015). Principle 15: Precaution. In J. E. Viñuales (Ed.), The Rio Declaration on Environment and Development: A Commentary (p. 404). Oxford University Press.

UN WSSD. (2002). Letter dated 6 August 2002 to the United Nations, Annex: ILA New Delhi Declaration of Principles of International Law Relating to Sustainable Development, A/CONF.199/8.

UNFCCC. (1992). United Nations Framework Convention on Climate Change. UNTS 1771, p. 107.

UNGA. (1992). Report of the United Nations Conference on Environment and Development (Annex I), A/CONF.151/26 (Vol. I).

Wilbrandt-Gotowicz, M. (2020). The Future of the Code of Administrative Procedure in the Context of the Europeanization of Administrative Procedures. Państwo i Prawo, (6), 60–84.

Wouters, J. (2019). The role of general principles in a multi-layered legal setting. In M. Andenas, M. Fitzmaurice, et al. (Eds.), General Principles and the Coherence of International Law (pp. 195–201). Brill.

Yang, T. (2019). The emergence of the environmental impact assessment duty as a global legal norm and general principle of law. Hastings Law Journal, 70(2), 525–574.

Jerzy Lachowski / Natalia Dańko

Can artificial intelligence be criminally liable?

1. Introduction

The relationship of artificial intelligence (hereinafter AI) to criminal law is not infrequently addressed in criminal law doctrine. Considerations include whether artificial intelligence can be the subject of criminal liability, how the manufacturer, seller or user of an AI-based device should be liable if harm is caused to a third party with the help of such a device. While there is no doubt that the actions of AI or its use may lead to negative consequences, such as the death of a human being, damage to health, destruction in the area of protected information, the question of whether artificial intelligence itself can be held criminally liable is contentious. This issue is all the more intriguing when it is pointed out that AI may be able to learn and then make decisions based on the information gathered.

The question formulated in the title can only be answered after a systematic juxtaposition of the essence of artificial intelligence with the elements in the structure of the crime. It will then be easy to put forward a thesis on whether it is possible today to hold artificial intelligence criminally responsible. Suppose this question is answered in the negative. In that case, it is worth going one step further and considering what changes would have to be made to the structure of the crime to make such liability possible or what other models of artificial intelligence liability might be. The considerations in this paper will aim to address the issues signalled.

2. The essence of artificial intelligence (AI)

In the literature, artificial intelligence (AI) is a branch of computer science that creates simulators of human thinking in computer programmes. AI is commonly divided into weak and strong forms. Weak AI allows for the simulation of human thinking within narrow task domains. At the same time, strong AI, learning from external stimuli, is considered capable of autonomous, human-like reasoning and generalised problem-solving (Gnas, 2021).

In Regulation (EU) 2024/1689 of the European Parliament and of the Council of 13 June 2024 (commonly referred to as the Artificial Intelligence Act), an "AI system" is defined as:

> "a machine-based system that is designed to operate with varying levels of autonomy and that can demonstrate an element of adaptability after deployment, and that, for either explicit or implicit purposes, infers how to generate outputs such as predictions, content, recommendations, or decisions that can influence physical or virtual environments" (AI Act, Art. 3(1)).

The regulation identifies three essential features distinguishing AI from traditional software: inference capability, autonomous operation, and adaptability (Flisak, 2024).

According to Encyclopaedia Britannica, artificial intelligence refers to the ability of a computer or robot controlled by a computer to perform tasks typically associated with intelligent beings. These include reasoning, discovering meaning, generalising, and learning from past experiences. Learning in AI can occur via trial and error, or through the abstraction of principles from prior data and situations. More advanced systems can adapt their responses based on previously encountered conditions (Britannica, 2024). Pei Wang (2019) notes that it is important to distinguish between systems whose behaviour is fully determined at the design stage and those capable of learning independently post-deployment. This distinction underpins many legal and ethical debates surrounding AI autonomy and accountability. Weak AI (also called Narrow AI) can only function within a clearly defined range of tasks—such as autonomous driving, medical image analysis, data sorting, image or text generation, or chess playing—and does not possess generalised intelligence. In contrast, strong AI, also known as Artificial General Intelligence (AGI) or Human-Level Machine Intelligence (HLMI), is expected to perform any intellectual task that a human can perform (Kerrigan et al., 2022).

Theoretical discussions also include Artificial Superintelligence (ASI), which would possess capabilities surpassing human intelligence—including creativity, emotional understanding, and social reasoning. Although ASI does not exist, many scholars predict its emergence within the 21st century, though estimates vary (Atkinson, 2019).

AI is increasingly embedded into diverse physical systems and consumer devices like cars or humanoid robots. Scholars such as Radutnyj (2019) have outlined the hypothetical capabilities of advanced AI-equipped robots: perfect memory, rapid data processing, independent learning and self-improvement, situation awareness, emotional judgment, strategic planning, and autonomous decision-making. Such traits could far exceed human abilities in many domains.

Given that humans are held criminally responsible for their actions, a provocative question arises: should intelligent systems, capable of greater cognition and action than humans, also be held accountable similarly? This question lies at the heart of emerging debates on AI responsibility and liability (Gnas, 2021; Atkinson, 2019).

3. The problem of committing an act by artificial intelligence

The basic element in the structure of a crime is the act. The legislator does not provide a statutory definition of this concept, and its essence has therefore been developed within the criminal law doctrine. Notably, the three principal conceptions of an act formulated in the literature all refer inherently to human behaviour.

The first is the causal conception, which defines an act as a series of physical movements that change the external world, triggered by a causal force—namely, the impulse of will initiating the decision-making process (Pohl, 2013, p. 222–225).

The second is the finalist conception (finalism), according to which an act is any intentional human conduct. This view holds that an act consists of will-controlled and goal-directed behaviour. Thus, consciousness and will are its essential components, and it is will that both determines and directs the perpetrator's actions (Mącior, 1971, p. 976; Pohl, 2013, p. 228).

The third is the sociological conception, which defines an act as human behaviour that has social relevance and impacts legal goods recognised in the social order. Here, two components must be distinguished: the objective element (human conduct) and the subjective element (the capacity to perceive external stimuli and control one's will) (Kaczmarek, 2006, p. 27).

All three conceptions—causal, finalist, and sociological—are intrinsically anthropocentric. They presuppose human qualities such as consciousness, intent, and will, which artificial intelligence does not possess. Consequently, applying these traditional models to AI raises significant theoretical obstacles.

However, if one were to hypothetically extend these models to include non-human actors—i. e., systems simulating human-like behaviour, such as artificial intelligence—the question arises as to which conception, if any, might justify treating AI as capable of committing an act in the criminal law sense.

The sociological conception seems ill-suited to this extension, as it hinges on the capacity to control will—a feature AI fundamentally lacks. While AI systems can respond to external stimuli, all actions are algorithmically programmed without volitional control. Similarly, the finalist conception, emphasising intentionality and goal-directed behaviour, is problematic for AI since it presupposes a conscious will guiding action.

Only the causal conception might offer a potential avenue, as it requires merely that behaviour result in a physical change in the world. Under this view, one could argue that AI can produce effects, such as when an autonomous vehicle causes an accident resulting in injury. Nevertheless, even here, problems persist. First, relying solely on a naturalistic view of the act (i.e., causation without volition) risks reverting criminal law theory to a pre-modern framework from the 19th century that lacks the normative sophistication of current doctrine. Second, even within a causal framework, the will remains an implicit precondition: it directs movement that causes external change (Pohl, 2013, p. 224).

AI lacks this will. It operates on pre-coded logic and learned statistical models, not through self-generated intentional states. Thus, even when AI causes real-world effects, it does so in a way that lacks the underlying mental elements traditionally required to define an act in criminal law.

4. The issue of the realisation of the elements of a criminal act by artificial intelligence

According to Article 115 § 1 of the Polish Criminal Code (kodeks karny, hereinafter "kk"), a criminal act contains the elements set out in a statute. Among these elements, it is essential to distinguish between the objective side and the subjective side of the offence.

Undoubtedly, artificial intelligence (AI) can contribute to fulfilling elements constituting the objective side of a criminal act. It is conceivable that an AI could cause the death of a human being, inflict bodily harm, or cause significant damage to digital infrastructure—e.g., through modification or deletion of IT data. Of course, this does not imply that AI can similarly fulfil the subjective elements of every offence under the Criminal Code.

The real challenge arises concerning the subjective side of the criminal act, which can be realised either in the form of intentionality (umyślność) or unintentionality (nieumyślność). Intentionality in criminal law includes two key components: consciousness and will (Budyn-Kulik, 2015, p. 76).

In psychological terms, consciousness is understood as the reflection of external reality within the human psyche, including self-awareness, which enables the planning and control of behaviour (Tomaszewski, 1977, p. 173). It is shaped by personal characteristics, memory, imagination, experience, and the functioning of the brain and sensory organs (Budyn-Kulik, 2015, p. 77; see also

Giezek, 2013, pp. 20–23). Essential conditions for consciousness include attention and the ability to engage with one's environment and interpret stimuli.

While the psychological concept of consciousness is expansive, in criminal law, consciousness is understood more narrowly—as the awareness and processing of information specifically within the context of the legal elements of a prohibited act (Budyn-Kulik, 2015, p. 85, 111).

Will, too, is viewed differently in criminal law than in psychology. In both cases, however, it relates to decision-making. Within criminal law, will is defined as a mental disposition towards the legally relevant reality described in the elements of an offence. Under Article 9 § 1 kk, will may take the form of either wishing (chcenie) or consenting (godzenie się) to the occurrence of certain consequences (Budyn-Kulik, 2015, pp. 257–263).

In contrast, unintentional commission of an offence occurs when there is no intent to commit a prohibited act. However, the act arises due to a breach of precautionary principles required by the circumstances, provided the act was or could have been foreseen (Article 9 § 2 kk). This includes: conscious negligence, in which the perpetrator wishes to avoid a prohibited act but fails due to insufficient care; unconscious negligence, where the perpetrator is unaware of the risk and believes they are acting correctly (Giezek, 2013, p. 196ff.).

It is, however, impossible to attribute intentionality to AI in the sense required by criminal law. While AI systems receive and process external data, which could prima facie resemble consciousness, their responses are algorithmic and automated, not guided by volitional processes. There is no will as understood in psychological or legal terms. AI does not want or consent to consequences in a way that reflects a mental attitude toward legally relevant reality.

Furthermore, AI cannot possess consciousness in the full psychological sense, as it lacks true self-awareness, imagination, or the capacity to plan and control its behaviour as a human does. Nor can AI be said to foresee the commission of an offence in the way required for unintentionality. Foresight implies a form of prospective thinking and mental anticipation that AI systems—reacting strictly to data inputs via predetermined or learned algorithms—do not possess.

In summary, even if AI can meet the objective criteria for a criminal act, its inability to satisfy the subjective prerequisites—particularly intent—precludes holding it liable in the traditional criminal law framework.

On the other hand, it is possible to imagine a breach of the precautionary principle constituting an unintentional act and artificial intelligence's reception of information from the external environment. However, it is difficult to attribute to such systems either conscious or unconscious unintentionality within the meaning of criminal law.

Attributing conscious negligence is impossible because there are no grounds for attributing to AI any foreseeability of the possibility of committing a criminal act in the context of an alternative intention. Nor does it appear possible to attribute the general capacity for foreseeability to an AI system. Foreseeability implies that the thought of a prohibited act arises before its commission—thus enabling the actor to refrain from risky behaviour potentially. Such prospective cognition is central to both forms of negligence and cannot be identified in systems governed solely by input–output algorithms.

These considerations lead to the conclusion that, in general, the liability of artificial intelligence—within the current framework of Polish criminal law—could only be based on the realisation of the material (objective) elements of the criminal act, and not its subjective components.

This interpretation is also dominant in foreign legal doctrine, where it is consistently emphasised that, due to the lack of true consciousness and free will, artificial intelligence cannot fulfil the subjective side of a criminal act and therefore cannot bear criminal liability in the traditional sense (Mongillo, 2023, p. 81; Gless/Silverman/Weigend, 2016, p. 424). Nevertheless, some dissenting voices in the literature suggest otherwise.

An often-cited example is the Random Darknet Shopper case, involving a bot developed for an art project, which was programmed to autonomously make random weekly purchases on the darknet using $100 in Bitcoin. Among its purchases were fake branded goods and drugs (specifically, 10 ecstasy pills). The bot's creators were briefly investigated for criminal liability, but the proceedings were later dropped. Advocates for AI liability interpret this case as proof that the bot demonstrated intentional behaviour: it scanned the darknet, evaluated prices, and proceeded to buy illicit substances—an action that would trigger criminal responsibility in a human agent (Lagioia & Sartor, 2020, pp. 441–448, 452).

However, this reasoning seems insufficient to justify criminal liability for AI. There is no indication that the bot understood the legal meaning of its actions, let alone that it wanted or consented to violating the law. The execution of a pre-programmed routine—however sophisticated—is not equivalent to a mental act of volition or legal awareness.

Even Gabriel Hallevy, a prominent proponent of AI criminal liability, has suggested that AI could be attributed a form of specific intent (when it is programmed to pursue a particular purpose), and even more plausibly, forms of recklessness (conscious inadvertence) or negligence (unconscious inadvertence), which do not require intent in the strict sense (Hallevy, 2010, pp. 21–22). Nevertheless, Hallevy's theory diverges significantly from the traditional understanding of culpability in Polish criminal law, where the subjective side requires either will or prospective thinking—both of which AI systems inherently lack. Programming AI with a particular goal cannot be equated with the AI wanting that goal. The essence of programming is precisely the absence of will: AI systems act because they are designed to, not because they choose to.

5. Can artificial intelligence be attributed with guilt?

The Criminal Code does not define the concept of guilt. However, at least several concepts have been formulated in the doctrine attempting to clarify its essence.

Firstly, the oldest is the psychological conception of guilt, which views guilt as the mental attitude of the offender towards the act. In the case of the will theory, this attitude may consist in wishing or condoning the criminal act. In the case of the theory of imagination, it may additionally involve anticipation that the criminal act may occur. However, this concept has failed to explain the nature of negligence, in which there is no mental relation to the act at all (Lachowski, 2017, pp. 653 et seq.; Kowalewska-Łukuć, 2019, pp. 40 et seq.; Zakrzewski, 2016, pp. 98–103).

Secondly, there is the complex theory of guilt, which views guilt as the alleged mental attitude of the perpetrator toward the committed act. Although it adds an element of judgment to the concept of guilt (i. e. the "allegedness"), it still suffers from the same flaw as the psychological concept, as it too fails to deal with negligence (Zakrzewski, 2016, pp. 104ff.; Kowalewska-Łukuć, 2019, pp. 51–57).

Thirdly, the pure normative theory now predominates. This theory defines guilt as an accusation against the offender because, given the opportunity to behave lawfully, the offender chose to behave unlawfully (Kowalewska-Łukuć, 2019, pp. 59–61).

Fourthly, guilt is considered a relation of culpability. The first element is a human being, the subject of the act; the second is the state of affairs produced by that subject; and the third is temporal relativity. The idea is that a certain subject is culpable under certain conditions (Patryas, 1988, p. 192). This approach was slightly modified by M. Rodzynkiewicz, who argued that the first element of the relation may not be the subject, but the act itself, and the second element the specific criminal law system in which guilt functions (Rodzynkiewicz, 1992, p. 17)

Fifthly, the functional concept of guilt (developed by S. Stomma) treats guilt as a fiction: punishment is determined by preventive considerations. Thus, we assign guilt not because it exists in any ontological sense, but because it serves social functions like deterrence and norm reinforcement (Stomma, 1947, pp. 11 et seq.).

Sixthly, there is the discursive conception of guilt, which sees its essence in violating a kind of social contract. Guilt is therefore a lack of respect for this implicit agreement that underlies legal norms and societal cooperation (Barczak-Oplustil, 2005, p. 84).

Applying these concepts to artificial intelligence, it must be concluded that AI cannot be attributed guilt under the psychological or complex theories. Both depend on processes inherent to the human psyche—processes that, although artificially imitated, do not humanly exist in AI. Similarly, AI cannot be found guilty under the normative theory, which assumes human capacities such as maturity and sanity. While AI may be able to distinguish between lawful and unlawful conduct (due to programming), these other prerequisites remain unmet. Only two of the four conditions for guilt in this view could potentially apply to AI—which is insufficient.

However, the functional and discursive theories of guilt open a different path. Under the functional view, guilt serves an instrumental purpose: if attributing guilt to AI systems can serve deterrent or normative functions (e.g. via regulation or strict liability regimes), then such attribution may be justified—even if it is fictional. Similarly, in the discursive view, an AI that causes harm may be seen as having violated the social contract, assuming (as a theoretical fiction) that AI can participate in such a contract.

6. Higher than negligible degree of social harm caused by artificial intelligence

Finally, the issue of the degree of social harm of artificial intelligence behaviours exhausting at least the subjective elements of the criminal act stipulated in the Act remains to be considered. The resolution of this problem will be easier or more difficult depending on which conception of the degree of social harm we accept. Three basic concepts have been formulated in the doctrine in this respect.

Firstly, it should be mentioned the holistic (universal) approach, which consists in the fact that in assessing the degree of social harmfulness of an act, the totality of the circumstances related to it is taken into account, i.e. not only the elements of the criminal act, but also other elements in the structure of the offence, such as, for example, guilt, as well as those lying outside it, in particular relating to the person of the perpetrator (Świda, 1970; Buchała, 1970).

Secondly, it is necessary to distinguish the subjective approach, according to which it is an objective category, depending only on objective elements, as a rule expressed in the elements of the subjective side of the criminal act (Kaczmarek, 1968). Among the assessment criteria, the nature and value of the infringed good, the nature and amount of the damage caused, the gravity of the obligations violated by the perpetrator, the type of tool used are indicated (Cyprian, 1952; Lernell, 1954; Mioduski, 1955).

Thirdly, the last concept is the object-object approach, otherwise known as the comprehensive approach, which assumes that assessing the degree of social harm results from the interplay of objective and subjective factors (Olszewski 1958, Marek 1966). It also allows for considering subjective elements related to the act, particularly those related to the subjective side of the prohibited act. The Polish legislator adopts this concept under Article 115 § 2 of the CC.

It seems impossible to relate the comprehensive view of the degree of social harmfulness of an act adopted based on Article 115 §2kk to artificial intelligence. This is because artificial intelligence cannot be attributed to an intention consisting of an element of will, which characterises the human psyche. The form of such intent also belongs to the assessment of the degree of social harmfulness of the act. Furthermore, it is impossible to relate motivation to artificial intelligence, since it operates based on algorithms, in an automated manner. For the same reasons, a universal, holistic concept, which considers not only subjective elements related to the subject, is not compatible with artificial intelligence.

On the other hand, it is possible to assess the degree of social harm of the behaviour of artificial intelligence based on the subject concept for the same reasons for which it is possible to attribute the realisation of the subject elements of a criminal act. After all, it is possible in this case to assess the infringed legal good, the circumstances related to the perpetrator's act, the harm threatened or caused by the artificial intelligence, the type of precautionary rules violated and the degree of their violation.

7. Can artificial intelligence be penalised?

The essence of criminal punishment is a personal inconvenience borne by the perpetrator of a crime as retribution for the crime committed and as an expression of condemnation towards their act (Gardocki, 2011). There are several theories of punishment, understood as justifications for their application, with contemporary views primarily pointing to three objectives of punishment: justice, individual prevention, and general prevention.

Justice-based rationalisation originally viewed punishment as just retribution or moral restitution. In contrast, the contemporary justice goal of punishment is expressed in terms of proportionality to the degree of guilt and the gravity of the crime (Marek, 2007). Individual prevention, the justification for punishment, is understood as an impact on the offender intended to protect society from their return to crime. This form of prevention may be carried out by intentional and systematic influence on the offender's attitude to life, aimed at directing them towards compliance with the legal order in the future (rehabilitation) (Utrat-Milecki, 2009), or by making it more difficult or impossible to commit a repeat offence through the imposition of a sentence—especially a long-term one—or appropriate penal measures.

General prevention, on the other hand, aims at influencing society. In the past, the rationale for punishment within this framework was primarily the deterrent effect of punishment (general negative prevention). In contrast, contemporary views understand punishment as a positive message addressed to society. This message reaffirms the effective validity of the legal and social order and serves as a mechanism for shaping socially acceptable behaviours (Utrat-Milecki, 2009).

A review of contemporary rationalisations of punishment shows that applying criminal punishment to artificial intelligence would not achieve these objectives. First, since criminal punishment is understood as an inconvenience, imposing it on AI misses the point—AI does not experience inconvenience. Further, punishment does not fulfil the goal of justice, as this rationalisation requires the punishment to be proportional to guilt. However, as discussed earlier, the concept of guilt in Polish criminal law cannot be attributed to AI.

Similarly, the goal of individual prevention cannot be realised. AI cannot reflect on its behaviour or change it based on such reflection. It lacks consciousness and internal moral reasoning, which are necessary to calculate benefits and harms like humans do ("it is profitable for me, it is not profitable for me"). However, one might argue that the objective of individual prevention could be pursued in the sense of physically preventing AI from committing further offences—by disabling or even "destroying" the system. Such a measure would eliminate the risk of recurrence.

The issue with this approach is that it shifts the rationale from punishment to mere incapacitation. This idea of "rendering harmless" is understood as physically preventing the perpetrator from continuing criminal behaviour, primarily through removal from society. This approach, which enjoys some popularity in common law countries, is rooted in risk assessments rather than guilt or the moral blameworthiness of the act. It abandons the classical paradigm of punishment based on guilt and the damage caused by the offence, does not address the need to shape socially desirable attitudes, and aligns more closely with the logic of protective or preventive measures (Utrat-Milecki, 2009).

The literature therefore stresses that punishing artificial intelligence would be punishment in name only, since criminal punishment could not achieve the objectives set for it. It would thus negate the very idea of criminal punishment (Picotti, 2023). The foregoing brings to mind the historical notion of criminal liability of animals, against which the goals of punishment also could not be meaningfully realised. However, it must be remembered that the criminal responsibility of animals was not a manifestation of naïve anthropomorphisation, but arose from the social need to satisfy justice. Since an animal caused harm, it had to suffer punishment—such reasoning also emerges in the context of artificial intelligence. If AI causes harm, the natural expectation of society may be to "punish" it.

However, other views suggest that punishment of AI is both permissible and possible, provided that the sanctions of criminal law are appropriately adapted. For instance, Hallevy (2010) proposes that the death penalty for AI could be translated into deleting its controlling software; imprisonment could become a temporary deactivation or exclusion from use; suspended imprisonment might not require adaptation at all; and community service—akin to the Polish concept of restriction of liberty by performing unpaid, controlled social work—could be both possible and valuable, since AI could perform various beneficial tasks for society. If AI has no assets, a fine could be substituted with unpaid labour directed at the public interest (Hallevy, 2010; Lagioia & Sartor, 2020).

In contrast, some authors argue that any consideration of punishing AI should be deferred until the emergence of strong artificial intelligence (Artificial General Intelligence, AGI), characterised by self-awareness. Only then—when an entity has internal consciousness and understanding—would the application of punishments be able to achieve specific goals beyond mere symbolic action (Gless, Silverman, & Weigend, 2016; Picotti, 2023).

8. A different model of liability for the acts of artificial intelligence

Criminal law currently does not allow artificial intelligence to be held criminally liable. For this reason, the literature has proposed that a different liability model be developed for acts committed by AI systems. This issue remains largely theoretical, as the sophistication of current AI systems is limited. In most contemporary cases, when a criminal act occurs through the action of AI, it is possible to trace a human cause—typically an error on the part of the designer, developer, or user. Likewise, when AI is used simply as a tool by a human to commit a crime, attribution of liability remains straightforward (Grandi, 2023).

The challenge arises with more advanced AI systems—those that respond autonomously to external stimuli and make independent decisions that harm persons or property. As AI capabilities evolve, these issues will increasingly complicate the legal landscape. Traditional criminal law institutions, such as causality between act and effect (Mamak, 2019), especially the subjective side of liability, will become obstacles to holding AI designers, producers, distributors, or users criminally accountable. Even the concept of unconscious negligence may not suffice in these cases, as it still requires that the perpetrator could have foreseen the wrongful outcome. It would be unreasonable to expect that an AI creator or developer could foresee every conceivable operational scenario, particularly the most unlikely ones (Grandi, 2023). To impose such a burden would be to move toward a form of strict liability that is purely objective—an approach that violates the foundational principle of nulla poena sine culpa (no punishment without fault) and, by extension, the principle of human dignity in criminal law.

Various alternative models have therefore been proposed in the legal literature. In the United States, some scholars advocate for strict liability for AI developers. However, this approach is generally rejected in many continental European jurisdictions, where criminal liability is typically grounded in fault. In addition, defining who qualifies as the "producer" of AI poses difficulties. AI development is usually a collective process involving multiple contributors with varying competencies—programmers, data scientists, engineers—making the attribution of liability even more complex (Picotti, 2023).

Another suggestion involves applying existing rules on product liability to cases involving AI. This approach treats AI as a potentially hazardous product, similar to how manufacturers can be liable for defective goods. In some countries, such as Germany and the Czech Republic, this analogy is gaining traction and has legal acceptance (Beck & Gerndt, 2023; Picotti, 2023). However, in many jurisdictions, this analogy remains controversial or underdeveloped.

Another proposed solution that seems most promising is creating a liability model along the lines of collective entities' liability for acts committed by AI. The rationale for introducing such liability lies in the development and production of advanced AI systems are unlikely to be undertaken by individuals; it is difficult to imagine that an ordinary person could independently design and produce such a system (Mongillo, 2023). In order to hold collective entities liable for criminal acts committed by AI, many jurisdictions—including Poland—would need to either reform their current collective liability regimes or create an entirely new parallel framework.

The existing Polish model of corporate criminal liability is secondary. According to the Ustawa o odpowiedzialności podmiotów zbiorowych za czyny zabronione pod groźbą kary (Act on the Liability of Collective Entities for Prohibited Acts Punishable by Penalty, 2023), a prerequisite for holding a collective entity liable is the prior establishment—by a final conviction or equivalent decision—of the commission of a prohibited act by an individual acting on behalf of or in the interest of the collective entity. This condition, however, renders such a liability model ineffective in the case of criminal acts committed by AI, given the earlier demonstrated difficulties in attributing such acts to individuals.

Two alternative approaches to corporate liability are proposed under this model. First, a collective entity could be held criminally liable for producing or deploying an AI system that subsequently causes a criminal offence, where the basis for liability would be a failure to exercise due diligence or to implement appropriate risk mitigation measures. However, critics argue that this model may impose an unrealistic obligation to foresee the unforeseeable, particularly as AI behaviour becomes increasingly complex and autonomous (Mongillo, 2023).

Second, a more structured and arguably more practical model would impose liability on collective entities for breaches of AI production and post-market monitoring regulations, regardless of whether a criminal offence actually occurs. Under this model, the rules for safe AI development and deployment would be codified in advance, and violations would initially trigger administrative sanctions, in line with the ultima ratio principle of criminal law. Only after a suitable evaluation period would criminal penalties be considered for more serious or repeated violations (Mongillo, 2023).

The catalogue of sanctions under this second model could include fines, bans on AI system production or use, prohibitions on research activities, mandatory destruction of the AI system, or even supervisory measures imposed on the company involved. This approach aligns with the regulatory strategy adopted at the EU level under Regulation (EU) 2024/1689 (AI Act), which introduces harmonised rules governing the marketing, deployment, and use of AI systems in the European Union. The AI Act classifies systems by risk level and accordingly imposes obligations on developers, importers, distributors, suppliers, and users. It prohibits certain practices outright—for example, manipulative AI systems—and subjects violations to high administrative fines, akin to those imposed under the General Data Protection Regulation (GDPR) (Regulation (EU) 2024/1689, 2024).

A concept similar to the collective entity model is assigning a Responsible Person to each AI system—this could be the manufacturer, supplier, or user—who would be personally liable in case of a failure to meet regulatory obligations (Abbott & Sarch, 2019).

It is worth emphasising that while legal models are currently being developed to assign responsibility for AI's actions to human agents, no serious efforts have been made to construct models in which AI is the legal subject of responsibility.

9. Summary

The currently widely accepted structure of the offence does not allow artificial intelligence to be held criminally responsible. This is because the subjective element of the act cannot be established in the light of the sociological concept of the act. At the level of the criminal act's elements, it is impossible to attribute intentional or unintentional intent to artificial intelligence. The notion of guilt in the purely normative sense and the subjective element of social harmfulness based on the provision of Article 115 §2kk also does not correspond to artificial intelligence.

For artificial intelligence to be held criminally responsible, it must grant it legal personality and create a parallel, separate model of criminal responsibility dedicated only to it. In the light of the considerations that have been made so far, the reflection arises that in a new model of criminal responsibility relating only to artificial intelligence, it would be necessary to disregard the subjective elements present in the case of human responsibility and to reduce the premises of criminal responsibility of artificial intelligence to objective (subjective) elements. Thus, such liability would only come into play if the material elements of a specific criminal act were exhausted. This would have to be liability without fault, after all, the currently largely accepted concept of fault in purely normative terms does not correspond to the essence of artificial intelligence. This leads to the conclusion that such liability could be structured along the strict liability model in common law. In such a case, the subjective elements of liability recede into the background; they do not matter after all, what matters is the material side of the committed act. The question arises, however, whether such a model of criminal liability would be consistent with the provision of Article 42(1) of the Constitution, which requires criminal liability based on guilt.

It is also problematic to impose a penalty on artificial intelligence, or more precisely on an object equipped with artificial intelligence in modern terms. Its application is based on guilt according to the nulla poena sine culpa principle, which in purely normative terms cannot be attributed to artificial intelligence. One would have to attribute fault in such a case in functional or discursive terms. Nevertheless, also in such a case, applying a penalty, which after all must involve an ailment, would be problematic. An artificial intelligence would not feel this ailment. The only sanction that could be imagined, based on an objectivised model of artificial intelligence liability, would be its forfeiture by destruction or, alternatively, its prohibition from functioning in commerce. Only in this case would the protective function of criminal law be fulfilled.

Another possible solution to the problem of artificial intelligence liability is to create a model of AI liability along the lines of corporate liability. Such a solution would have to involve basing this liability on the principle of risk, or strict liability, as it could not be linked to the prior commission of a criminal act by a person acting on behalf or for the benefit of a collective entity, as it is currently the case in many legal systems, including Poland.

References

Abbott, R., & Sarch, A. F. (2019). Punishing artificial intelligence: Legal fiction or science fiction? UC Davis Law Review, 53, 367–414.

AI Act. (2024). Regulation (EU) 2024/1689 of the European Parliament and of the Council of 13 June 2024 laying down harmonised rules on artificial intelligence. OJ L 2024/1689.

Atkinson, D. (2019). Criminal liability and artificial general intelligence. The Journal of Robotics, Artificial Intelligence & Law, 2(5), 335–338.

Barczak-Oplustil, A. (2005). Sporne zagadnienia istoty winy w prawie karnym. Zarys problemu [Controversial issues of the essence of guilt in criminal law: An outline of the problem]. Czasopismo Prawa Karnego i Nauk Penalnych, (2), 84.

Beck, S., & Gerndt, S. (2023). German report on traditional criminal law categories and AI. In L. Picotti & B. Panattoni (Eds.), Traditional criminal law categories and AI: Crisis or palingenesis? (RIDP 94.1, pp. 216–217). Siracusa: AIDP.

Britannica. (2024). Artificial intelligence – Reasoning, algorithms, automation. Encyclopaedia Britannica. Retrieved May 17, 2024, from https://www.britannica.com.

Buchała, K. (1970). Społeczne niebezpieczeństwo czynu jako dyrektywa sądowego wymiaru kary. Wrocław–Warszawa–Kraków: KSP.

Budyn-Kulik, M. (2015). Umyślność w prawie karnym i psychologii. Teoria i praktyka sądowa [Willfulness in Criminal Law and Psychology: Theory and Judicial Practice]. Warsaw: Wolters Kluwer.

Cyprian, T. (1952). Wina w projekcie KK. Nowe Prawo, (10), 16.

Flisak, D. (2024). Akt w sprawie sztucznej inteligencji. LEX/el.

Gardocki, L. (2011). Prawo karne. Warsaw: C.H. Beck.

Giezek, J. (2013). Świadomość sprawcy czynu zabronionego [The Awareness of the Perpetrator of a Criminal Act]. Warsaw: Wolters Kluwer.

Gless, S., Silverman, E., & Weigend, T. (2016). If Robots Cause Harm, Who Is to Blame? Self-Driving Cars and Criminal Liability. New Criminal Law Review, 19(3), 412–436.

Gnas, A. (2021). Odpowiedzialność za roboty inteligentne. Internetowy Kwartalnik Antymonopolowy i Regulacyjny, (6), 69.

Grandi, C. (2023). Positive obligations (Garantestellung) grounding criminal responsibility for not having avoided an illegal result connected to the AI functioning. In L. Picotti & B. Panattoni (Eds.), Traditional criminal law categories and AI: Crisis or palingenesis? (RIDP 94.1, pp. 69–73). Siracusa: AIDP.

Hallevy, G. (2010). I, Robot – I, Criminal: When Science Fiction Becomes Reality: Legal Liability of AI Robots Committing Criminal Offenses. Syracuse Science & Technology Law Reporter, 22, 21–35.

Kaczmarek, T. (1968). Materialna istota przestępstwa i jego znamiona. Wrocław: Ossolineum.

Kaczmarek, T. (2006). O czynie ludzkim i jego znaczeniu w prawie karnym (na marginesie książki Władysława Mąciora). In Rozważania o przestępstwie i karze. Wybór prac z okresu 40-lecia naukowej twórczości (p. 27). Warsaw.

Kerrigan, C., Rab, S., Kenny, S., Payne, C., & Allen, J. G. (2022). Chapter 3: Introduction to AI. In C. Kerrigan (Ed.), Artificial Intelligence: Law and Regulation (p. 31). Cheltenham.

Kowalewska-Łukuć, M. (2019). Wina w prawie karnym [Guilt in criminal law]. Warsaw: Wolters Kluwer.
Lachowski, J. (2017). In R. Dębski (Ed.), System prawa karnego. Tom 3. Nauka o przestępstwie [System of criminal law. Vol. 3: Science of crime] (pp. 653–676). Warsaw: C.H. Beck.
Lagioia, F., & Sartor, G. (2020). AI systems under criminal law: A legal analysis and a regulatory perspective. Philosophy & Technology, 33(3), 435–463.
Lernell, L. (1954). Niektóre zagadnienia kodyfikacji prawa karnego. Państwo i Prawo, (2–3), n.p.
Mamak, K. (2019). Rewolucja cyfrowa a prawo karne [Digital revolution and criminal law]. Kraków: Wydawnictwo Uniwersytetu Jagiellońskiego.
Marek, A. (1966). W sprawie społecznego niebezpieczeństwa czynu. Nowe Prawo, (2), 199.
Marek, A. (2007). Prawo karne. Warsaw: C.H. Beck.
Mącior, W. (1971). O finalizmie w prawie karnym. Państwo i Prawo, (6), 976.
Mioduski, K. (1955). Społeczne niebezpieczeństwo czynu jako zagadnienie terminologii. Wojskowy Przegląd Prawniczy, (3), 24–25.
Mongillo, V. (2023). Corporate criminal liability for AI-related crimes: Possible legal techniques and obstacles. In L. Picotti & B. Panattoni (Eds.), Traditional criminal law categories and AI: Crisis or palingenesis? (RIDP 94.1, pp. 83–86). Siracusa: AIDP.
Olszewski, M. (1958). Czy utrzymać pojęcie społecznego niebezpieczeństwa czynu w prawie karnym. Państwo i Prawo, (3), 433–434.
Patryas, W. (1988). Interpretacja karnistyczna. Studium metodologiczne [Criminal interpretation: A methodological study]. Poznań: Wydawnictwo Naukowe UAM.
Picotti, L. (2023). Traditional criminal law categories and AI: Crisis or palingenesis? General report. In L. Picotti & B. Panattoni (Eds.), Traditional Criminal Law Categories and AI: Crisis or Palingenesis? (RIDP 94.1, pp. 17–18). Siracusa: AIDP.
Pohl, Ł. (2013). System Prawa Karnego. Tom 3. Nauka o przestępstwie. Zasady odpowiedzialności (R. Dębski, Ed.). Warsaw: C.H. Beck.
Radutnyj, O. E. (2019). Adaptation of criminal and civil law in view of scientific-technical progress (artificial intelligence, DAO and digital human). Problems of Legality, (144), 144.
Regulation (EU) 2024/1689 of the European Parliament and of the Council of 13 June 2024 laying down harmonised rules on artificial intelligence and amending various EU legal acts (Artificial Intelligence Act), OJ L, 12.7.2024.
Rodzynkiewicz, M. (1992). Pojęcie winy w prawie karnym – próba analizy krytycznej na tle ujęcia relacyjnego [The concept of guilt in criminal law: A critical analysis in the context of a relational approach]. Ruch Prawniczy, Ekonomiczny i Socjologiczny, 54(3), 17–27.
Stomma, S. (1947). Fikcja winy [The fiction of guilt]. Państwo i Prawo, (10), 11–15.
Świda, W. (1970). Prawo karne. Część ogólna. Warszawa: Państwowe Wydawnictwo Naukowe.
Tomaszewski, T. (1977). Świadomość [Consciousness]. In T. Tomaszewski (Ed.), Psychologia [Psychology] (p. 173). Warsaw: PWN.
Ustawa o odpowiedzialności podmiotów zbiorowych za czyny zabronione pod groźbą kary [Act on the Liability of Collective Entities for Prohibited Acts Punishable by Penalty], Dz. U. 2023, poz. 659.

Utrat-Milecki, J. (2009). Kara. Teoria i kultura penalna: perspektywa integralnokulturowa. Warsaw: Wydawnictwo Naukowe Scholar.

Wang, P. (2019). On defining Artificial Intelligence. Journal of Artificial General Intelligence, 10, 54.

Zakrzewski, P. (2016). Stopniowanie winy w prawie karnym [Graduation of guilt in criminal law]. Warsaw: Wolters Kluwer.

Kinga Bączyk-Rozwadowska / Damian Kaczan

Artificial Intelligence as a Challenge for Modern Medicine and Law

1. Introduction

Artificial intelligence (AI) has captivated scientists and science fiction writers for many years. "Some of the earliest significant AI concepts emerged" in the first half of the 20th century. However, owing to technological and equipment limitations, they were rooted more in theory and did not offer practical application (Buchanan, 2005; Devarapalli, 2018; Biczysko-Pudełko & Szostek, 2019; Chłopecki, 2018).

However, as scientific and technological advancements have accelerated, AI systems have permeated nearly every facet of modern life—transportation, industry, communications, and notably, healthcare. In recent years, AI systems have proved effective in the medical field. Scholarly work in both medical and legal disciplines highlights AI's growing integration into healthcare, with concepts such as "medical artificial intelligence" and "black-box medicine" becoming distinct areas of study (Buch et al., 2018; Zalewski, 2020).

AI has emerged as a valuable asset not only for healthcare providers but also for patients. AI-driven medical devices enhance and support medical professionals' work, expediting diagnostic and therapeutic processes. By harnessing AI, healthcare teams can swiftly identify underlying causes of health issues, analyse test results with greater precision, and select optimal treatment pathways (Buch et al., 2018). AI-powered technology enables healthcare practitioners to address intricate, challenging cases that would otherwise demand significant time and effort—or, in some situations, might not be solvable at all without AI support. Medical equipment integrated with AI algorithms also contributes to cost reductions in healthcare facilities. By providing efficient data and image storage and display capabilities, such as with radiology images, facilities can minimize the need to print results or maintain large teams of specialized staff, such as radiology technicians and medical administrative personnel. These operational efficiencies also extend to patient management systems, with AI-driven voicebots autonomously scheduling appointments, notifying patients when test results are available, and managing patient flow in medical queues.

AI systems offer additional conveniences for patients beyond accelerated diagnoses and more efficient treatment. Shortened diagnostic and therapeutic procedures mean that patients experience less pain and discomfort, and with faster recovery times, they can more quickly resume daily activities and return to work. Furthermore, AI allows specialists—whose availability is often limited—to serve a greater number of patients, dedicating sufficient time to each, thereby increasing access to essential healthcare services.

However, the integration of AI in medicine also introduces significant risks. Cyber threats, such as viruses and hacker attacks, can disrupt system operations, cause technical failures, or lead to the theft of sensitive patient data. Additionally, errors stemming from faulty programming, inherent algorithmic inaccuracies, or improper handling by operators can result in serious personal injuries or health complications. These errors may also infringe on patient rights, including the right to bodily integrity and confidentiality (Kaczan, 2022). The increasing automation of healthcare services may also prompt patient apprehension, with concerns that diminished personal interaction with physicians could lead to impersonal treatment, lacking empathy, conversation, and the psychological comfort traditionally provided in patient care. As AI reliance grows, there is a risk that medical professionals will become more dependent on AI-generated outputs for clinical decision-making. Over time, this could erode their clinical judgement and expertise.

Integrating AI-based systems into medical practice presents significant challenges for contemporary medicine and legal frameworks. A critical area requiring careful examination is the impact of AI on the obligations placed on doctors, specifically regarding compliance with applicable law and professional standards of deontological ethics. Furthermore, it is essential to analyse the legal implications of potential non-compliance, particularly in the light of recent advancements within EU legislative frameworks.

2. Definition of Artificial Intelligence and Its Function in Medicine

There is no universally accepted definition of artificial intelligence (AI) in legal scholarship. For analytical purposes, sociological and technical perspectives provide useful frameworks. From a sociological standpoint, AI encompasses computer programmes that perform tasks traditionally associated with human intelligence. This view suggests that AI enables machines to emulate human cognitive functions, allowing them to perform tasks that require a learning process and consider new circumstances while solving a problem (Kisielewicz, 2011). To varying degrees and extents, these systems can function autonomously and dynamically interact with their environment (Ciszewski, 2024).

In computer science, AI is defined as computer systems that analyse vast datasets, make decisions, and execute tasks based on that analysis. These systems can learn from collected data and continue learning as they operate, thereby constantly refining decision-making processes and expanding their knowledge bases (Ciszewski, 2024; Zalewski, 2020).

The definitions above illustrate that artificial intelligence is characterized by its ability to simulate advanced communication, creating an impression of self-awareness and an understanding of the external world. AI can pursue goals by leveraging identified patterns in ways that give an appearance of creativity. These capabilities stem from human-designed code that guides the actions and responses of AI systems, which typically operate through a physical medium, such as a robot or other device (Jankowska, 2015; Różanowski, 2007).

The degree of autonomy and the type of information AI can process allow us to differentiate between "weak" and "strong" AI. Weak AI refers to systems designed to emulate human-like intelligence, but with a controlled level of autonomy, subject to oversight by developers. In contrast, strong AI describes systems capable of truly independent thought and decision-making, comparable to human cognition and displaying self-awareness. All known AI solutions worldwide fall under the category of weak AI, and there is ongoing scientific debate regarding the feasibility of achieving strong AI (Bar, 2020).

The EU legislator carried over the understanding of AI outlined above into the Artificial Intelligence Act of 13 June 2024. Article 3(1) of the Act defines an "AI system" as a "machine-based system that is designed to operate with varying levels of autonomy and that may exhibit adaptiveness after deployment, and that, for explicit or implicit objectives, infers, from the input it receives, how to generate outputs such as predictions, content, recommendations, or decisions that can influence physical or virtual environments" (AI Act, 2024).

Radiology and dermatology were among the first medical fields to adopt AI systems on a large scale. In radiology, AI algorithms demonstrated a remarkable capacity to interpret lung X-rays, achieving accuracy rates that exceeded those of experienced radiologists. Similarly, in dermatology, AI analysed images of approximately 130,000 different skin conditions, enabling it to diagnose skin cancers with exceptional precision and speed, often outperforming specialists (Lakhani & Sundaram, 2017; Wałachowska 2020).

Today, AI systems are effectively used to detect conditions such as cancer, stroke, diabetes, epilepsy, eye diseases, and numerous other medical issues (Dong et al., 2021). In cardiology, pulmonology, internal medicine, and paediatrics, "intelligent stethoscopes" assist clinicians by monitoring patients' heart and respiratory systems. Using anonymised data, these devices can accurately detect specific health issues. Additionally, AI systems can generate comprehensive patient records and profiling treatment needs. Virtual medical assistants, including voicebots and chatbots, have also become widespread. These tools interact with patients by asking questions about their symptoms, helping to narrow down potential diagnoses and suggesting treatment options (Singer, 2024).

For instance, Poland has developed the world's first robot designed to diagnose epilepsy—Ictal®—which leverages advanced machine learning algorithms and is equipped with a vast dataset of epilepsy types and treatments. Similarly, AI-powered voicebots, such as the Symptom Checker implemented by the Polish Ministry of Health, guide patients through structured interviews, generate personalized health report and recommend further steps.

3. The Role of the Doctor Amid the Growing Importance of Artificial Intelligence in Medicine

The increasing reliance on artificial intelligence (AI) in healthcare raises critical questions about the evolving role of physicians and other medical professionals. Specifically, it examines how much human expertise and skills can—or should—be supplemented or replaced by AI-powered devices. Clarifying these boundaries is essential, given the risks AI poses and the potential harm patients may suffer if AI is misapplied in treatment. As clinical experience demonstrates, the consequences of such failures can be significant and severe.

As new technologies advance, it is neither feasible nor desirable to envision a healthcare system in which all diagnostic and therapeutic tasks are carried out solely by humans without AI support, nor a system wholly reliant on AI. The role of a healthcare professional remains critical, even as advanced technologies become widespread. There are areas where, by nature, machines cannot supplant human expertise, and, in parallel, doctors are bound by their duty to provide care with due diligence under Article 4 of the Law on the Professions of Doctor and Dentist and Article 355 § 2 of the Civil Code, and in alignment with deontological standards established in the Medical Code of Ethics (KEL, 2024).

The nature of the doctor–patient relationship is also a key consideration. This relationship is founded on patients' trust in their doctors, entrusting them with their health and life based on confidence in their knowledge and competence. Practice demonstrates that the quality of this relationship often has a profound impact on the treatment process and frequently serves as a cornerstone of effective therapy (Świderska, 2007; Szpara, 1999).

The significance of a patient's direct relationship with their physician is evident regarding the right to be informed about one's condition and proposed treatment (Articles 31–34 of the UZL). Intelligent machines, including voicebots or chatbots, cannot—and from a legal standpoint must not—replace a human when determining the scope and manner of information communicated to a patient, as stipulated in Article 31 of the UZL. This is because effective communication should consider the nature of the diagnosed condition, the patient's specific health status, and any complexities in the patient's circumstances.

This provision of information is central to the doctor–patient relationship. When conveyed appropriately—in terms of scope, method, and format—it enables the patient to assess a proposed treatment's potential benefits and risks, thereby facilitating informed consent or refusal. A physician is generally obligated to inform the patient of the typical risks associated with treatment, which commonly arise under similar circumstances and which the patient might reasonably anticipate (Nesterowicz, 2019). Moreover, the information must be tailored to the patient's needs, including their age, emotional state, intellectual capacity, and ability to comprehend the info (Pickering, 2021).

An AI system may also fall short when a patient refuses a treatment that carries absolute medical indications, necessitating an expansion of the scope of provided information and explaining the risks of opting out (Bączyk-Rozwadowska, 2011). It is equally challenging to envision AI making nuanced, case-by-case decisions to limit the scope of information for the patient's benefit—a practice known as therapeutic privilege (Article 31(4) of the UZL; Article 18 of the KEL). Such decisions require a human sensitivity to the patient's mental and emotional state, often communicated through subtle cues like facial expressions or gestures. While AI can be trained to recognize patterns in human behaviour and respond predictably to specific statements or actions, it fundamentally lacks the empathy, intuition, and flexibility required to handle critical moments in patient care. In particularly sensitive or distressing situations, a doctor's ability to convey understanding, compassion, and support is irreplaceable. From both practical and legal perspectives, only a human being (a doctor) can fulfil the legal obligation to inform patients thoughtfully and tactfully, especially those experiencing high emotional tension (Świderska, 2007).

Medical devices equipped with AI also require ongoing oversight from their operators (doctors) and those responsible for maintaining the system, such as IT specialists and software developers. It is crucial that qualified individuals continuously monitor these systems to prevent and quickly address potential errors. This oversight aims to promptly detect and address anomalies, unexpected outputs, and other signs of malfunction. In cases where such issues arise, the doctor must be prepared to halt the use of the system, disregard algorithmic recommendations, and manually adjust or correct the AI-generated results. These actions are mandated under Article 355 § 2 of the Civil Code and Article 4 of the UZL. AI systems without careful human supervision pose a significant risk of harm, including critical errors such as misidentifying a patient or providing inaccurate diagnoses. For example, improper pixel calibration in a scan could lead to a failure to detect a disease or result in a false diagnosis of a disease that does not exist. System update issues might cause the AI to display information or images for a different patient from the one intended.

Additionally, errors in processing written descriptions could lead to the misinterpretation of conditions, whereby alcohol misuse could be mistaken for addiction or lumbago for generic back pain. There is also the risk of breaching medical confidentiality if patient data is mishandled. While not all anomalies and irregularities can be detected, even with the highest degree of diligence (exactissima diligentia), the law imposes sanctions for cases in which a doctor or other system operator could reasonably have identified and addressed a defect, malfunction, or error (Czochra & Bar, 2019).

Artificial intelligence in medicine brings an additional concern: physicians and other healthcare personnel may develop an undue reliance on automated AI systems, particularly in diagnostic processes. This dependency can sometimes lead doctors to ignore conflicting information or even disregard their own clinical observations and judgements. This tendency to place excessive trust in AI —a phenomenon known as automation bias—is especially pronounced in diagnostics, where some practitioners may mistakenly assume that an "intelligent system is always right" (Cummings, 2004). Doctors must remain vigilant to the risks of automation bias and actively work to mitigate favouritism toward AI-derived results. Due to the so-called black-box medicine issue, AI operates on cause-and-effect relationships that are not fully transparent. In contrast, a doctor's role, as mandated by Article 355 § 2 of the Civil Code, is to exercise due diligence and provide care based on clinical assessments informed by their knowledge and experience, always prioritizing patient well-being and health needs (*salus aegroti suprema lex esto*) (Nguyen, 2024). For this reason, in cases of doubt, doctors should rigorously verify AI-generated results, adhering to the principle of limited trust.

On the other hand, automation bias may lead to situations where excessive reliance on AI will reduce situational awareness, erode clinical skills, and lead to a loss of practical experience. Over time, the assumption that AI will always produce the correct diagnosis may deter some doctors from pursuing further education and skill development (Cummings, 2004). Ultimately, this erosion of expertise will likely adversely affect patient care.

4. AI Act and Its Impact on Medical Malpractice Liability

Legislators respond differently to irregularities in healthcare depending on whether they affect the rights of a specific individual or the collective rights of a wider group of patients. Importantly, collective rights are not merely the sum of individual claims but reflect the potential or actual infringement of patient rights in comparable situations (Judgement of the Supreme Administrative Court of 28 September 2021, II GSK 363/21; Judgement of the Supreme Administrative Court of 23 April 2014, II OSK 2826/12). This distinction is equally relevant in the context of improper use of artificial intelligence (AI) in medical practice. With the implementation of the Artificial Intelligence Act (AI Act), and complementary EU regulations, it is essential to consider how legal frameworks governing individual and collective patient rights may evolve.

Traditionally, patients whose rights were infringed upon by a medical error had the right to pursue damages through national civil law (Safjan, 2012). The AI Act introduces another mechanism: Article 85 provides patients the right to file a complaint to the relevant market surveillance authority. However, this administrative path does not override judicial options, as it is established without prejudice to other administrative or judicial remedies. There is no hierarchy between national and EU procedures; both remain available concurrently.

Although Articles 57(12) and 60(9) of the AI Act mention liability, they do so only in narrow contexts—specifically, liability related to "experimentation taking place in the AI regulatory sandbox" and "testing in real-world conditions." These provisions are limited to a reference to "applicable Union and national liability law" and do not create new forms of liability (Enqvist, 2023; Biasin et al., 2023). The AI Act, therefore, makes only marginal reference to indemnity and refrains from establishing a standalone liability regime. This suggests that the EU legislature intended only to influence civil liability systems indirectly.

Thus, the professional obligations of individuals and institutions deploying AI —whether in software development or commercial medical practice—remain governed by stricter existing national standards, where applicable. Paragraph 9 of the AI Act's preamble explicitly preserves the primacy of such standards.

In conclusion, the implementation of the AI Act will not remove or reduce patients' ability to seek compensation under traditional fault-based regimes. They may still base liability claims on the established legal standard of a physician's duty of care—defined under Article 355 § 2 of the Polish Civil Code and Article 4 of the Law on the Professions of Doctor and Dentist (UZL). That duty now arguably includes a due diligence obligation in choosing, supervising, and applying AI tools in clinical settings.

The Artificial Intelligence Act (AI Act) is a regulation that directly applies to all EU Member States. Thus, if a physician or their employing institution—referred to as a "deployer" under Article 3(4) of the AI Act—fails to comply with its provisions, such behavior is unlawful per se, even without additional national legislation (Van Kolfschoten & Van Oirschot, 2024; Biasin et al., 2023; Bublitz et al. 2024). This classification of unlawfulness is significant because, under Polish civil law, a finding of fault is typically required to link a medical injury to damages, including cases of so-called organizational fault (Articles 415–416 of the Civil Code; Article 4(1) of the Patients' Rights and Patients' Rights Ombudsman Act [UPP]) (Bączyk-Rozwadowska, 2012, 2021).

However, in the context of AI, patients may struggle to successfully pursue these legal remedies—particularly due to the "black-box" nature of AI decision-making, which often obscures causal mechanisms (Wałachowska, 2018). The EU is drafting an AI Liability Directive to address this challenge, which proposes a novel framework for civil claims.

Under this draft directive (2022/0303/COD), a "claim for damages" includes non-contractual, fault-based civil claims arising from an AI system's harmful output or a failure to generate an output when one was expected. Articles 3 and 4 of the draft set out two rebuttable presumptions to ease the burden of proof on plaintiffs:

1) That the deployer did not exercise due diligence.
2) That there is a causal link between the deployer's conduct and the harm caused by AI system (European Commission, 2022).

Under Article 4 of the AI Act, deployers must proactively develop AI-related competencies among their personnel. This obligation should be evaluated case-by-case, considering the healthcare professional's role, existing knowledge, and the potential impact of the AI system's use. Particularly for high-risk AI systems —such as those used in diagnostic or therapeutic tools—Article 14(1–2) mandates that deployers must ensure supervisors can "prevent or minimize the risks to health, safety, or fundamental rights."

This obligation aligns with Article 8 of the UPP, which requires that doctors receive comprehensive training in the use of medical technologies (Journal of Laws, 2024). Article 26(2) of the AI Act further specifies that human oversight should be exercised by „natural persons who have the necessary competence, training and authority". Notably, the deployer is not required to train doctors to understand every technical detail of AI systems (cf. Article 14(4)); it is sufficient that they have reliable access to qualified IT professionals when necessary.

The legal requirements outlined in the previous section are not directly imposed on end-users, such as doctors—unless the doctor independently operates a medical practice and thereby assumes the status of a "deployer" under Article 3

(4) of the AI Act. Nonetheless physicians, should be held to complementary expectations. As previously outlined, they cannot remain indifferent to the growing presence of AI in medical practice. Instead, acquiring knowledge of AI-based systems and developing competence becomes a natural component of the obligation to maintain continuous medical professional development, as established on the basis of Article 3(1b) and Article 18 of the UZL (Bagaria & Chhabra, 2024; Rączka, 2015).

For high-risk AI systems, the deployer must implement technical and organizational safeguards to ensure the software's use aligns with its instructions for use. These safeguards must be coupled with continuously monitoring the AI system's operation. These duties are in addition to the obligations imposed by national or EU law. According to Article 26(1)(3)(5) of the AI Act, deployers must suspend the use of such systems when continued operation—even if aligned with provided instructions—would pose unjustifiably high risks concerning the potential benefits (Article 3(19) of Regulation 2019/1020).

Accordingly, while these provisions do not explicitly bind doctors, one may reasonably infer that healthcare professionals are legally obligated to follow the instructions for use associated with high-risk AI systems when deployed in patient care. Nevertheless, as the AI Act does not override national or EU regulations concerning professional conduct, doctors must prioritize their duties under Article 4 of the UZL and Article 8 of the UPP—providing care under the best available medical knowledge, professional integrity, and due diligence (Girdwoyń, 2024). In certain situations, these obligations may require abstaining from using AI.

The EU legislator emphasizes in paragraph 9 of the AI Act's preamble that "all rights and remedies provided pursuant to Council Directive 85/374/EEC (10) remain unaffected and fully applicable". However, the AI Act does not reproduce this reference in its operative clauses. Therefore, it does not impose obligations on Member States to extend strict product liability to manufacturers of AI systems as standalone goods (Wałachowska, 2020). Nonetheless, there is a clear legislative shift in this direction.

According to Article 4(1) in conjunction with Article 2(2) of the Directive 2024/2853, the term "product" includes software, except for „free and open-source software that is developed or supplied outside the course of a commercial activity". This definition suggests that AI systems used in healthcare fall within the directive's scope which is consistent with the objectives of the EU legislator expressed in recitals 3, 13 and 40 of the preamble.

Notably, the directive extends the scope of compensable damage to include "medically recognised damage to psychological health". Such harm might arise if a doctor—excessively reliant on AI—fails to fulfil the obligation to properly inform the patient, especially regarding the limitations of the AI's recommendations. Although strict liability under this directive would fall on the manufacturer or other economic operator (Article 8), doctors involved in training AI systems—for example, by contributing patient data—may still face regressive liability claims from their employers (e.g., under Articles 114–122 of the Polish Labour Code) if their actions contributed to harm (Pyrzyńska & Bocheńska, 2022).

In Polish law, violations of collective patient rights arising from using AI systems are subject to intervention by the Patients' Rights Ombudsman (Rzecznik Praw Pacjenta) under Articles 59–67 of the UPP. This process targets "practices that violate the collective rights of patients," defined as organized actions or omissions by healthcare entities that are both illegal and aimed at limiting or depriving patients of their rights.

As detailed earlier, the criterion of illegality under the UPP may be fulfilled under long-term systemic failures, such as:

1) Continued use of AI despite serious concerns about the risk-benefit ratio,
2) Absence of sufficient human oversight,
3) Inadequate training of medical staff who oversee or interact with AI tools,
4) Disregard for the instructions for use.

However, proving intentional limitation or deprivation of rights remains difficult —especially under conditions influenced by the so-called black-box effect inherent to AI systems, which obscures transparency and interpretability (da Fonseca et al., 2024; Wengler 2012). Furthermore, even the most robust safeguards cannot entirely eliminate risks related to cyberattacks, technical failures, or flawed training data.

Over time, increased AI proficiency in the healthcare sector may allow more precise determinations of whether a provider has willfully failed to fulfill organizational duties—e.g., by prioritizing cost-cutting over patient rights (Judgment of the Supreme Administrative Court of 28 September 2021, II GSK 363/21). If such a violation is established, Patients' Rights Ombudsman issues an administrative decision, ordering cessation of unlawful conduct and possibly specifying corrective actions and deadlines. The decision is subject to immediate enforcement (Article 64(1), (3) and (4) UPP).

Under Article 99(1) of the AI Act, "Member States shall lay down the rules on penalties and other enforcement measures (…) applicable to infringements of the AI Act by operators". Solutions adopted for this purpose "may also include warnings and non-monetary measures" and "shall be effective, proportionate and dissuasive".

The Polish framework satisfies these expectations in part: under Article 68 UPP, administrative fines of up to PLN 500,000 (~€116,000) may be imposed for non-compliance with Patients' Rights Ombudsman orders (Wałachowska, 2021).

Still, existing laws may be insufficient where intent to infringe patient rights cannot be proven. As such, expanding the Patients' Rights Ombudsman's powers to include public warnings or individual notifications regarding AI systems is recommended. Such a mechanism would facilitate more robust enforcement, making it harder for healthcare entities to claim ignorance or lack of intent. While this would not automatically prove violation of collective patient rights, it would strengthen the evidentiary position of regulatory authorities in future proceedings.

5. Conclusions

AI-enabled devices have become integral to modern healthcare, expediting diagnostics, enhancing treatment efficacy, and improving the efficiency of patient care. Both healthcare providers and patients gain significantly from the integration of artificial intelligence.

However, as the analysis indicates, the role of human professionals, particularly doctors, remains essential despite AI's growing autonomy and influence. Algorithms cannot replace a physician's duty to inform the patient, nor can they assume decisions on therapeutic privilege. This is currently unfeasible both technically (to ensure comprehensive implementation of this duty) and legally, given the wording of Article 31 of the UZL. Furthermore, despite confidence in AI systems, there is little doubt that in a medical emergency, patients prefer to interact with a human who brings knowledge, experience, empathy, and emotional intelligence to their care.

The use of intelligent devices also involves inherent risks, especially the potential for AI-related errors. Therefore, it is critical to maintain rigorous oversight and inspection of AI tools, applying a principle of limited trust and recognizing the impact of automation bias. Neglect in this area can result in severe, often irreversible, consequences for patients. The EU legislature is working to establish appropriate frameworks for damage compensation related to AI in healthcare, yet domestic laws still lack provisions that fully address AI's unique challenges. Consequently, in disputes involving AI-related healthcare issues, courts may need to apply laws designed without considering AI technologies. Thus, once again, legal systems are struggling to keep pace with advances in medical science.

References

Bagaria, V., & Chhabra, H. (2024). The balancing act: Adopting AI and robotics in medicine with cautious optimism. Journal of Clinical Orthopaedics and Trauma, 57, 1.

Bar, G. (2020). In L. Lai & M. Świerczyński (Eds.), Prawo sztucznej inteligencji [Artificial Intelligence Law]. Warsaw: Legalis.

Bączyk-Rozwadowska, K. (2011). Prawo pacjenta do informacji według przepisów polskiego prawa medycznego [The patient's right to information according to the provisions of Polish medical law]. Studia Iuridica Toruniensia, 9, 81–87.

Bączyk-Rozwadowska, K. (2021). Odpowiedzialność cywilna za szkody wyrządzone w związku z zastosowaniem sztucznej inteligencji w medycynie [Civil liability for damages caused in connection with the use of artificial intelligence in medicine]. Przegląd Prawa Medycznego, 3–4, 14–20.

Biasin, E., Yaşar, B., & Kamenjašević, E. (2023). New cybersecurity requirements for medical devices in the EU: The forthcoming European Health Data Space, Data Act, and Artificial Intelligence Act. Law, Technology and Humans, 5(2), 44–47.

Biczysko-Pudełko, K., & Szostek, D. (2019). Koncepcje dotyczące osobowości prawnej robotów – zagadnienia wybrane [Concepts regarding legal personality of robots – chosen aspects]. Prawo Mediów Elektronicznych, 2, 9–15.

Borysiak, W. (2020). Kilka uwag o pojęciu należytej staranności w stosunkach regulowanych przez prawo medyczne [Some remarks on the concept of due diligence in relations regulated by medical law]. Studia Prawa Prywatnego, 3, passim.

Bublitz, C., Molnár-Gábor, F., & Soekadar, S. (2024). Implications of the novel EU AI Act for neurotechnologies. Neuron, 112(12), 3013–3016.

Buch, V., Ahmed, I., & Maruthappu, M. (2018). Artificial intelligence in medicine: Current trends and future possibilities. British Journal of General Practice, 68(668), 143–144.

Buchanan, B. (2005). A (Very) Brief History of Artificial Intelligence. AI Magazine, 26(4), 53–60.

Chłopecki, A. (2018). Sztuczna inteligencja. Szkice prawnicze i futurologiczne [Artificial Intelligence – Legal and Futurological Sketches]. Warsaw: Wolters Kluwer.

Ciszewski, B. (2024, September 24). Sztuczna inteligencja w medycynie: roboty rozpoznają już choroby płuc i mózgu [Artificial intelligence in medicine: robots already recognize lung and brain diseases]. HomoDigital. https://homodigital.pl/czy-roboty-zastapia-lekarzy-sztuczna-inteligencja-w-medycynie/.

Cummings, M. (2004). Automation bias in intelligent time-critical decision support systems. In 1st Intelligent Systems Technical Conference, Collection of Technical Papers (Vol. 2, pp. 557–562). Massachusetts Institute of Technology.

Czochra, M., & Bar, D. (2019). Śmierć pacjenta wywołana zastosowaniem sztucznej inteligencji w technologiach medycznych – analiza prawnokarna [Patient death caused by the use of artificial intelligence in medical technologies – Criminal law analysis]. Studia Prawnicze: rozprawy i materiały, 2, 71–84.

da Fonseca, A., de Sequeira, E., & Xavier, L. (2024). Liability for AI driven systems. In H. Antunes et al. (Eds.), Multidisciplinary perspectives on artificial intelligence and the law (pp. 299–300). Cham: Springer.

Devarapalli, P. (2018). Machine learning to machine owning: Redefining copyright ownership from the perspective of Australian, US, UK and EU law. European Intellectual Property Review, 40(11), 722–730.

Draft of the Directive of the European Parliament and of the Council on adapting non-contractual civil liability rules to artificial intelligence, (2022/0303/COD).

Directive (EU) 2024/2853 of the European Parliament and of the Council of 23 October 2024 on liability for defective products and repealing Council Directive 85/374/EEC (Directive 2024/2853), Official Journal of the European Union, L 2024/2853.

Dong, L., Yang, Q., Zhang, R. H., & Wei, W. B. (2021). Artificial intelligence for the detection of age-related macular degeneration in color fundus photographs: A systematic review and meta-analysis. EClinicalMedicine, 35, 100865.

Enqvist, L. (2023). 'Human oversight' in the EU Artificial Intelligence Act: What, when and by whom? Law, Innovation and Technology, 15(2), 155–181.

European Commission. (2022). Proposal for a Directive on adapting non-contractual civil liability rules to artificial intelligence. https://eur-lex.europa.eu/legal-content/EN/TXT/?uri=CELEX:52022PC0496.

European Parliament. (2024). Legislative resolution of 12 March 2024 on the proposal for a directive on liability for defective products. COM(2022) 495 final. Retrieved from https://eur-lex.europa.eu/legal-content/EN/TXT/?uri=CELEX:52022PC0495.

European Union. (2024). Regulation (EU) 2024/1689 of the European Parliament and of the Council of 13 June 2024. Official Journal of the European Union, L 2024, 1689.

Girdwoyń, A. (2024). Należyta staranność lekarza [Due diligence of the doctor]. Warszawa: Legalis.

Jankowska, M. (2015). Podmiotowość prawna sztucznej inteligencji [Legal entity of artificial intelligence]. In A. Bielska-Brodziak (Ed.), O czym mówią prawnicy, mówiąc o podmiotowości [What Do Lawyers Mean When They Talk About Subjectivity?] (pp. 171–180). Katowice: UŚ.

Journal of Laws. (2024). Ustawa z dnia 6 listopada 2008 r. o prawach pacjenta i Rzeczniku Praw Pacjenta [Patients' Rights and the Patients' Rights Ombudsman Act], item 581.

Judgement of the Supreme Administrative Court of 23 April 2014, II OSK 2826/12 (PL).

Judgement of the Supreme Administrative Court of 28 September 2021, II GSK 363/21 (PL).

Judgement of the Supreme Administrative Court of 29 November 2016, II OSK 1908/16 (PL).

Kaczan, D. (2022). Odpowiedzialność odszkodowawcza za funkcjonowanie sztucznej inteligencji w medycynie [Liability for damages for the functioning of artificial intelligence in medicine]. Annales Universitatis Paedagogicae Cracoviensis. Studia de Cultura, 14(2), 145–152.

KEL. (2024). Kodeks Etyki Lekarskiej [Medical Code of Ethics]. Adopted by the 16th Extraordinary National Medical Congress on 18 May 2024. Retrieved September 24, 2024, from https://nil.org.pl/dokumenty/kodeks-etyki-lekarskiej.

Kisielewicz, A. (2011). Sztuczna inteligencja i logika: Podsumowanie przedsięwzięcia naukowego [Artificial Intelligence and Logic: A Summary of a Scientific Project]. Warsaw: PAN.

Lakhani, P., & Sundaram, B. (2017). Deep learning at chest radiography: Automated classification of pulmonary tuberculosis by using convolutional neural networks. Radiology, 284(2), 574–582.

Law on the Professions of Doctor and Dentist of 5 December 1996 (2024). Journal of Laws, item 1287.
Nesterowicz, M. (2019). Prawo medyczne [Medical Law] (12th ed.). Toruń: Towarzystwo Naukowe Organizacji i Kierownictwa.
Nguyen, T. (2024). Chat GPT in medical education: A precursor for automation bias? JMIR Medical Education, 10, e50174. https://doi.org/10.2196/50174.
Pickering, B. (2021). Trust but verify: Informed consent, AI technologies, and public health emergencies. Future Internet, 13(5), 20. https://doi.org/10.3390/fi13050020.
Pyrzyńska, A., & Bocheńska, A. (2022). Relacje między systemem prawa cywilnego a systemem prawa pracy – czy wyłącznie oddziaływanie jednokierunkowe? [Relations between the civil law system and the labour law system – is it just a one-way interaction?]. In R. Szczepaniak (Ed.), Problemy pogranicza prawa cywilnego [Boundary problems of civil law]. Warszawa: Legalis.
Rączka, G. (2015). Article 18. In L. Ogiegło (Ed.), Ustawa o zawodach lekarza i lekarza dentysty. Komentarz [Law on the Professions of Doctor and Dentist. Commentary] (pp. 294–299). Warszawa: Wolters Kluwer.
Regulation (EU) 2019/1020 of the European Parliament and of the Council of 20 June 2019 on market surveillance and compliance of products and amending Directive 2004/42/EC and Regulations (EC) No 765/2008 and (EU) No 305/2011 (Regulation 2019/1020), Official Journal of the European Union L 2019., No. 169, p. 1.
Regulation (EU) 2024/1689 of the European Parliament and of the Council of 13 June 2024 laying down harmonised rules on artificial intelligence and amending Regulations and Directives (AI Act), Official Journal of the European Union, L 2024/1689.
Różanowski, K. (2007). Sztuczna inteligencja: rozwój, szanse, zagrożenia [Artificial Intelligence: Development, Opportunities, Threats]. Zeszyty Naukowe Warszawskiej Wyższej Szkoły Informatyki, 2, 109–116.
Safjan, M. (2012). In System Prawa Prywatnego. Tom 1. Prawo cywilne – część ogólna [Private Law System. Volume 1: Civil Law – General Part] (pp. 32–52). Warsaw: C.H. Beck.
Singer, E. (2024, September 24). The slow rise of the robot surgeon. MIT Technology Review. https://www.technologyreview.com/s/418141/the-slow-rise-of-the-robot-surgeon/.
Szpara, J. (1999). Prawo do informacji medycznej w relacjach pacjenta z lekarzem [The right to medical information in patient-doctor relations]. Prawo i Medycyna, 4, 135.
Świderska, M. (2007). Zgoda pacjenta na zabieg medyczny [Patient consent to medical procedure]. Toruń: Dom Organizatora.
Van Kolfschoten, H., & Van Oirschot, J. (2024). The EU Artificial Intelligence Act (2024): Implications for healthcare. Health Policy, 149, 1–4.
Wałachowska, M. (2018). In M. Fras & M. Habdas (Eds.), Kodeks cywilny. Komentarz. Tom III. Zobowiązania. Część ogólna (art. 353–534) [Civil Code. Commentary. Volume III: Obligations. General Part (Articles 353–534)]. Warszawa: LEX.
Wałachowska, M. (2020). In L. Lai & M. Świerczyński (Eds.), Prawo sztucznej inteligencji [Artificial Intelligence Law]. Warsaw: Legalis.
Wałachowska, M. (2021). Naruszenie prawa do dokumentacji medycznej [Violation of the right to medical records]. Gdańskie Studia Prawnicze, 1, 92–98.

Wengler, L. (2012). Praktyki naruszające zbiorowe prawa pacjentów. Wprowadzenie do problematyki [Practices that violate patients' collective rights: An introduction to the issue]. In T. Bąkowski & K. Żukowski (Eds.), Studia prawnoadministracyjne. Księga Jubileuszowa Profesora Eugeniusza Bojanowskiego [Administrative Law Studies: Jubilee Book for Professor Eugeniusz Bojanowski], Gdańskie Studia Prawnicze, 28, 377–378.

Zalewski, T. (2020). In L. Lai & M. Świerczyński (Eds.), Prawo sztucznej inteligencji [Artificial Intelligence Law]. Warsaw: Legalis.

Agnieszka Laskowska-Hulisz

Artificial intelligence (AI) in civil proceedings – selected issues

1. Introduction

In the Polish legal literature, the problem of the possibility of using artificial intelligence (AI – Artificial Intelligence), including in civil proceedings, has been raised for several years (Goździaszek, 2015; Lai & Świerczyński, 2020). However, the national legislator has not introduced any specific regulations.

To date, the Polish legal literature has also failed to develop a universally accepted definition of the term "artificial intelligence" itself (Płocha, 2020). The term is used for several applications, often related to machine learning (ML) systems. However, machine learning is a broader term than artificial intelligence and encompasses all solutions based on algorithms capable of building their conclusions based on available information.

As for the legal definition of AI, it is contained in Regulation (EU) No. 2024/1689 of the European Parliament and of the Council of 13 June 2024 on laying down harmonised rules on artificial intelligence (Artificial Intelligence Act) (Regulation 2024/1689, 2024). According to Article 3(1) of this Regulation, an "AI system" means a machine system that is designed to operate with varying levels of autonomy when deployed and that may exhibit adaptability when deployed and that, for explicit or implicit purposes, infers how to generate, based on received inputs, outputs such as predictions, content, recommendations or decisions that may affect the physical or virtual environment.

Referring to the distinction in the literature between weak AI and strong AI, it should be pointed out that the EU legislator refers to weak AI. Currently, we are dealing with weak AI, while scientists are developing strong AI, which would be a "human imitation" (Kościółek, 2019; Kerrigan et al., 2022). Today's technical capabilities allow the development of machine learning algorithms and prototype solutions that fall into weak AI. While it is anticipated that weak AI systems will be developed and find practical applications in the next few/some years, it appears that the creation of strong AI environments is beyond the capabilities of current science (Płocha, 2020).

Polish law has no legal regulation concerning the use of artificial intelligence in civil proceedings. On the other hand, regulation concerning AI has been introduced, as indicated above, in European Union law and concerns, inter alia, the use of AI in the administration of justice. Systems related to the administration of justice according to Article 6(2) of Regulation No. 2024/1689 in conjunction with Annex III(8) to the Regulation are, in principle, classified as high-risk systems, unless there are derogations referred to in Article 6(3) of the same Regulation (Regulation 2024/1689, 2024).

Therefore, this article is worth pointing out to what extent EU law allows the use of AI in civil proceedings and what doubts this regulation may raise under Polish law.

2. European Union law regulation of the use of AI in civil proceedings

In Annex III (point 8) of Regulation 2024/1689, the EU legislator categorises AI systems used for the administration of justice and democratic processes as high-risk systems and defines them as AI systems intended to be used by or on behalf of a judicial authority to assist the judicial authority in investigating and interpreting the facts and the law and in applying the law to a particular factual situation, or to be used similarly in alternative dispute resolution.

In doing so, the EU legislator introduced several conditions that high-risk systems should meet, such as operating risk management systems (Art. 9 of Regulation 2024/1689), implementing certain data management rules (Art. 10 of Regulation 2024/1689), having technical documentation on the AI system (Art. 11 of Regulation 2024/1689), having technical systems for automatic recording of events (Art. 12 of Regulation 2024/1689), have clear instructions for the operation of the AI system (Article 13 of Regulation 2024/1689), ensure human supervision of the AI system (Article 14 of Regulation 2024/1689), design and modify the AI system to ensure accuracy, robustness and cyber security (Article 15 of Regulation 2024/1689). In addition, in Regulation 2024/1689, the EU legislator has imposed several obligations on high-risk AI system providers and adopters.

By way of derogation from paragraph 2 of Article 6(3) of Regulation 2024/1689, an AI system referred to in Annex III shall not be considered high-risk where it does not pose a significant risk of harm to the health, safety or fundamental rights of individuals, including by not significantly affecting the outcome of the decision-making process. This situation occurs when any of the following conditions are met:

a) An AI system is designed to perform a narrowly defined procedural task;
b) AI system is designed to improve the outcome of a previously completed human activity;
c) the AI system is designed to detect patterns of decision-making or deviations from patterns of previously made decisions and is not intended to replace or influence a previously completed human assessment – without appropriate human review; or
d) the AI system is designed to perform preparatory tasks in the context of an assessment relevant to the use cases listed in Annex III.

Notwithstanding the above, an AI system referred to in Annex III shall always be considered a high-risk system where the system profiles natural persons.

3. Can AI be treated as a subject of proceedings or a tool used in civil proceedings?

There is some debate in the literature about granting AI legal capacity. AI has no free will of its own, no emotions of its own, cannot define its purpose, has no interests of its own, and cannot direct its behaviour. Admittedly, in terms of AI's purpose, it is pointed out in the literature that it has a goal of action, but in the case of weak AI, this is a goal originally hatched not by AI, but by its designer. However, AI's possession of a goal does not determine that AI is capable of possessing an interest. This is because interest is related to the ability to feel, which AI does not possess. Artificial intelligence 'wants' or 'does not want' what results from the software, and is indifferent to what remains outside the scope of the processes the creator plans. Artificial intelligence has no feelings of its own. It cannot independently distinguish between right and wrong, or just and unjust. The AI designer can program it as they wish, but can also make mistakes in the process and lead to situations where the AI's actions are unpredictable (Uliasz, 2019).

It must therefore be assumed, although this view is debatable, that even a strong AI does not meet the material conditions for the grant of legal capacity that have been observed in legislation to date. The mere intellectual capacity (even exceeding human capacity) to acquire and process information in a goal-oriented activity does not make an AI a human-like 'creation'. It remains a system, machine, device, automaton or software. It is an object, not a subject. It is artificial and should serve man as a tool to facilitate and assist his activity (Uliasz, 2019). Besides, granting legal capacity to AI would detach liability for this application from the person who created it; there could be a problem with enforcement of claims, as AI has no assets.

The replacement of a human judge by AI also raises reasonable doubts about the compliance of such a solution with the Constitution of the Republic of Poland. A properly formed court, which is a component of the constitutional right to a court (i.e., Article 45(1) of the Constitution), in its current form eliminates, in principle, the possibility of artificial intelligence exercising the judiciary (Szanciło & Stępień-Załucka, 2023).

An additional argument to reinforce the view that artificial intelligence should not be treated as a subject of proceedings, but as a tool to support the administration of justice, is the EU regulation—namely Regulation 2024/1689—including Annex III to that regulation, which shows that the acceptable scope of the use of artificial intelligence in judicial proceedings by the EU legislator is limited to assigning it the role of a tool to support the administration of justice, rather than replacing it (Regulation 2024/1689, 2024).

For these reasons, it seems that granting AI legal subjectivity would not be the right solution. Regardless of the functions to be granted to AI in civil proceedings, it should be treated as an object—a tool to assist the judicial authorities—and not as a subject of civil proceedings. AI cannot therefore replace the human judge. Instead, it can be a tool used in civil proceedings by judges to perform certain repetitive activities, and the results of its work should be subject to the control of judges. This position corresponds with the provisions of Annex III to Regulation 2024/1689, which makes it clear in paragraph 8 that AI is only intended to be a tool to assist judicial authorities in examining and interpreting the facts and the law and in applying the law to a specific factual situation or to be used similarly in alternative dispute resolution (Regulation 2024/1689, 2024).

4. Can AI as an assistive tool conduct proceedings, issue judgments, or can it only perform other activities that do not involve adjudicating civil cases?

Considering the provisions of Regulation 2024/1689 on the role of AI in the administration of justice by the authorities called upon to do so, it is therefore necessary to consider what scope of activities can be entrusted to AI in assisting the administration of justice.

Currently, the use of artificial intelligence in the legal field, theoretically, is possible in three different categories of applications—firstly, for the construction of expert systems; secondly, for the construction of legal information retrieval systems; and thirdly, for the construction of automatic decision systems (Dymitruk & Gołaczyński, 2019).

Referring to the areas of application of artificial intelligence outlined above, it is also possible to make a general division of legal artificial intelligence into two categories: legal retrieval systems and legal analysis systems. The former can be equated with commercial legal applications already on the market, while the latter can determine the legal consequences of specific facts. Among legal analysis systems, we distinguish between adjudication machines and legal expert systems, which are divided into rule-based systems, case-based systems, and hybrid systems (Dymitruk & Gołaczyński, 2019).

Transferring these considerations to civil proceedings and the activities undertaken by judges in them, it should be noted that AI can undoubtedly be helpful in the work of a judge. It can be used to search for and analyse judicial case law and the views of academics on the cases which are the subject of the proceedings or selected specific issues related to that subject. It can indicate, among other things, trends in case law, similarities and differences between theses formulated by the courts or views of representatives of science. AI can also be used to analyse changes in the law, including differences and similarities between changing regulations. AI can also analyse similarities and differences between different factual situations. AI in the role of court assistant can therefore be a tool used in the work of a judge, not making decisions on its own, not making rulings and consequently not taking responsibility for them. AI in the role of a helper will reduce the responsibilities of judges, but will not relieve them of responsibility for their decisions, nor will it affect the model of the civil process and the procedural rights guaranteed to litigants in it (Bieliński, 2019). Any decision made by a judge will be their decision for which they will be held responsible, and this presupposes that the judge, when making a decision based on the results of the AI work, will review and evaluate them and, consequently, make a decision of which they are convinced of the validity.

AI can also be used to calculate court fees, to settle court costs, and to examine the formal conditions of letters filed on forms. However, any AI ruling should be appealed to the court to allow the court to check its correctness. In this way, doubts about the accountability of rulings made by AI could be avoided and, consequently, the condition of human verification of its work would be met.

In addition, the literature proposes as a short-term goal related to the possibility of using artificial intelligence in court proceedings the introduction of an automatic speech recognition system that will produce a written report during an e-trial, programs for the preparation of joint sentences in criminal cases, and the use of a so-called chatbot that could successfully replace front office staff. The digitisation of court files and, in the long term, programs to replace assistant judges and court registrars have been identified as medium-term goals (Kotalczyk, 2021).

It is also worth considering whether AI can be used in non-judicial dispute resolution proceedings, such as mediation. It seems that a mediator can use AI as a tool to develop different proposals for resolving a dispute, to compare different cases and develop results based on this to help mediate or draft a settlement. In out-of-court proceedings, if a settlement is reached, it is concluded by the parties, who decide on the proposals presented to them, verify the results of the AI work, and decide whether to accept them. In addition, for example, a settlement concluded before a mediator, in order to have the force of law equal to a court settlement, must be approved by the court (Article 18315 of the Code of Civil Procedure), which is another "human" stage of verification of its content.

One variant of artificial intelligence highlighted in the literature is the electronic judge. An electronic judge is a variant of artificial intelligence—the most far-reaching form of such intelligence in law. However, artificial intelligence in the judiciary cannot be equated exclusively with an electronic judge with human mental characteristics, the so-called judgment machine (Dymitruk & Gołaczyński, 2019).

Whether AI can independently conduct civil proceedings and issue judgments, we can answer this question in the current state of the law—no. A justice system using AI is a high-risk system. It requires a number of conditions to be met as set out in Regulation 2024/1689 provisions, unless there are derogations regulated in Article 6(3) of Regulation 2024/1689. Meeting these conditions by, among others, those using AI requires work, time, and a lot of financial resources. As stated in Annex III to Regulation 2024/1689, paragraph 8), an AI system used in the administration of justice is intended to assist judicial authorities in the examination and interpretation of facts and laws and the application of the law to a specific factual situation, not to replace them. The EU legislator in Article 7 of Regulation 2024/1689 has admittedly reserved the possibility of amending this annex, including the classification of high-risk AI systems, but this is a matter for the future. Therefore, it cannot be ruled out that the scope of permissible use of AI systems in civil proceedings may be broader over time.

It would therefore be necessary to consider whether it is advisable to introduce legal regulations allowing AI to issue rulings and, if so, in which cases. It would seem that the conduct of proceedings by AI and the issuing of a ruling by it could only apply to a specific type of case heard in civil proceedings, at first instance. AI could conduct adjudication proceedings in simple, repetitive cases, e.g. payment of rent or bills (Kotalczyk, 2021), in which the plaintiff would assert monetary claims of a limited amount. These claims would arise from undisputed facts and would be supported by documentary evidence held by the plaintiff and indicated in the statement of claim. The proceedings in question would not require an evidentiary hearing, would not involve complex legal issues, and would be limited to judicial confirmation of the defendant's obligation to pay the plaintiff the amount specified in the judgment, arising from repetitive, typical facts and documentary evidence supporting them.

However, a prerequisite would be that judges should qualify cases for such AI proceedings. It would seem that the statement of claim should be written on a form containing options to choose from on the model of the statement of claim in European injunction proceedings. Evidence would not be attached to the statement of claim. In these proceedings, the AI would not take evidence but issue a judgment based on the statement of claim filed. Such a solution would help to speed up proceedings in many simple and obvious cases. AI, on the other hand, cannot replace a human judge in complex or unusual cases involving the emotions of the parties or participants in the proceedings, or in those where issues such as good or bad faith, compliance with the rules of comity, or degree of fault are being examined (Kaczmarek-Templin, 2022; Płocha, 2020).

Artificial intelligence could also be used in simple cases based on certain patterns in registry and land and mortgage proceedings (Kościółek, 2019).

Decisions made by AI, irrespective of the type of proceedings they were made, would be subject to appeal before the court. The lodging of an appeal would result in the case being referred back to the court of first instance. Consequently, if the defendant did not agree with an AI decision, he or she would have the right to refer the case to the court, which should hear it under procedural guarantees. In doing so, AI would not be treated as a judge, but as a tool used by the judicial authorities. In my opinion, such a solution would also not violate the parties' procedural rights and would not relieve judges of their responsibility for the rulings made. Especially as similar solutions admittedly involving the court are currently in place—namely the electronic writ of payment procedure and the European order for payment procedure—and are working well (Dymitruk & Gołaczyński, 2019).

To summarise this part of the discussion, introducing AI into civil proceedings must not lead to AI replacing human judges. If AI is introduced into civil proceedings, it will not be as a quasi-judge, but as a tool to support the judiciary in carrying out the actions chosen by the legislator.

AI should be introduced into civil proceedings with due caution and prudence. This process should be preceded by introducing a number of changes to the Code of Civil Procedure provisions, aimed at simplifying and then automating selected activities of civil proceedings. After all, it should be borne in mind that AI is only an artificial algorithm, which may be wrong, which may fail, which may be vulnerable to hacking attacks and, above all, which will not replace such an essential element as life experience and will not ensure a comprehensive consideration of the evidence gathered in the case, which well-prepared and experienced judges guarantee.

On the other hand, it is difficult to accept the solution that one AI issues a ruling, while another AI recognises an appeal against such a ruling. In the case of allowing certain procedural actions to be performed by AI, it seems necessary to include a human being in supervising how AI performs the actions and to extend the State Treasury's liability for mistakes made in civil proceedings also by AI.

5. Conclusions

The introduction of AI into civil proceedings may involve not only changes in the right direction, but also several risks. AI can also facilitate the work of judges by assisting them in searching for necessary rulings, analysing changes in the law or views of doctrine. With so many changes to the law, a rich body of academic work and the courts, it is very labour- and time-intensive for judges to investigate these areas, translating into case deadlines.

AI can help speed up the adjudication of cases, relieve the burden on judges and courts and reduce the cost of proceedings. However, AI can make mistakes, break down, be vulnerable to hacking attacks, have faulty software.

However, as far as the risks are concerned, they exist not only when AI replaces the judge in adjudicating a case, but also when it performs an auxiliary, supportive function for the judge. The unreflective use of AI can lead to adjudication according to a set pattern, without thinking about the case or a broader analysis of the differences between cases. Relying, whether in adjudication or other so-called supportive activities, entirely on AI can lead to accepting as the only valid solution proposals developed by AI, which are based on certain patterns and do not consider the subtle differences between cases.

For these reasons, to avoid these risks, as indicated above, it is necessary, firstly, to treat AI as a tool to support the judiciary, and secondly, to create the possibility for judges to verify the results of AI work. It seems that the introduction of AI to some extent into civil proceedings in the future is highly likely. However, this should be a comprehensively considered decision and preceded by significant changes and not only to the Code of Civil Procedure. In doing so, introducing AI into civil proceedings should not restrict a party's right to a fair trial, including the right to be heard.

References

Bieliński, A. (2019). Potential areas of application of artificial intelligence in civil proceedings—does it currently have a raison d'être and are we ready for such solutions? In K. Flaga-Gieruszyńska, J. Gołaczyński, & D. Szostek (Eds.), Sztuczna inteligencja, Blokchain, cyberbezpieczeństwo oraz dane osobowe (p. 62). Warsaw: C.H. Beck.

Dymitruk, M., & Gołaczyński, J. (2019). Elektroniczny sąd a sztuczna inteligencja w prawie polskim [Electronic court and artificial intelligence in Polish law]. In K. Flaga-Gieruszyńska, J. Gołaczyński, & D. Szostek (Eds.), Sztuczna inteligencja, Blokchain, cyberbezpieczeństwo oraz dane osobowe. Zagadnienia wybrane (pp. 51–54). Warsaw: C.H. Beck.

Goździaszek, Ł. (2015). Perspektywy wykorzystania sztucznej inteligencji w postępowaniu sądowym. Przegląd Sądowy, (10), 46–60.

Kaczmarek-Templin, B. (2022). Artificial intelligence (AI) and prospects for its use in civil court proceedings. Studia Prawnicze. Dissertations and Materials, (2), 66.

Kerrigan, C., Rab, S., Kenny, S., Payne, C., & Allen, J. G. (2022). Introduction to AI. In C. Kerrigan (Ed.), Artificial Intelligence: Law and Regulation (pp. 31–36). Cheltenham: Edward Elgar.

Kościółek, A. (2019). Wykorzystanie sztucznej inteligencji w sądowym postępowaniu cywilnym. In K. Flaga-Gieruszyńska, J. Gołaczyński, & D. Szostek (Eds.), Sztuczna inteligencja, Blockchain, cyberbezpieczeństwo oraz dane osobowe. Zagadnienia wybrane (pp. 67–75). Warsaw: C.H. Beck.

Kotalczyk, M. (2021). Artificial intelligence in the service of the Polish court - proposed solutions. Iustitia, (2), 61–66.

Lai, L., & Świerczyński, M. (Eds.). (2020). The Law of Artificial Intelligence. Warsaw: C.H. Beck.

Płocha, E. A. (2020). On the concept of artificial intelligence and the possibilities of its application in civil proceedings. Prawo w Działaniu. Sprawy Cywilne, 44, 274–283.

Regulation (EU) 2024/1689 of the European Parliament and of the Council of 13 June 2024 laying down harmonised rules on artificial intelligence. Official Journal of the European Union, L, 12.7.2024.

Szanciło, T., & Stępień-Załucka, B. (2023). Sędzia robotem a robot sędzia w postępowaniu cywilnym w ujęciu konstytucyjnym i procesowym. Prawo i Więź, 4(47), 218–232.

Uliasz, M. (2019). Artificial intelligence as an artificial legal person. In K. Flaga-Gieruszyńska, J. Gołaczyński, & D. Szostek (Eds.), Artificial Intelligence, Blockchain, Cyber-Security and Personal Data. Zagadnienia wybrane (pp. 29–30). Warsaw: C.H. Beck.

Maciej Serowaniec

The role of the European Semester in promoting green energy and modern technologies in the EU Member States[1]

1. Introduction

The European Semester is one of the key mechanisms for economic policy coordination in the European Union. Created in response to financial instability following the global financial crisis and the ensuing debt crisis in the euro area, the European Semester was originally designed to monitor fiscal discipline and promote macroeconomic stability. Over time, however, it has evolved into a comprehensive tool that covers an increasingly wide range of policy priorities across the EU, including social and environmental objectives. Through this mechanism, the EU seeks to promote sustainable economic growth and ensure that all Member States collectively pursue long-term strategic goals that transcend national boundaries.

The European Semester operates as part of an annual economic policy guidance and surveillance cycle, during which the European Commission presents recommendations tailored to each Member State. These recommendations, known as country-specific recommendations (CSRs), are based on in-depth reviews of each country's fiscal and economic conditions and its progress towards broader EU goals. They initially focused on economic indicators, but now also include an assessment of environmental sustainability and digital progress. As a result, the European Semester has become an essential instrument for implementing the European Green Deal and the Digital Decade strategy, which emphasise the EU's commitment to achieving climate neutrality and digital leadership by mid-century (European Commission, 2020).

The European Semester's main objective is to promote green energy and modern technologies in the Member States. This shift reflects the EU's broader goal of reducing greenhouse gas emissions by at least 55% by 2030 (compared to

1 This article is the result of research conducted within the National Science Centre funded project 'CONCILIA: Democratic legitimacy in the post-crisis economic governance of the European Union' (Grant Agreement No 2021/43/D/HS5/2022).

1990) and achieving net zero emissions by 2050. The European Green Deal, adopted in 2019, sets out this ambitious roadmap to transform Europe into the world's first climate-neutral continent. The Semester therefore serves as a key tool in aligning national policies with these goals, providing targeted guidance to Member States in areas such as renewable energy development, energy efficiency and reducing dependence on fossil fuels (European Commission, 2020). At the same time, it encourages investment in cutting-edge technologies, including artificial intelligence, digital infrastructure and smart city solutions, which are essential for a sustainable and competitive economy in the 21st century.

This article aims to assess the effectiveness of the European Semester as a tool for promoting green energy and technological modernisation across the EU. In particular, it will address the following research questions: (1) How has the European Semester supported the promotion of green energy in the Member States? (2) What role has the Semester played in developing modern technologies in the EU? (3) How effective is the European Semester in supporting compliance with the goals of the European Green Deal and Digital Decade strategies?

2. Policy Instruments under the European Semester for Green Energy and Technology

The European Semester coordinates economic, social and environmental policies through various instruments to guide and assess Member States' progress towards EU goals. As the EU has integrated green energy and technology objectives into its policy agenda, the European Semester has been adapted to ensure compliance with these evolving priorities.

The Annual Growth Survey (AGS) is the main policy instrument of the European Semester, setting economic priorities and policy direction for the coming cycle. Each year, the AGS provides a macroeconomic overview and highlights key priorities such as sustainability, digitalisation and competitiveness. Identifying green and digital transformation as pillars of economic growth, the AGS encourages Member States to adopt policies and reforms to support these areas, aligning national objectives with the EU's overarching sustainable development goals. For example, in the Annual Growth Survey 2020, "Green Deal" and "digital transformation" were identified as central to the EU's growth strategy, advocating reforms that support clean energy, resource efficiency and the development of digital infrastructure (European Commission, 2020). Embedding these priorities in the Annual Growth Survey, the European Semester sets a core agenda that encourages Member States to pursue green energy projects and deploy advanced technologies in line with the EU's climate and digital goals.

The country-specific recommendations (CSRs) are tailored to each Member State and serve as the European Commission's main tool to guide national reforms. Published annually, the CSRs provide practical recommendations for achieving fiscal discipline, sustainable growth and compliance with the EU's climate and technology goals. In recent years, CSRs have increasingly focused on renewable energy integration, energy efficiency and digital transformation. For example, the 2021 Polish country-specific recommendations highlighted the need to increase the share of renewable energy and improve energy efficiency in line with the objectives of the European Green Deal. Similarly, Spain received country-specific recommendations recommending increased investment in digital infrastructure to support environmental and economic resilience (European Commission, 2021). These recommendations are not binding, but are essential to guide national policies and ensure that each Member State is progressing towards the EU's sustainability and digitalisation goals. It is worth noting that the CSRs reflect the twin goals of environmental and economic sustainability, balancing fiscal sustainability with environmental and technological progress. By targeting the needs of individual countries, the CSRs also address the different capacities and economic structures of Member States. For example, recommendations for advanced countries such as Germany may focus on pioneering clean-technology innovations, while less developed economies receive guidance on expanding their basic energy and digital infrastructure.

Scholars note that the Semester is a tool of economic governance and an evolving mechanism of integration, especially relevant in times of crisis (Serowaniec, 2015; Serowaniec, 2023). This legal and governance dimension has grown even more significant with recent challenges such as the COVID-19 pandemic and the war in Ukraine, which required flexible yet coordinated responses. Furthermore, the Semester plays a critical role in shaping structural reforms in transitioning economies within the EU, balancing between cohesion and competition (Myant, 2018).

The policy instruments of the European Semester—AGS, CSR, and NRP—form an interlinked framework guiding the EU's transformation towards a sustainable and digital economy. These instruments enable the European Commission to target national policies towards common environmental and digital objectives, while considering national contexts. Using these tools, the European Semester has enhanced the EU's ability to coordinate Member States' responses to climate change and digitalisation, creating a more united and resilient European Union.

3. The impact of the European Semester on the promotion of green energy

The European Semester has become a key platform for promoting green energy in EU Member States, aligning national policies with the European Green Deal's ambitious climate and energy goals. As part of its annual review process, the European Semester issues country-specific recommendations (CSRs), often including green energy-related directives such as increasing renewable energy production, improving energy efficiency and reducing dependence on fossil fuels. The European Semester has contributed to significant progress through structured guidance, financial incentives, and policy coordination. This section examines how the Semester has influenced green energy initiatives, highlights achievements in different Member States and assesses its impact on the EU's broader energy and climate goals (Directorate-General for Energy, 2020).

Country-specific recommendations (CSRs) are one of the key tools of the European Semester to influence national energy policies. Issued annually, the CSRs provide tailored advice for each Member State based on assessing its economic and environmental status. Since adopting the European Green Deal in 2019, country-specific recommendations have increasingly focused on climate targets, particularly developing renewable energy sources and improving energy efficiency. For example, in 2020, the CSR for Germany highlighted the need to phase out coal and increase renewable energy capacity, aligning with Germany's energy transition strategy to replace fossil fuels with renewables by 2038 (European Commission, 2020a). Similarly, Poland received recommendations to diversify its energy mix, reduce its dependence on coal and improve energy efficiency, particularly in the residential sector, which relies heavily on coal for heating (European Commission, 2020b). These recommendations guide Member States in developing national energy policies, facilitating alignment with EU-wide climate and energy targets.

The recommendations of the European Semester have led to a significant increase in investment in renewable energy across the EU. In particular, solar, wind and biomass projects have expanded in Member States traditionally relying on fossil fuels. Greece, for example, has made notable progress in increasing its share of renewable energy, following the Semester's recommendations to reduce dependence on coal and invest in solar and wind energy. By 2022, Greece generated almost 50% of its electricity from renewable sources—a significant improvement from previous years (International Energy Agency, 2023).

In addition to developing renewable energy sources, the European Semester promoted energy efficiency as a key aspect of the EU's climate strategy. Countries such as Hungary and Romania implemented energy efficiency programmes in line with Semester recommendations, particularly in the building sector where energy consumption is high. These programmes included retrofitting residential buildings with energy-efficient technologies to lower energy use and reduce greenhouse gas emissions (International Energy Agency, 2022).

While the European Semester has successfully steered many Member States toward adopting renewable energy and improving energy efficiency, challenges remain. The Semester's reliance on soft law, which lacks enforcement power, means implementation is not guaranteed. In addition, Member States' differing economic conditions may limit their ability to carry out ambitious green energy policies. For example, Central and Eastern European countries, including Poland and Hungary, have faced difficulties reducing their dependence on coal due to economic constraints and local resistance. These Member States argue that abandoning coal threatens jobs and raises energy prices, complicating compliance with the Semester's recommendations (Maltby & Mišík, 2021).

4. The development of modern technologies within the European Semester

The European Semester has become an essential instrument not only for achieving economic stability, but also for achieving the EU's digital transformation goals. As the EU seeks to increase its global competitiveness, it has identified developing and deploying modern technologies as a priority area, recognising that technological modernisation is essential for a sustainable, efficient and resilient economy. In recent years, the European Semester has increasingly emphasised investments in digital infrastructure, artificial intelligence (AI) and clean energy technologies. These investments are guided by the Digital Decade strategy, which aims to strengthen the EU's technological sovereignty and digital capabilities by 2030, and the European Green Deal, which includes technology as a key enabler of green transformation.

One of the main roles of the European Semester in technology development is to promote investment in digital infrastructure. The COVID-19 pandemic highlighted the importance of reliable digital networks and connectivity, as remote working, e-commerce and online education became essential for economic and social continuity. Recognising this, the recommendations of the European Semester increasingly prioritise the development of high-speed broadband networks, 5G networks and cloud infrastructure to support the EU's vision of a highly connected and technologically advanced continent. Investment in these areas is seen as fundamental to digital innovation and economic resilience, enabling seamless connectivity for businesses and individuals. Germany and Spain, for example, received CSRs that emphasised accelerating 5G deployment and investment in high-speed digital infrastructure to improve connectivity in urban and rural areas (European Commission, 2021a). These guidelines align with the EU's goal of achieving full 5G coverage in all populated areas by 2030.

The European Semester also plays a key role in enhancing the EU's leadership in artificial intelligence (AI) and the data economy, essential for increasing productivity and fostering innovation across sectors. AI can potentially increase efficiency, from automating production processes to optimising energy consumption, while the data economy creates opportunities for new business models based on data sharing and analysis. For example, in 2021, the European Commission issued recommendations encouraging France to increase its AI research and development capacity, focusing on ethical and safe applications of AI (European Commission, 2021b). The EU's Coordinated Plan on Artificial Intelligence complements the efforts of the European Semester by providing a roadmap for the development of AI ecosystems, including public-private partnerships and support for innovation centres (European Commission, 2018). Similarly, Finland has been recognised for integrating AI into its public administration, in line with the Semester's recommendations to improve data analytics and digital governance capabilities (European Commission, 2021c). By developing a data-driven economy and promoting ethical AI, the European Semester helps Member States take advantage of technological advances while protecting privacy and data in line with EU values.

Successful digital transformation requires access to advanced technology and a skilled workforce capable of using it effectively. The European Semester therefore highlights the need for Member States to invest in digital skills training and education. The EU aims to foster an inclusive digital economy that enables everyone to benefit from technological advances by enhancing digital competencies and equipping citizens with the necessary skills to use new technologies. In Estonia, often considered a digital leader in the EU, the European Semester has encouraged further investment in digital education and e-government initiatives, building on strong existing digital infrastructure (European Commission, 2021d). Similarly, Poland has received recommendations to improve digital skills education, focusing on general education and vocational training to support workforce adaptability in a rapidly changing labour market (European Commission, 2021e). These efforts are integral to closing the digital divide that risks emerging from unequal access to education and technology across the EU.

5. Case studies in promoting sustainable energy and digital modernisation

The European Semester focusing on sustainable energy and digital modernisation has influenced several successful initiatives in EU Member States. By analysing specific case studies, we can understand how the European Semester has influenced the implementation of green energy and advanced digital infrastructure projects, as well as the key lessons learned from overcoming the challenges of these developments. This section examines two notable cases: Portugal's renewable energy transformation and Estonia's digital leadership. Both examples illustrate the role of the European Semester in leading Member States towards greater sustainability and technological innovation, while highlighting areas where the EU could improve policy coordination and support.

Portugal has become one of Europe's leaders in renewable energy, making significant progress in solar, wind and hydropower (Vieira et al., 2024). This transformation closely aligns with the recommendations of the European Semester and the EU's broader climate goals, including the European Green Deal target of climate neutrality by 2050 (European Commission, 2023a). Portugal's progress on renewable energy is an example of how a combination of European Semester guidelines, strategic investment and national commitment can foster a successful green energy transition. As part of the European Semester, the European Commission has consistently recommended that Portugal increase its renewable energy capacity to reduce dependence on imported fossil fuels and improve energy security. Portugal's National Energy and Climate Plan (NECP) sets a target for renewable energy to account for 80% of the country's electricity production by 2030, which aligns with the European Semester's country-specific recommendations (CSR) and the EU's renewable energy targets (European Commission, 2023a). Portugal has made significant progress in wind and solar energy, with around 54% of its electricity coming from renewable sources from 2020, a notable increase compared to previous years. This success is primarily attributed to proactive policies, competitive auctions for renewable energy projects and EU structural funds to boost infrastructure for clean energy (European Investment Bank, 2025). The recommendations of the European Semester also encouraged Portugal to modernise and increase its hydroelectric capacity, leading to significant upgrades to existing dams and construction of new facilities to improve efficiency (European Commission, 2023a). Portugal's success can be attributed to the effective use of EU funds under the European Structural and Investment Funds (ESIF) and targeted investments under the Recovery and Resilience Facility (RRF), including energy storage solutions and grid modernisation.

Estonia stands out as one of the most digitally advanced countries in the world, mainly due to its innovative e-government systems and digital infrastructure. The European Semester has actively supported Estonia's digital ambitions, recommending increased digital connectivity and fostering innovation across sectors (European Commission, 2023b). Estonia's digital success started with foundational investments in e-government and digital services in the early 21st century. However, recent recommendations of the European Semester have encouraged further advances in digital infrastructure, including 5G deployment, cybersecurity and artificial intelligence (AI) (European Commission, 2022b). The Estonian Digital Agenda 2030, in line with the EU Digital Decade, aims to expand digital access in rural and urban areas, supported by EU structural funds and the RRF. A key driver in Estonia's success has been the *e-Estonia* initiative, which delivers nearly universal digital services—enabling citizens to vote, access healthcare, and manage finances online. This digitalisation has helped reduce administrative costs, enhance transparency and improve public service delivery (OECD, 2022). The European Semester further recommended strengthening Estonia's cybersecurity and cross-border digital interoperability, vital for ensuring resilience and EU-wide compatibility (Salumaa-Lepik, & Nisu,, 2024). Estonia also accelerated implementation of 5G and AI projects with support from the European Commission, using resources from the Digital Europe Programme and the RRF to develop a nationwide data-sharing platform and a cyber defence training centre (European Commission, 2023b).

The case studies of Portugal and Estonia illustrate the European Semester's role in stimulating significant progress in green energy and digital transformation. These examples show that clear, long-term policy commitments—when paired with effective use of EU resources—can yield substantial progress in sustainability and innovation. They also underscore the importance of tailoring EU-wide goals to local contexts and allowing flexibility to address diverse economic and infrastructural challenges across Member States.

6. Conclusions

While the European Semester has significantly influenced policy alignment across the EU, especially in areas such as green energy and technological modernisation, it also faces several persistent challenges. These challenges relate primarily to the effectiveness of its recommendations, disparities in Member States' capacities, and the availability and use of funding and implementation mechanisms. Several criticisms highlight the Semester's reliance on 'soft law', its one-size-fits-all nature, and its misalignment with national priorities. The European Semester functions through recommendations and guidelines rather than legally binding directives, using a soft law approach to promote compliance among Member States. While this flexible framework is designed to respect national sovereignty and accommodate diverse economic realities, it also results in largely voluntary implementation.

This voluntary nature has led to varying levels of commitment across Member States, particularly concerning climate and digitalisation objectives. For example, countries with more developed renewable energy sectors like Germany and Denmark have shown more substantial alignment with the Semester's green energy recommendations. In contrast, economies heavily reliant on coal or with limited technological infrastructure—such as Poland—have been slower to align with the EU's green transition agenda, often citing economic and social concerns. This inconsistent compliance leads to fragmented progress, ultimately hampering the EU's collective ability to reach its climate neutrality and digitalisation targets.

Another critical challenge is political resistance at the national level. Although the European Semester promotes green and digital reforms, these priorities can sometimes clash with local political and economic agendas. Member States with close political or financial ties to the fossil fuel sector—such as Poland and Hungary—have historically resisted stringent climate policies out of concern for employment, energy costs, and regional economic stability. Similarly, short-term economic pressures may lead governments to deprioritise digital investments, particularly during downturns or periods of fiscal austerity.

Despite these limitations, the European Semester remains a valuable tool for promoting policy coherence and supporting strategic investment in sustainable growth. However, enhancing its impact will require addressing several structural issues: the dependency on non-binding instruments, inadequate funding for implementation, national-level resistance, and a lack of rigorous accountability mechanisms.

The European Semester is expected to play an increasingly important role in shaping the EU's green and digital future. To overcome the limitations of soft law, the EU could introduce more robust enforcement tools within the Semester framework. One possibility is to require Member States to adopt binding commitments in their national reform programmes, including specific performance indicators and consequences for non-compliance. This would bolster the Semester's authority and promote greater policy convergence.

Additionally, more sophisticated monitoring and evaluation mechanisms could improve transparency and accountability. A centralised EU digital platform to track Member States' progress in real-time would enable the comparison of key metrics—such as renewable energy expansion, energy efficiency gains, and digital infrastructure coverage—while supporting peer learning.

Finally, sustained investment in research and development will be critical to drive innovation in green and digital technologies. Allocating targeted resources under the European Semester to support the development of hydrogen, battery storage, and artificial intelligence would strengthen the EU's position as a global leader in sustainable and digital transformation.

References

Directorate-General for Energy. (2020). *National Energy and Climate Plans (NECPs) Overview.* Luxembourg: Publications Office of the European Union.

European Commission. (2018). *Coordinated Plan on Artificial Intelligence.* Brussels: European Union.

European Commission. (2020). *Annual Sustainable Growth Strategy.* Brussels: European Union.

European Commission. (2020a). *Country Report: Germany 2020.* Brussels: European Union.

European Commission. (2020b). *Country Report: Poland 2020.* Brussels: European Union.

European Commission. (2021). *Country-Specific Recommendations 2021 for Poland.* Brussels: European Union.

European Commission. (2021a). *Country-Specific Recommendations for Germany*, 2021. Brussels: European Union.

European Commission. (2021b). *Country-Specific Recommendations for France*, 2021. Brussels: European Union.

European Commission. (2021c). *Country-Specific Recommendations for Finland*, 2021. Brussels: European Union.

European Commission. (2021d). *Country-Specific Recommendations for Estonia*, 2021. Brussels: European Union.

European Commission. (2021e). *Country-Specific Recommendations for Poland*, 2021. Brussels: European Union.

European Commission. (2023a). *Portugal 2023 Country Report.* Brussels: European Union.

European Commission. (2023b). *Estonia 2023 Country Report.* Brussels: European Union.

European Investment Bank. (2025). *Portugal financing from EIB Group surpasses €2 billion in 2024 with record investment in green financing and sustainable energy.*

International Energy Agency. (2022). *Hungary 2022. Energy Policy Review.* International Energy Agency.

International Energy Agency. (2023). *Greece 2023. Energy Policy Review.* International Energy Agency.

Maltby, T. & Mišík, M. (2024). *Energy Transitions in Central and Eastern Europe: The Political Economy of Climate and Energy Policy.* Cambridge: Cambridge University Press.

Myant, M. (2018). The limits to dependent growth in East-Central Europe. Revue de la régulation. *Capitalisme, institutions*, pouvoirs, (24).

OECD. (2022). *Digital Economy Outlook: Estonia.* Paris: OECD Publishing.

Salumaa-Lepik, K., & Nisu, N. (2024). European Values, artificial intellligence and e-governance in Estonia and EU. *Internet of Things*, 101278.
Serowaniec, M. (2015). Odpowiedzialność integracyjna parlamentów narodowych w dobie kryzysu gospodarczego w strefie euro. *Studia z Zakresu Nauk Prawnoustrojowych. Miscellanea*, 5, 163–177.
Serowaniec, M. (2023). The debudgetisation of public finances in Poland after Covid-19 and the war in Ukraine. *Politics and Governance*, 11(4), 62–72.
Vieira M., et al. (2024). Onshore wind in Portugal: History, supporting policies, economic viability and future perspectives. *Energy Reports*, Volume 11, 3406–3423.

List of authors

Bączyk-Rozwadowska Kinga – Faculty of Law and Administration, Nicolaus Copernicus University in Toruń, Department of Insurance and Medical Law, e-mail: kbaczyk@umk.pl, ORCID: 0000-0001-6545-2671

Cilak Małgorzata – Faculty of Law and Administration, Nicolaus Copernicus University in Toruń, Department of Public Finances Law, e-mail: mcilak@umk.pl, ORCID: 0000-0003-1429-8429

Daśko Natalia – Faculty of Law and Administration, Nicolaus Copernicus University in Toruń, Department of Criminal Law, e-mail: ndasko@umk.pl, ORCID: 0000-0001-9122-4883

Drewek Marcin – Faculty of Law and Administration, Nicolaus Copernicus University in Toruń, Department of Civil Law, e-mail: drewek@umk.pl, ORCID: 0000-0003-3485-4090

Janowska Kinga – Faculty of Law and Administration, Nicolaus Copernicus University in Toruń, Student Scientific Group of Energy Law

Kaczan Damian – Faculty of Law and Administration, Nicolaus Copernicus University in Toruń, Department of Insurance and Medical Law, e-mail: d.kaczan@umk.pl, ORCID: 0000-0002-1741-0669

Karpus Karolina – Faculty of Law and Administration, Nicolaus Copernicus University in Toruń, Department of Environmental Protection and Public Economic Law, e-mail: kkarpus@umk.pl, ORCID: 0000-0002-3575-7949

Kościelak Aleksandra – Faculty of Law and Administration, Nicolaus Copernicus University in Toruń, Student Scientific Group of Energy Law

Kuczyński Tomasz – Faculty of Law and Administration, Nicolaus Copernicus University in Toruń, Department of Department of Administrative Law, e-mail: t.kuczynski@umk.pl, ORCID: 0000-0002-9936-1951

Kustra-Rogatka Aleskandra – Faculty of Law and Administration, Nicolaus Copernicus University in Toruń, Department of Theory of Law and State, e-mail: a_kustra@law.umk.pl, ORCID: 0000-0002-1153-8717

Lachowski Jerzy – Faculty of Law and Administration, Nicolaus Copernicus University in Toruń, Department of Criminal Law, e-mail: lachowsk@umk.pl, ORCID: 0000-0002-6669-2105

Laskowska-Hulisz Agnieszka – Faculty of Law and Administration, Nicolaus Copernicus University in Toruń, Department of Commercial Law, Maritime Law and Civil Procedure Law, e-mail: agalas@umk.pl, ORCID: 0000-0002-2834-9306

Majka Paweł – Faculty of Law and Administration, University of Rzeszów, Department of Public Finances Law, e-mail: pmajka@ur.edu.pl, ORCID: 0000-0003-4315-4133

Rączka Piotr – Faculty of Law and Administration, Nicolaus Copernicus University in Toruń, Department of Department of Administrative Law, e-mail: racz ka@umk.pl, ORCID: 0000-0002-1097-5712

Serowaniec Maciej – Faculty of Law and Administration, Nicolaus Copernicus University in Toruń, Department of Department of Constitutional Law, e-mail: mserowaniec@umk.pl, ORCID: 0000-0003-4693-7977

Wantoch-Rekowski Jacek – Faculty of Law and Administration, Nicolaus Copernicus University in Toruń, Department of Public Finances Law, e-mail: rekowski@umk.pl, ORCID: 0000-0002-1606-7790

Wilmanowicz-Słupczewska Martyna – Faculty of Law and Administration, Nicolaus Copernicus University in Toruń, Department of Public Finances Law, e-mail: mws@umk.pl, ORCID: 0000-0003-1847-9905